Prentice-Hall, Englewood Cliffs, New Jersey 07632

Roy R. Behrens

University of Wisconsin—Milwaukee

Illustration as an Art

Library of Congress Cataloging-in-Publication Data

BEHRENS, ROY R.
    Illustration as an art.

    Includes index.
    1. Visual perception.   2. Communication in art.
I. Title.
N7430.5.B44   1986   741.6   85-16896
ISBN 0-13-451428-9

Editorial/production supervision: Patricia V. Amoroso
Interior design: Judith A. Matz-Coniglio
Manufacturing buyer: Harry P. Baisley
Page layout: Irene L. Poth

COVER ILLUSTRATION: Pastel illustration (*detail*) made in 1983 by **Gary Kelley** for Hellman Design Associates. The work in its entirety is reproduced in this book as Figure 1–32. Courtesy the artist.

The author is grateful to Robley Wilson, Jr., *The North American Review,* and the University of Northern Iowa for permission to use brief passages and several illustrations from his earlier book, *Art and Camouflage: Concealment and Deception in Nature, Art and War* (Cedar Falls, Iowa: North American Review, University of Northern Iowa, 1981).

In addition, the following illustrations were originally published as covers or short story illustrations in various issues of *The North American Review:* Figures 1–35, 1–38, 1–57, 2–18, 2–24, 2–41, 3–19, 3–23, 3–25, 3–88, 3–93, 4–4, and 4–9.

**In memory of
Chester Gottlieb Heinrich Behrens**

© 1986 by Prentice-Hall
A Division of Simon & Schuster, Inc.
Englewood Cliffs, New Jersey 07632

Printed in the United States of America

10 9 8 7 6 5 4 3 2 1

ISBN 0-13-451428-9 01

PRENTICE-HALL INTERNATIONAL (UK) LIMITED, *London*
PRENTICE-HALL OF AUSTRALIA PTY. LIMITED, *Sydney*
PRENTICE-HALL OF CANADA INC., *Toronto*
PRENTICE-HALL HISPANOAMERICANA, S.A., *Mexico City*
PRENTICE-HALL OF INDIA PRIVATE LIMITED, *New Delhi*
PRENTICE-HALL OF JAPAN, INC., *Tokyo*
PRENTICE-HALL OF SOUTHEAST ASIA PTE. LTD., *Singapore*
EDITORA PRENTICE-HALL DO BRASIL, LTDA., *Rio de Janeiro*
WHITEHALL BOOKS LIMITED, *Wellington, New Zealand*

Contents

Foreword *by Robley Wilson, Jr.* *vi*
Preface *viii*

Chapter 1 Illustration as Design *1*

Similarity Grouping *1*   Visual Confusion and Fusion *6*
Planned Confusion *8*   Similarity and Difference *13*
Concealment by Design *18*   Meditation and Ecstasy *22*
Esthetics and Visual Art *24*

Chapter 2 Illustration as Invention *47*

Feats of Association *47*   Cabbages and Kings *55*
Categorical Patterns *63*   Species and Genera *70*
The Factor of Attention *73*

Chapter 3   Illustration as Representation

82

Fooling the Eye *82*   Zeuxis and Parrhasius *86*
Differing Perspectives *90*   Realism and Attention *94*
Physiognomic Resemblance *97*   Innate Responses *100*
Glance Aversion *100*   The Anatomy of Cuteness *103*
The Taxonomy of Style *105*   The Relativity of Realism *108*
Art as a Partisan Model *113*   This Is Not the Thing Itself *116*
The Necessity of Difference *118*   Models and Photography *126*
The Realism of Pavlov *141*   Fooling the Mind *142*
Conditioning in Advertising *144*

Chapter 4   Techniques, Materials, Tools, and Styles *158*

Chapter 5   Information Sources *177*

General Reference *178*   Art Reference *178*
Bibliographies *179*   Design, Esthetics, and Anesthetics *179*
Underlying Visual Rhymes *180*   Embedded Pictorial Content *180*
Pictorial Representation *181*   Color Theory *182*
Visual Thinking *183*   Creativity and Idea Production *183*
Editorial and Advertising Illustration *184*
Scientific and Biological Illustration *184*
Zoological Illustration *184*   Botanical Illustration *185*
Medical Illustration *185*   Science Fiction Illustration *186*
Cartographic Illustration *186*   Archaeological Illustration *186*
Architectural Illustration *186*   Interior Design Graphics *186*
Fashion Illustration *186*   Technical Illustration *187*

Computer Illustration *187*   Animation *187*

Caricature and Cartooning *188*   Children's Book Illustration *188*

Illustrators *189*   Graphic Production Skills *189*

Techniques and Materials *189*   Art Law and Copyright *190*

Getting a Job *190*   Magazines and Journals *190*

Annual Collections of Exemplary Illustrations *190*

Copyright-Free Picture Sources *191*

Catalogs of Art Supplies *191*   Library Guide for Illustrators *192*

Index *195*

Foreword

Astronomers are bragging that they have found the outer boundary of the universe: it is marked by pickets of quasars, which stand at the very edge of everything like buoys whose signals are not lights, not bells, not solemn foghorns, but marvelous patterns of radio frequencies.

The edge of the universe. If that isn't the last frontier, I quit.

As a child—eleven or twelve, lying in the dark, insomniac beyond my years—I tried to imagine the dimensions of the universe, tried to contain its shape and reach in the room of my mind. I gave the job up when awesome, unmanageable fear began churning my stomach. Then I called out for my mother, who sat beside me and stroked my forehead and persuaded me that I shouldn't let the universe scare me.

She might have been right. It doesn't seem to scare science or theology. Or art.

Probably the universe is so well designed, you wouldn't notice its boundaries. By the time you arrived at a quasar,

probably every direction away from it would be back toward the universe's center. Wherever that is. (Did my mother know?)

Dimension.
Pattern.
Example.

Some of the things "illustration" is about.

We design, and we have designs on. This is more than playing with prepositions. Maybe the difference is between discovering order and imposing order. I think the former is a good thing, and the latter isn't, necessarily.

Roy Behrens is a magician (it seems to me) at discovering order, no matter how it tries to conceal itself. He might also be pretty good at imposing order, but I don't know about that. What he does in the privacy of his mind is his own business. What he does in the following pages is yours and mine.

I don't know what your experience will be as you read

this book. My experience has been that I've learned to see better. I'm not what you would call a "visual person." Ever since I was a child, scared off by the universe and my failed vision of it, I have been a "verbal person." Words; not pictures. Grammar; not visual relationships. Genre; not medium.

Art galleries are wasted on me.

Now along comes Roy to tell me that even "verbal" and "visual," if not the same thing, at least are scarcely separable. An image is an image, manipulate it how you will. There must be connections, but there needn't be boundaries. The imagination is infinite and eccentric.

It must be something like the old variation on "Who was that lady I saw you with last night," in which two magicians are the actors:

Who was that lady I sawed with you last night? That was no lady. That was my half-sister.

This book is a lot better than that joke.

ROBLEY WILSON, JR.

Robley Wilson, Jr. is editor of *The North American Review* (the nation's oldest magazine) and Professor of English at the University of Northern Iowa. He has published three collections of short stories: *The Pleasures of Manhood, Living Alone,* and *Dancing for Men,* which won the 1982 Drue Heinz Literature Prize. He was a Guggenheim Fellow in 1983–1984. Under his editorship, *The North American Review* has received the National Magazine Award for Fiction in 1981 and 1983.

Preface and Acknowledgments

I teach illustration. I also practice it a lot. It is in my mind not a job but rather a way to discover oneself, a way of finding where we fit, a means of knowing where we stand. It can be on turbid days what sonar is to bats at night. It is a way to transmit signs, to ricochet symbols outside of ourselves, and by that to locate the edges of things. It is, as Abraham Maslow would say, a means of *self-actualization,* a tool for constructing a meaningful life.

*   *   *

. . . creative art education, or better said, Education Through Art, may be especially important not so much for turning out artists or art products, as for turning out better people.

Abraham Maslow, *The Farther Reaches of Human Nature* (New York: Penguin Books, 1976).

*   *   *

Illustration is make-believe. It is a parrot, a dummy, a dupe. It is of value and interest because (unlike the claim of soft drink ads) it is *not* the real thing. It is retinal ventriloquism. It is a puppetry of the eye, a sleight of line that makes it seem that things which are present are absent, and that things which are absent are present. I find it especially baffling that it does this with even more impact at times than we would derive from the actual thing.

There is no book that I know of that deals with every aspect of illustration. This book is no exception. It is intended to play up those aspects which are critical to the practice of illustration as a fine and exemplary goal to pursue. It is an introduction to *illustration as an art,* as something you might live to do, regardless of whether you do it to live, as something of value regardless of cost.

*   *   *

My purpose in providing art experience for others is to make it possible for each person to explore and learn to use his own aesthetic sense, not because the creation of products in art media is of tremendous importance in every life, but because . . . the

viii

aesthetic sense is also the moral sense, *and the sense of self—of being.*

Frances Wilson, "Human Nature and Aesthetic Growth," in C.E. Moustakas, ed., *The Self* (New York: Harper & Row, Pub., 1956).

* * *

This volume is purposely widely addressed to those who are artists and those who are not, since I believe that everyone (regardless of whether or not they plan to become professional illustrators) could grow in a genuine personal sense from a better knowledge of the ways in which mere lines and shapes appear to stand for things in life. Even if we are not practicing illustrators, there is a much more general sense in which everyone "illustrates" daily—through gestures, demeanors, graffiti, or even the shoes and the hats that we wear.

There are seemingly countless books that deal with illustration. The present book is a carefully targeted try to amalgamate some of their contents, to make sense of some of the things that they say. It should be a valuable supplement to the leading periodicals (*Communication Arts, Print, Graphis,* and *U&lc*), to the excellent volumes already in print (most of which are listed in Chapter 5, Information Sources), and to the annual collections, which are inspiring archives for experts, beginners, and browsers.

* * *

The clarification of visual forms and their organization in integrated patterns as well as the attribution of such forms to suitable objects is one of the most effective training grounds of the young mind.

Rudolf Arnheim, "Gestalt Psychology and Artistic Form," in L.L. Whyte, ed., *Aspects of Form* (Bloomington: Indiana University Press, 1966).

* * *

Arthur, Lord Balfour, the British statesman, was once quoted as having advised that a person "has only half learned the art of reading who has not added to it the even more refined accomplishments of skipping and skimming." I find that undoubtedly useful advice, and most of this book is arranged in

a way that it can be scanned or browsed or thumbed in a purposely purposeless manner. There are all kinds and species of cursory bits, including expedient glossary terms, quotations from artists whose works are discussed, annotated diagrams, and so on. On the other hand, I would not recommend skimming the first three chapters because they are an attempt to paint the three attributes of excellent illustration: quality, originality, and appropriateness. They are listed in this book as *esthetic design, invention,* and *representation.*

* * *

A book ought to be like a man or a woman, with some individual character in it . . . with some blood in its veins and speculation in its eyes and a way and a will of its own.

John Mitchel, *Jail Journal,* 1854.

* * *

When a book and a head collide and a hollow sound is heard, is it always the fault of the book?

Georg Christoph Lichtenberg.

* * *

As I embarked on this book, I had just completed *Design in the Visual Arts* (Prentice-Hall, 1984), a guidebook for courses in basic design. This book was begotten from that one. And as that book is an introduction to "patternmaking" (or composition), this book is an introduction to "picture-making" (or representation). They are indispensable to one another, and they slightly overlap, since visual esthetic invention is the main concern in both. They are a bit like Siamese twins. They are flexibly joined at a chapter or two, and yet they are separate entities too.

This book took several years to write. During part of that period, I team-taught various courses with Craig Ede, Connie Gage-Kivlin, and Stephen Samerjan, three gifted artists and teachers at the University of Wisconsin–Milwaukee. I learned a lot from working with them, and undoubtedly some of the things that I learned have helped to shape this volume. I am grateful for the opportunity to have taught with these three people, and for their patience in working with me.

As in my previous book on design, the majority of the photographs of artworks, especially the work of my students, were kindly prepared (if not with a lack of amusement and pranks) by my friend and compatriot, Edward Tom Geniusz. He is the peerless curator of the superbly diverse collection of slides in the UWM Department of Art. His dedication is legendary.

My indebtedness also remains to my friend and mentor, Robley Wilson, Jr., whose renown as a writer continues to grow. I am thankful for his foreword, as well as for the vital fact that it was he who enabled my students to publish the best of their artworks.

Much of this book's usefulness depends on its appearance. I am especially grateful then to the illustrators, students, and other artists whose works I have included. I was honestly surprised by the enthusiasm with which they responded to what was nearly a blind request, and I hope they are pleased with the outcome.

In 1980, long before this book began, I was fortunate to receive a summer faculty research grant from the Graduate School at the University of Wisconsin–Milwaukee, in order to experiment with the illustration of fiction. It was an invaluable prelude to this.

As a teacher, I am especially sensitive to the ways in which a person learns, directly or indirectly, from the support and affection of friends. I am tempted to include a lengthy roll of teachers, students, and colleagues who have contributed to my growth. It may suffice to list a few, including Dean and Gerry Schwarz of Luther College, Cheng Hsi-ling of the University of Northern Iowa, Gordon and Lynn Mennenga of De Pauw University, John Volker of the University of Illinois at Urbana–Champaign, Amy Marein of the University of Wisconsin–Whitewater, Kathleen Holder of the University of Arkansas at Little Rock, Guy Davenport of the University of Kentucky at Lexington, Lewis and Barbara Snyder, my mother, and my family.

I am also thankful for the trust and continued alliance of my editor at Prentice-Hall, Norwell Therien, Jr. He saw the promise of this book at a time when it could have been doubted. I am grateful to his assistant, Jean Wachter, to the copyeditor, Bob Mony, and to the staff at Prentice-Hall. I am especially thankful to Pattie Amoroso, my production editor, who has been remarkably helpful and kind.

Finally, I cannot forget that one does not build books alone. In this case, the primary carpenter other than me was my astute and beautiful wife, Mary Snyder Behrens. It was she who did some of the troublesome stuff, so that I could give my time to refining the thoughts and the wording. It was a very long labor this time. But it was a literal labor of love, and the project has only enlivened our bond.

ROY R. BEHRENS

Chapter 1

Illustration as Design

Similarity Grouping

There are a number of variations on an ancient proverb, of which the most familiar are "like will to like" and "birds of a feather flock together," or, as I have sometimes heard, "hedgehogs live among the thorns because they too are prickly." In other words, *things that are alike attract;* and the corollary is, of course, *things that are unlike repel,* or at least do not attract.

This proverb dates from ancient Greece (at least seven centuries before Christ), where it appears in a line from the *Odyssey* in which the poet Homer says that "the gods bring like to like."

It is ironic that Homer was blind, because a variant of this thought (*things that look alike attract*) may be the one reliable guide to what is considered esthetic in visual art. As rephrased by Rudolf Arnheim: "The relative degree of similarity in a given perceptual pattern makes for a corresponding degree of connection or fusion."

This rule was applied to human perception shortly before World War I by **Gestalt** psychologists in Germany. Since then it has gone by a number of names, including the *principle of perceptual organization,* the *law of similarity grouping* (the

Visual statements such as illustrations which do not involve esthetic judgments and which are merely literal descriptions of reality can be neither intellectually stimulating nor visually distinctive.

Paul Rand, *Thoughts on Design* (New York: Van Nostrand, 1970).

1

GESTALT A school of holistic psychology, chiefly concerned with perception, that originated in Germany about 1910. The original Gestaltists (Max Wertheimer, Wolfgang Köhler, and Kurt Koffka) investigated figure-ground relationships, developed the principles of perceptual organization (which are principles of design), and stressed the contextual nature of things ("the whole is greater than the sum of its parts"). Now, the term usually means the whole effect, the structure or total arrangement of things, rather than parts. Thus, artists often squint to view their work or look at it from far away in order to see the general layout instead of the details. The usual synonyms for Gestalt are "structure" or "organization."

SIMILARITY GROUPING In visual perception, the theory that things that look alike will be seen as belonging together (which produces unity), while those that are dissimilar will be seen as belonging apart (which produces variety). However, no two things are inherently similar or different, since any two things may appear to belong together, depending on the traits we stress. An apple may be grouped with a fire engine if the emphasis is on redness, or it may be grouped with a ball if the emphasis is on roundness.

FIGURE 1–1 We tend to group on the basis of similarities and differences, which allows us to distinguish the numbered figure from the ground in a test for color blindness. This is an innate ability—that is, one that is not taught. In this example, the squares form a *4* to the extent that they are similar to each other, while they are dissimilar to (on the basis of color and shape) the background field of blackened dots. In general, all illustrations contain **figure-ground** relationships.

term used here), *unit-forming factors,* and so on. In books on art, it is most often listed as a principle of esthetic design. But again, it simply means that things that look alike attract.

This is nothing new, of course. In one way or another, whether consciously or not, all artists and nonartists already know (to some degree) that parts tend to form a group, that they tend to make a shape, to the extent that they resemble one another.

It is because of this strange pull (this principle of **similarity grouping**) that we see constellations, or that we can separate the dotted **figure** from the **ground** in a test for color blindness (see Figures 1–1 and 1–2). We respond to the law of perceptual attraction as surely as we respond to the law of gravity. It is the foremost law of sight. It is especially important in art, since it is the basis of structure in art, or what is usually called **design.** This law is the chief concern of painting, drawing, printmaking, sculpture, and photography, whenever the intention is to make an esthetic arrangement. It is of great importance, then, in the practice of graphic design, the main components of which are typography and illustration (see Figures 1–3 to 1–8).

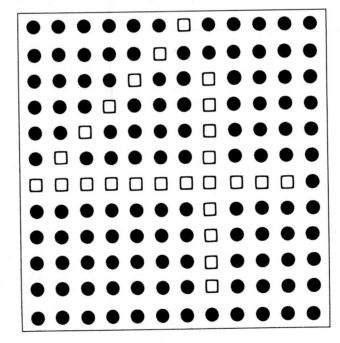

FIGURE 1–2 Whenever we look at the heavens at night, we tend to see groups, or constellations, of stars. The brighter stars are more likely than others to form constellations. But constellations are not fixed groupings; they vary to some extent from culture to culture. This woodcut of the major stars and constellations of the northern hemisphere was designed by **Albrecht Dürer** in 1515. Reproduced from *Symbols, Signs, and Signets* by Ernst Lehner (New York: Dover Publications, 1969) from the Dover Pictorial Archives.

FIGURE 1–3 Since Picasso has been quoted more frequently than any other artist, it seemed fitting to one artist to make a portrait of him out of words. On one occasion Picasso recalled that "when I was a child, my mother said to me, 'If you become a soldier you'll be a general. If you become a monk you'll end up as the pope.' Instead I became a painter and wound up as Picasso." This typographic portrait doubly represents the man by literally making a "typeface." **Paul Siemsen** constructed the picture by juggling the intricate tensions of attraction and detachment (the effects of *similarity grouping*) that result from the juxtaposition of four different sizes, values, and weights of a type style called Korinna. Copyright © 1978 by Word/Form Corporation. Courtesy the artist.

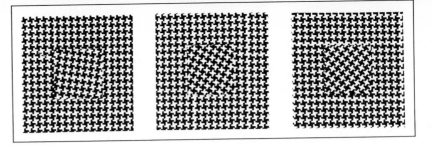

FIGURE-GROUND   The theory that any perceptual field (one in which a shape is seen) must have at least two features: A salient portion called *figure* (what is focused on) and an indistinct portion called *ground* (what is behind or surrounding the figure). In a very general sense, all artworks as well as all human expressions embody figure-ground relationships.

DESIGN   When something is designed, it is "put together" with some goal in mind. Everything that is not entirely accidental is, to some extent, designed. *Design is organization.* There are as many varieties of design as there are ways to organize.

Units which resemble each other in shape, size, direction, color, brightness, or location will be seen together.

Rudolf Arnheim, "Gestalt Psychology and Artistic Form," in L.L. Whyte, ed., *Aspects of Form* (Bloomington: Indiana University Press, 1951).

Visual elements which are similar (in shape, size, color, etc.) tend to be seen as related.

Richard Zakia, *Perception and Photography* (Rochester, N.Y.: Light Impressions, 1979).

FIGURE 1–4   The conspicuousness of a shape depends in part on the degree to which it differs from the surrounding context (or ground). The background is the same in each of these figure-ground patterns, but the figural squares are slightly turned, resulting in three different effects. Viewed from a distance of about one foot, some of them appear to be three-dimensional fields, either convex or concave.

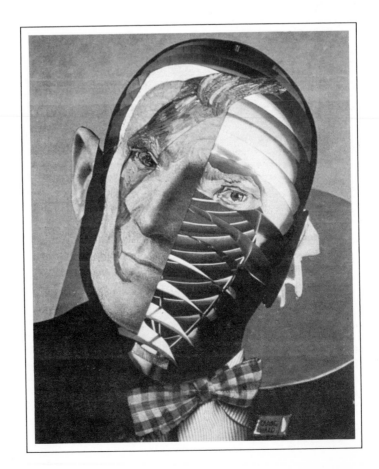

FIGURE 1–5   A shape is partly determined by its context. In this collage portrait by the American illustrator **Carol Wald,** there are fragments of a painting that nearly everyone is familiar with, and yet they are not easy to see within this odd surrounding. Parts of the face are derived from a self-portrait by Vincent Van Gogh. The illustration was commissioned in 1977 by *New York Magazine* but never used. The art director was Judith Fendelman. The original, entitled *Inner Man,* is in the collection of Sandra Ringlever, Grand Rapids, Michigan. Courtesy the artist.

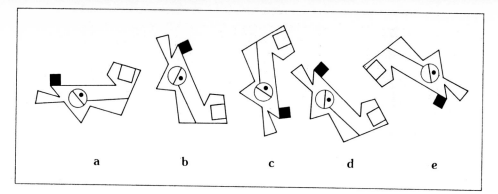

a   b   c   d   e

FIGURE 1–6 The readiness to look at shapes in terms of their structural features (or **design elements**) is basic to visual esthetic design. It is also essential to **visual thinking.** In this visual-spatial abilities task from a hypothetical IQ test, the subject is requested to find the two configurations that differ from the other three. Which two things do not belong? For other examples of questions like this, see *Know Your Own I.Q.* by H. J. Eysenck (Middlesex, Eng.: Penguin Books, 1962).

FIGURE 1–7 Although legibility is not synonymous with esthetic quality, it is an important concern in design, especially in type design. The central problem in designing a typeface is inventing an alphabet (or font) that balances similarity with difference. Each letter must be different from every other letter so that no two will be confused. On the other hand, all letters must be sufficiently alike that they appear to belong to the font. As might be expected, some typefaces are excellent and others are dreadful. These examples range from the virtually unreadable to the superlegible.

ORCHESTRA BOLD

SHANGRI-LA

Helvetica Medium

ROCK OPERA

Lubalin Graph Med.

THUNDERBIRD

DESIGN ELEMENTS In psychology these are called *grouping attributes.* They are the visible features by which things are judged to be either like or unlike other things. Such attributes include hue, value, intensity, shape, texture, number, proportion, size, density, angle of axis, distance from the picture plane, and so on.

VISUAL THINKING The kind of thinking artists use in the composition of shapes, colors, and other visual attributes. It is not done "in the head." It is done by rearranging actual things at hand—for example, by manipulating the elements of a Rubik Cube. Tracings, roughs, and thumbnail sketches are common ways of practicing visual thinking in art.

APPARENT MOVEMENT The illusion that a number of motionless things, perceived in a sequence, are a single moving thing.

Similarity of any kind—of shape, color, size, illumination, character of line and edge, and texture—will promote the impression of coherence and hence of unity.

Edmund Burke Feldman, *Art as Image and Idea* (Englewood Cliffs, N.J.: Prentice-Hall, 1967).

A most valuable and widely used device for achieving visual unity is repetition.

David Lauer, *Design Basics* (New York: Holt, Rinehart & Winston, 1979).

Repetition of identical or similar lines, shapes, forms, textures, values, or colors creates a predictable pattern: a coherent visual structure.

Paul Zelanski and Mary Pat Fisher, *Design* (New York: Holt, Rinehart & Winston, 1984).

We tend to group units on the basis of proximity or of similarity—i.e., two shapes situated close to each other are seen together as a visual whole even though they may be dissimilar; but more insistent is the linking together of similar units, similar shapes or colors. . . .

Maurice de Sausmarez, *Basic Design: The Dynamics of Visual Form* (London: Herbert Press, 1983).

Everything is known as a figure in a ground or not at all.

Guy Davenport, "Pyrrhon of Elis," in *Trois Caprices* (Louisville, Ky.: Pace Trust, 1981).

Design is the organization of parts into a coherent whole.

Marjorie Elliott Bevlin, *Design Through Discovery* (New York: Holt, Rinehart & Winston, 1984).

. . . many illustrators and artists are not visual people. They're essentially verbal people who have gotten into the field of illustration and painting. Really visually oriented people are rare.

Robert Weaver, illustrator, in an interview in *Print* (1978).

The closer two or more visual elements are, the greater the probability is that they will be seen as a group or pattern.

Richard Zakia, *Perception and Photography.*

FIGURE 1–8 Similarity grouping is the principle behind the illusion of **apparent movement,** by which pictures seem to move. In motion pictures, thousands of individual stills, projected in rapid succession, appear to be a single moving image. Apparent movement is also responsible for the trail of blinking lights that circle a theater sign. These photographs are not film stills; they are a single selection from the work of the nineteenth-century American photographer **Eadweard Muybridge,** who captured motion by photographing his subjects with a row of still cameras with rigged shutters. Muybridge's famous photographs (all 9,000 or so) are an inexhaustable information source for all branches of visual art, especially illustration. Reproduced from *Animals in Motion* by Eadweard Muybridge (New York: Dover Publications, 1957), from the Dover Pictorial Archives.

Visual Confusion and Fusion

Things that are alike attract, while things that are unlike repel. Take, for example, the lettering on the spine of the dust jacket of *Cockpit,* a novel by Jerzy Kosinski (see Figure 1–9). The typography is confusing. A viewer tends not to read the spine as a work, *Cockpit,* by an author, Kosinski. Instead he or she tends to read it as COCKPIT KOSINSKI; the title and the author seem to belong together as a single unit. Such a reading is not implausible—we would not be too surprised to find a book entitled *Cockpit Kosinski,* or even to hear of an author who used that as a pseudonym. In the same way, one of the reasons we see some stars as forming a nameable group (for example, Orion or the Pleiades) is because they make simple, sensible shapes.

This occurs because the human mind assumes that "like will to like," that "birds of a feather flock together," that things that are alike attract. In other words, we read the spine of this novel as COCKPIT KOSINSKI because there are too many similarities between the title and the name.

What are those similarities? A graphic designer would tell us that the colors, light and dark values, and size and style of type are too much alike. Or, a common alternative way to avoid confusion between two things is to spread them out in space, just as thespacebetweentwowordsenablesonetoreadwithease. Indeed, more space was needed between the title and the author's name.

In addition, a poet might point out that the same sounds occur in both *Cockpit* and Kosinski (they both begin with "ko"), and that part of their pull is due to rhyme.

COCKPIT KOSINSKI

WET
CAUTION
FLOOR

An easy way to gain unity—to make separate elements look as if they belong together—is by proximity, or simply putting these elements close together.

David Lauer, *Design Basics.*

Photographers who do not pay attention to the background when photographing people or objects often find that, in the two-dimensional frame of a photograph, depth is collapsed and ground sometimes becomes figure. This effect is seen in photographs of people with fence posts growing from their heads.

Richard Zakia, *Perception and Photography.*

PROXIMITY GROUPING   In visual perception, the theory that things appear to belong together to the extent that they are near one another, regardless of their visual traits.

FIGURE 1–9   This is the typographic plan of the dust jacket spine of *Cockpit* by Jerzy Kozinski (Boston: Houghton Mifflin Company, 1975). Because of the visual similarities between the title and the name, and because they are so close in space, the line is likely to be read as COCKPIT KOSINSKI.

FIGURE 1–10   This sign is supposed to read "CAUTION wet floor." To reinforce that grouping, "wet" and "floor" have been made similar in size and style of typeface, while "CAUTION" is dissimilar in color and in size and style of type. However, because of their sequence, the sign is just as easy to read as "wet CAUTION floor."

Such correspondences make it likely that *two conventionally separate things will be perceived as being one,* and that they will be read incorrectly. This common mistake may remind you of the cliché traffic sign that reads SLOW CHILDREN, or the janitor's sign that says WET CAUTION FLOOR (see Figure 1–10), or that famous photograph of the Lone Ranger and Tonto in which a cactus seems to sprout from the top of the Lone Ranger's hat.

Such juxtapositions may not have been mistakes. They may have been intended flubs. But, assuming that they were mistakes, then they are all examples of inept uses of design, of unplanned attractions in which two things that should be kept apart were naively joined as one.

Planned Confusion

There are times, however, when likeness is used intentionally to create confusion. For example, an inventive musical group called Talking Heads released an album entitled *Speaking in Tongues.* The album cover (designed by David Byrne, the group's lead singer) was especially unusual because the title was arranged in the following manner:

SP   EAK   IN   GI   N

TO   NGU   ES

while the by-line of the group was arranged to read like this:

TA   LKI   N   GHE   ADS

Considering the title of the album and the reputation of the group, this is a case of intentional confusion, of determined displacement (or "planned incongruity," as the critic Kenneth Burke would say). The "birds" that one would group (TONGUES) have been pushed outside their normal flock (TO   NGU   ES), as if they were sitting on musical chairs (by coincidence, the cover shows four views of chairs).

Unlike the *Cockpit* book design, however, these errors have not produced plausible wholes (for example, NGU is not an English word, although it could be Vietnamese). And so, despite the static, the message is not hard to read, although it does require a double take.

We might also consider the case of the British vaudeville comedy star who used the name of Nosmo King. He had discovered his stage name while staring at a door one day. It was a double door on which had been printed NO SMOKING; when it was opened, he saw the new words NOSMO KING (see Figure 1–11).

Nosmo King brings to mind another example of confusion that arose from perceiving items in a normally unified pair as separate, unconnected entities. As a child, I was in the habit of misreading the two-part trademark that appeared on boxes of Smith Brothers Cough Drops. The label portrayed the founders of the company, William and Andrew Smith, almost—but not quite—side by side (see Figure 1–12). Beneath William it said TRADE, while beneath Andrew it said MARK. I spent some extra summer days, with cherry cough drops in my cheeks, wondering if Mrs. Smith had named her two sons Trade and Mark. This confusion occurred because the words were spaced too far apart and placed too close to the portraits. There was also a chance that this interpretation was plausible—it was conceivable, was it not, that Andrew's given name was Mark?

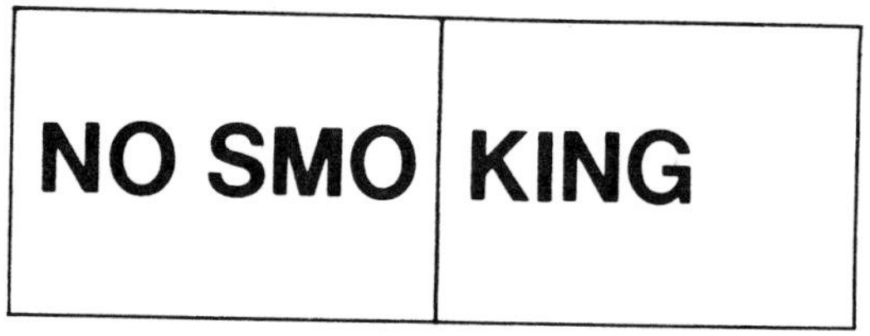

NO SMO | KING

FIGURE 1–11 The British psychologist R. L. Gregory, in his book *The Intelligent Eye* (New York: McGraw-Hill, 1970), recalls the story of Nosmo King, a British vaudeville comedian who discovered his professional name on a sign painted across a double door.

FIGURE 1–12 What were the names of the Smith Brothers? William and Andrew? Or Trade and Mark? The erroneous grouping occurs because of the distance between "Trade" and "Mark," because of the nearness of the brothers' portraits and the words, and because of the likelihood that the name of one of the brothers was Mark. Reproduced from *The 100 Greatest Advertisements* by Julien Lewis Watkins (New York: Dover Publications, 1959), from the Dover Pictorial Archives.

FIGURE 1–13 Are these portraits of twins, William and James? Or are they William James, shown twice? This rendition is loosely based on a similar drawing by the American conceptual artist and photographer Robert Cumming.

FIGURE 1–14 The tensions of attraction are almost at a stalemate in this "word search" puzzle, b e c a u s e t h e l e t t e r s a r e e q u a l l y s p a c e d. However, with some effort, we can isolate certain parts, and meaningful units like UBU and ROI begin to be perceived as things, in much the way that groups of stars are seen as constellations. Typographers and illustrators often use extended spacing (by simply spreading things apart) to make their work more puzzling and, by that, more involving.

Playful, intentional confusion occurs in a work by the American conceptual artist and photographer Robert Cumming (Figure 1–13). Cumming's drawing, a purposely crude-looking cartoon, juxtaposes two bearded heads, virtually identical and almost—but not quite—side by side. Beneath the head on the left was the word "WILLIAM," while under the head on the right was "JAMES." When I first saw this work, I could not keep from giggling in response to the unresolved tension. Just how was this work to read? Was it two twins named William and James? Or was it William James, shown twice? Other examples of playful confusion can be found in Figures 1–14 to 1–18.

CLOSURE A principle of perceptual organization in which patterns that are incomplete will be perceived as more nearly complete, because we prefer stable forms. The parlor game called "Telephone" (in which a phrase is radically changed as it is passed from ear to ear down a line of people) is a common example of this. Closure is discouraged in such explicit communications as military directives, or step-by-step assembly plans. It is desired in works of art because it promotes *empathy* (a complicity on the part of the viewer) and a vivid esthetic response. Patterns that are incomplete are retained in the memory longer.

In a sense, all good works of art are like a mystery novel. The pleasure comes from being given clues, not just the solution itself.

Marcia Eaton, *Art and Nonart* (East Brunswick, N.J.: Associated University Presses, 1983).

FIGURE 1–15 Articulation, legibility, and clarity are only a part of effective design. For purposes of esthetic communication, it is equally essential that an artwork be somewhat perplexing, that the message be hard to read, to insure that the viewer takes part in the work. This is a trade secret of the best illustrators. Thus, in this elegant poster, the designer and illustrator **McRay Magleby** has purposely spaced the letters apart in the title at the top. To structure an esthetic web, he has hidden rhyming shapes throughout the surface of the work in a kind of fugue or canon for the eye. For example, a circle is quietly used as theme and variation when the circle of the sun recurs in the French horn and in the "O" of "orchestra." Note the counterpart of squares (disguised as buckles on the shoes) and the repetitions of outline shapes, stripes, and gestural shadows, and so on. The poster was developed for the Brigham Young University Chamber Orchestra, 1975. Courtesy the BYU Department of Music.

FIGURE 1–16 In 1980, when the illustrator **David Gambale** was asked by Ambition Records to illustrate the jacket of an album, "13 Tracks of U.S. Rock," with the ambitious title of *Declaration of Independents*, he began with four large copies of an engraving of George Washington. The metamorphic sequence of facial distortions was made by marking on top of the Xeroxes with Neo-Color crayons. The arrangement of the words is purposely disturbing. When TRACKS and ROCK are split in half and the type is equally spaced, the effect of *proximity grouping* is used to create intended confusion. The art director was Steve Byram. Courtesy the artist.

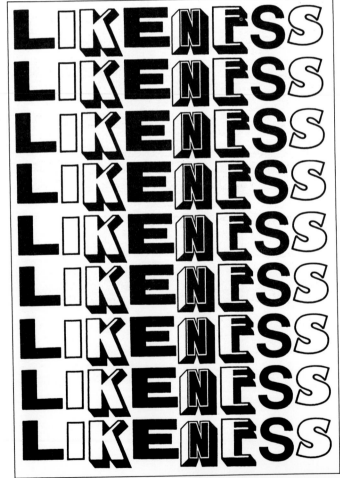

FIGURE 1–17 The apparent vibration throughout this design results from the conflicting attractions, horizontal and vertical. Because of their consistent height, as well as their meaningful function as words, the letters constellate as horizontal units. But due to the differing styles of type, there is an equally powerful pull to join them as vertical columns.

groupiNg
GROUPING
GR OUPING
GROUPIng
grouping

FIGURE 1–18 These permutations of the word "grouping" suggest the innumerable ways by which an arrangement of legible shapes can be made confusing by the interjection of differences. Esthetic arrangements are always a mix of legible clues and baffling gaps. A judicious amount of confusion, by which the work is made harder to read, insures that viewers will be drawn in by the process called **closure.**

Similarity and Difference

In the case of the dust-jacket spine, two normally separate units (*Cockpit* and Kosinski) were read as if linked (COCKPIT KOSINSKI). In the case of Talking Heads, parts that are normally married (TONGUES) were seen as being two or more (TO NGU ES). Too much attraction arises in the former case, too little in the latter. Too much similarity occurs in the first, too much distinction in the last.

With this antithesis in mind, let us briefly look at a psychological test called an **embedded figure** task (Figure 1–19). In this test, the subject is simultaneously shown two paired geometric shapes. One is a complex system of lines, the other

If a work of art strikes one as hopelessly dated, [it is] because it is spelt out in a too obvious, explicit manner. . . . To discover the principle of unity hidden in variety must be left to the beholder's imagination.

Arthur Koestler, *The Act of Creation* (New York: Macmillan, 1964).

When there's too much information, whether in an article or a poem, the mind rejects it.

Robert Weaver, illustrator, in an interview in *Print* (1978).

I enjoy drawings in which little information is given and the viewer must imagine the details.

Milton Glaser, *Graphic Design* (Woodstock, N.Y.: Overlook Press, 1973).

Art obviously depends upon incomplete communication. A work which is altogether explicit is not art, the audience cannot respond with their own creative act of the imagination, that leap of the faculties which leaves one an increment more exceptional than when one began.

Norman Mailer, novelist.

Popular novelists and other popular artists . . . suffer from being too easy to "read."

Marcia Eaton, *Art and Nonart.*

Painters consciously group visual elements to obtain unity in their paintings.

Robert McKim, *Experiences in Visual Thinking* (Monterey, Calif.: Brooks/Cole, 1980).

Artists can predict how most viewers' eyes will move; the fovea image jumps toward anything novel or emotionally stimulating. In viewing commercial art, there would be great similarity in the fovea paths followed by most individuals as they scan the advertisement.

Wilson Bryan Key, *Subliminal Seduction* (Englewood Cliffs, N.J.: Prentice-Hall, 1973).

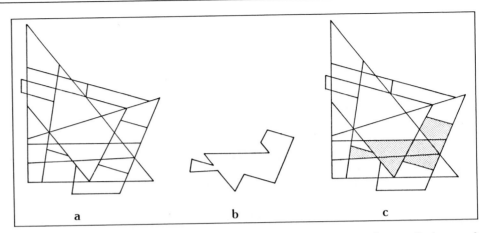

FIGURE 1–19   In embedded figure tasks, the subject is shown two shapes, of which one (*a*) is rather complex, while the other (*b*) is simpler and smaller. The object is to quickly find the latter inside of the former (as shown in *c*). In esthetics, the use of embedment is one way by which shapes can be implied rather than blatantly stated.

EMBEDDED FIGURES   Complex geometric shapes (commonly used in psychology tests) in which smaller shapes are hidden. The smaller shapes are hard to see because they make "good units" with (they are consistent with or similar to) the larger wholes in which they hide. In personality testing, people who score highly on the Embedded Figures Task (EFT) are referred to as "field independent" while those who find it difficult are called "field dependent." In general, the latter are assumed to have more difficulty in decoding camouflage, to be less analytic, and less able to ignore the effects of things outside of themselves.

is a simple shape. The point of the exercise is to overcome the confusion and find the simple shape within the larger complex whole. Because of all the alternate shapes that one could find within the maze of lines, and because the target shape is no more "wholesome" than anything else, this can be a perplexing test. For this reason, it is also called the "camouflaged figure" test, and indeed it is an excellent parallel to the camouflage of TONGUES, WILLIAM JAMES, NO SMOKING, or of TRADEMARK.

Certain kinds of intentional confusion are classified as camouflage, while other types are called *creativity*. The relationship between creativity and confusion was suspected long ago by no one else but William James. When someone asked what genius was, James defined it as the gift to see similarities within a field of differences, to perceive connections between things that had gone unlinked before.

Embedded figure diagrams, secret codes, and camouflage (military and natural) take advantage of the fact, as H. G. Barnett tried to show, that "under certain conditions, it is extremely difficult for a person to perceive similarity in diversity" (for example, to perceive TO NGU ES as TONGUES), just as it can be equally hard to perceive diversity in similarity (to read COCKPIT and KOSINSKI as being two separate units). Some research suggests that those who readily detect embedded figures tend to be more creative, humorous, and less compliant than those who do not score as high. One wonders if they can see through the labyrinth of military camouflage, as was claimed in World War II of soldiers who were colorblind (see Figures 1–20, 1–21, 1–22, and 1–23).

FIGURE 1–20 The figure of a sleeping man has been embedded in the land in this eighteenth-century engraving entitled *The Isle of Man: The Rocks of Scilly at a Distance.* Reproduced from a book of engravings originally published around 1790 by Bowles and Carver under the title *Catchpenny Prints* (New York: Dover Publications, 1970) from the Dover Pictorial Archives.

. . . when you look at a wall spotted with stains, or with a mixture of stones, if you have to devise some scene, you may discover a resemblance to various landscapes, beautified with mountains, rivers, rocks, trees, plains, wide valleys and hills in varied arrangement; or again you may see battles and figures in action; or strange faces and costumes, and an endless variety of objects, which you could reduce to complete and well-drawn forms. And these appear on such walls confusedly, like the sound of bells in whose jangle you may find any name or word you choose to imagine.

Leonardo da Vinci, *Notebooks.*

FIGURE 1–21 This is the cover illustration for *Kladderadatsch,* a German satirical journal founded in 1848. The magazine's name was invented when a dog knocked over a stack of plates. To mimic the crash of dishes, someone yelled out "*kladderadatsch!*" That became the magazine's name, and, in homage to its source, the face of the dog was embedded in the picture of the boy. The dog is on the boy's right cheek.

. . . Picasso one day went to look at his friend's latest work. Suddenly he became aware that there was a squirrel in the picture, and pointed it out to Braque, who was rather abashed at this discovery. The next day Braque showed him the picture again, after reworking it to get rid of the squirrel, but Picasso insisted he still saw it, and it took yet another reworking to banish the animal for good.

H. W. Janson, "Chance Images," in Philip Wiener, ed., *Dictionary of the History of Ideas* (New York: Scribner's, 1973).

Hidden anatomical details play an important part in art. The mind unconsciously, apparently, assimilates and structures unseen portions of the anatomy in a search for meaning.

Wilson Bryan Key, *Subliminal Seduction.*

SUBLIMINAL PERCEPTION The perception of structures that are too weak to be specifically identified but not too weak to have an influence on a person's mental processes. In the 1950s, it was claimed that certain movie theaters were inserting in their films single-frame advertisements such as "Drink Soda" and "Buy Popcorn," which, although they could not be consciously seen, somehow influenced the viewers' behavior. Subsequent research suggests that we are sensitive to some levels of embedded information, but it has not been confirmed that such sensitivity will lead a person to buy a product like popcorn. Many illustrations contain embedded structural traits (*underlying visual rhymes, broken continuity lines,* and so on) that make the works appear to be orderly and coherent, regardless of whether or not we are conscious of them.

FIGURE 1–22 In this ingenious cover design, **Alan Peckolick** has partially embedded the title by designing the type to look beardlike. This is an exquisite example of an illustration in which the typography and the illustration are literally inseparable. Courtesy the artist, from *Beards* by Reginald Reynolds (New York: Harcourt Brace Jovanovich, 1976).

PROJECTION The perception of coherent images in shapes arising by chance. When people are shown inkblots, for example, they may report that they see shapes. Or they may see shapes in clouds, in stains on walls, or on the surface of the moon. In other words, projection is an unwarranted closure. But it is not always easy to determine a case of projection. For example, when someone sees a picture of a human skull in an ice cube in an ad for alcohol, is that person "seeing things" (projecting) or is it a case of embedment?

FIGURE 1–23 Since the 1950s, it has been claimed that some advertisers hide messages in their ads. There are faces, it is said, embedded in the ice-cube shapes in certain alcohol ads, and "sex" is imprinted on crackers. This phenomenon is called **subliminal perception.** Some of these appear to be genuine cases of embedded figures; but many are probably **projections,** since even when they're pointed out, the shapes are still hard to discern. Even if the clues are clear, the shape might still arise from chance like figures in trees or faces in clouds. For example, in 1978, it was reported in the news that the skillet burns on a New Mexican housewife's tortilla resembled the face of Christ. Was this an embedded shape, or was it a **simulacrum?** This same question comes to mind in a print by **Albrecht Dürer,** entitled *Melencolia I,* dated 1514. Some people claim that they can see the features of a human face embedded in the textured rock (on the left above the dog). Others dismiss it as merely a random collection of shapes. This engraving is reproduced from *The Complete Engravings, Etchings, & Drypoints of Albrecht Dürer,* edited by Walter Strauss (New York: Dover Publications, 1972) from the Dover Pictorial Archives.

SIMULACRUM   A pictorial shape produced by accident or chance, such as figures in clouds, the Man in the Moon, rocks that seem to have faces, and so on.

BLENDING CAMOUFLAGE   Anesthetic visual fields in which a figure is concealed by making it so similar to its background or surroundings that it is no longer distinguishable as a separate thing. It is extreme similarity (unity without variety).

DAZZLE CAMOUFLAGE   Anesthetic visual fields in which a figure is concealed by breaking up its surface with a crazy quilt of shapes making it difficult to see the figure as one thing. This is an example of extreme variation (variety without unity).

FIGURE 1–24   Two major factors govern the extent to which an object can be seen: (1) the degree of visible contrast (difference) between the figure and the ground, and (2) the extent to which the figure is structurally integrated or consistent within its own borders. As would be expected then, in military and natural camouflage, the visibility of a figure is sabotaged in two main ways: through extreme similarity (*blending camouflage*) and extreme difference (*dazzle camouflage*). In this series of diagrams, high visibility of the figure is represented by diagram *a*. In blending camouflage (diagram *b*), there is a lack of difference between figure and ground. In dazzle camouflage (diagram *c*), the wholeness or continuity of the figure is destroyed by making it highly dissimilar within its own parameters. The most effective camouflage patterns are probably combinations of blending and dazzle (diagram *d*), in which a shattered figure also blends in with part of the ground. Most embedded figure diagrams seem to be combinations of blending and dazzle confusion effects.

Concealment by Design

There are two types of camouflage: one is called **blending,** the other **dazzle.** The first kind depends on too much similarity (too much attraction, if you will), the second on too much distinction (see Figure 1–24). Indeed, if we wrote out their names to look like the kinds of confusion they are, the first would be arranged like this:

BLENDINGCAMOUFLAGE

While the second would look like this:

dA z ZLecA mo UFLa GE

The first is comparable to COCKPIT KOSINSKI, SLOW CHILDREN, and WET CAUTION FLOOR. The second is related to TA LKI N GHE ADS, WILLIAM JAMES, NOSMO KING, and the brothers TRADE and MARK. To repeat, too much similarity occurs in the first kind of confusion, too much diversity in the last.

Camouflage—whether we find it in nature or war, and whether it dazzles or blends—is never entirely perfect, but it can work remarkably well because it is established on a universal human mental principle. As you should know by heart by now, that principle is: "like will to like." This principle is so universal, in fact, that a country going to war needn't worry that enemy soldiers might be so unschooled that they would not be deceived by traditional camouflage schemes. This rule is so essential to our lives that *if* there is a law in art, then surely this must be the one (see Figures 1–25, 1–26, 1–27, and 1–28).

a   b   c   d

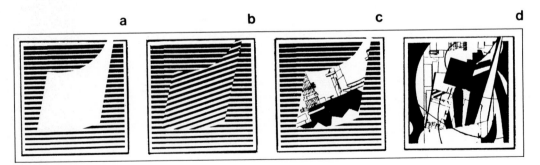

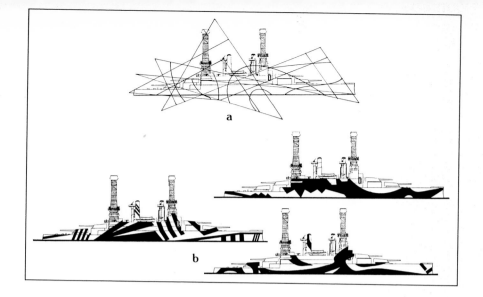

a

b

FIGURE 1–25 Military uses of visual deception are as ancient as warfare, but the systematic use of camouflage appears to have started in World War I in 1914. It was initially practiced by artists (some of whom were Cubists) in the French army. On the other side, the German army may have consulted Gestalt psychologists in designing their camouflage. The British and Americans (including many artists) were largely responsible for the development of ship camouflage, especially the dazzle plans (shown here in *b*), which were intended to confuse submarine torpedo gunners in their critical estimates of the speed, direction, and location of ships. The brightly colored dazzle schemes were so effective that less than 1 percent of dazzle-painted Allied ships were sunk by German torpedoes. At the time, much of the interest in and knowledge about military camouflage was due to the research of natural camouflage by the prominent American painter Abbott H. Thayer, whose book, *Concealing Coloration in the Animal Kingdom,* had been published in 1909. As diagram *a* shows, dazzle ship patterns might have been developed by superimposing an embedded-figure design onto the surface of a ship. For a more detailed account, see *Art and Camouflage: Concealment and Deception in Nature, Art and War,* by Roy R. Behrens (Cedar Falls: The North American Review, University of Northern Iowa, 1981).

FIGURE 1–26 A surprising number of prominent artists were directly involved in military camouflage (either as teachers or artists) during both world wars, including Arshile Gorky, László Moholy-Nagy, Ellsworth Kelly, Oskar Schlemmer, Roland Penrose (Picasso's biographer), and many others. In this photograph, dated July 12, 1918, U.S. Navy camouflage artists are applying dazzle patterns to experimental ship models. U.S. Navy Department photograph, National Archives and Record Service.

MIMICRY A special case of blending camouflage in which a thing is made to look so similar to another *kind* of thing that it is likely to be mistaken for it (for example, insects that resemble sticks). It is camouflage by disguise rather than by obliteration.

I was happy when, in 1914, I realized that the army had used the principles of my Cubist paintings for camouflage.

Georges Braque, quoted in Alexander Lieberman, *The Artist in His Studio* (New York: Viking, 1969).

Another thing that interested us enormously was how different the camouflage of the french looked from the camouflage of the germans, and then once we came across some very neat camouflage and it was american. The idea was the same but as after all it was different nationalities who did it the difference was inevitable. The colour schemes were different, the designs were different, the way of placing them was different, it made plain the whole theory of art and its inevitability.

Gertrude Stein, *The Autobiography of Alice B. Toklas* (New York: Vintage, 1961).

FIGURE 1–27 In her autobiography, which she inventively titled *The Autobiography of Alice B. Toklas*, Gertrude Stein reported what Picasso said in 1915 when he saw a convoy of French cannons, painted in dazzle patterns. "We invented that," he said, "It's Cubism." The cannon in this photograph has not been painted. Instead, it has been dazzled by the technique known as **osnaburg,** the use of overhanging nets into which strips of fabric have been interwoven. When the sun is shining, the image of anything beneath the net is visually disrupted by the shadows of the strips. In especially bright conditions, this is an effective way to make an object hard to read. From a U.S. Army photograph, 1943.

If a gun is covered with paint in such a way that one part of it will "fuse" with the bole of a tree, another with the leaves, a third with the ground, then the beholder will no longer see a unit, the gun, but a multiplicity of much less important objects.

Kurt Koffka, *Principles of Gestalt Psychology* (New York: Harcourt Brace, 1935).

In modern wars it has become a real art to make objects such as guns, cars, boats, etc., disappear by painting upon these things irregular designs, the parts of which are likely to form units with parts of their environment.

Wolfgang Köhler, *Gestalt Psychology* (New York: New American Library, 1947).

OSNABURG   In military camouflage, a portable means of producing dazzle camouflage in bright, sunlit places, by suspending overhead nets into which strips of fabric have been sewn. The shadows of the strips disrupt the shapes beneath the nets.

FIGURE 1–28   During World War I, Picasso jokingly remarked to the poet Jean Cocteau that the French army could make its soldiers harder to see if it dressed them in harlequin costumes. In fact, it was an excellent idea, as is witnessed by the fact that a number of natural forms are camouflaged by dazzle schemes, which make them somewhat similar to harlequins and crazy quilts. The harlequin duck is one example, the clown fish another. Other examples include these five butterflies in a painting by **E. A. Sequy,** the French designer and illustrator, *circa* 1920. Forty full-color plates of his paintings have been made available in *Seguy's Decorative Butterflies and Insects in Full Color* (New York: Dover Publications, 1977) in the Dover Pictorial Archives.

If [repetition is] persisted in, it easily degenerates into monotony and boredom, even hypnotic trance, which no longer permits controlled presentation of feeling, but opens instead the flood-gates of the irrational, which is neither recognizable life nor art.

Arthur Fallico, *Art and Existentialism* (Englewood Cliffs, N.J.: Prentice-Hall, 1962).

ANESTHETIC In modern parlance, an anesthetic is the cause of a total or partial loss of sensation, purposely induced by drugs. However, sensation can also be lost from prolonged encounters with forms that are either too repetitious (unity without variety) or too incoherent (variety without unity); for example, we tend to be "anesthetized" by driving on a freeway. In this sense, an anesthetic is the direct opposite of things that are *esthetic.*

MEDITATIVE TRANCE A state of *hypo*arousal characterized by a tranquil unresponsiveness to events outside the mind. It is reliably produced by prolonged exposure to monotonous forms. It is an anesthetic state, since it interferes with the direct perception of the kind, location, and timing of things.

ECSTATIC TRANCE A state of *hyper*arousal characterized by what appear to be seizures or fits, such as hallucinations, speaking in tongues (*glossalia*), and rapturous dance. It is an anesthetic state, since it interferes with the direct perception of the kind, location, and timing of things.

. . . the sensory mode of meditation makes little difference. The important effect is the state evoked by the process of repetition.

Robert Ornstein, *The Psychology of Consciousness* (New York: Penguin, 1975).

Meditation and Ecstasy

The goal of camouflage (whether it dazzles or blends) is to prevent us from sensing the kind, location, and timing of things that are outside of our bodies. In that restricted sense at least, the effects of camouflage are similar to the effects of an **anesthetic** (such as a drug that a surgeon would give). Anesthetics prevent a patient from sensing the kind, location, and timing of things (such as the blade of the surgeon's knife) that impinge upon the self. Anesthesia is thus the partial or total loss of sensation.

There are, however, states of anesthesia that can be induced *without* drugs. In ancient Greek medicine, for example, the Hippocractic cure for bacchanalian madness was dance. But long before the ancient Greeks and undoubtedly ever since, in virtually every part of the world, two reliable means have been used to entrance the mind: (1) sustained exposure to *extreme similarity,* such as monotonous chanting, resulting in a state of "hypoarousal"; and (2) sustained exposure to *extreme diversity,* such as spasmodic song and dance, resulting in a state of "hyperarousal."

You are familiar with both of these states. The first of these is sometimes known as a **meditative trance,** the second as **ecstatic trance.** Those who enter either trance (whether they are Balinese dancers, Masai warriors, Indian Yogis, Buddhist priests, Haitian voodoo worshippers, Pentecostal Christians, or more subdued practitioners of secular stress-avoidance techniques like Transcendental Meditation) are blessed (and afflicted) by a relative lack of connection with life, a state of partial anesthesia, a state of numbness (more or less) in which they cannot fully sense the kind, location, and timing of those ephemeral, sensuous ghosts that constitute one's life on earth.

There are a lot of examples of this, but let us be content with one: In 1937 the writer Arthur Koestler was captured by fascists while working in Spain as a correspondent for the *London News Chronicle.* He was accused of being a spy, abruptly imprisoned, and sentenced to death. In solitary confinement, he awaited execution at any moment because, indeed, as he could hear, prisoners from neighboring cells were being taken out and shot. Understandably, he developed fits of fear, or what are commonly described as severe anxiety seizures.

A detailed account of Koestler's ordeal is found in *Dialogue with Death,* his prison journal, in which he also talks about two effective means he found to numb the edge of his terror.

In one method, he chose a line from Thomas Mann, and "repeated the same verse thirty or forty times, for almost an hour, until a mild state of trance came on and the attack passed." This, as he was well aware, was the proven tactic of the Catholic rosary, "of the prayer-mill, of the African tom-tom, of the age-old magic of sounds." Trance was induced by extreme similarity.

In the second method, he would select an intricate concept ("such as Freud's theories about death and the nostalgia for death") and then free associate until, "after a few minutes, a state of feverish exaltation was evoked, a kind of running amok in the realm of reasoning, which usually ended in a day-dream." In this case, trance was induced by extreme diversity.

These two techniques, as Koestler states, were "anesthetizing" schemes. They are the two antitheses of the state of enlivened perception that is the result of **esthetic design** (see Figures 1–29, 1–30, and 1–31).

ESTHETIC DESIGN Patterns characterized by repetition with variation, by *unity with variety*. These occur not only in art but in natural forms as well and in all human pursuits, from football to cooking to teaching. Encounters with esthetic forms can be pleasant or unpleasant (they are not always beautiful), enthralling or disturbing; but in general they heighten our ability to perceive the kind, location, and timing of things. Works of art are not always esthetic, nor are they always intended to be. Often spelled "aesthetic."

"Aesthetic" derives from the Greek aisthetikos, pertaining to sense perception, and, although for centuries this meant that art was expected to be beautiful, today we extend the range of response to include the entire gamut of human reaction.

Marjorie Elliott Bevlin, *Design Through Discovery.*

FIGURE 1–29 In *Rococo to Cubism in Art and Literature* (New York: Vintage Books, 1960), Wylie Sypher listed the chief procedures Cubists used to make their paintings hard to read. He included "a breaking of contours, the passage, so that a form merges with the space about it or with other forms; planes or tones that bleed into other planes and tones; outlines that coincide with other outlines, then suddenly reappear in new relations; surfaces that simultaneously recede and advance in relation to other surfaces; parts of objects shifted away, displaced, or changed in tone until forms disappear behind themselves." This is not a Cubist work. It is an oil painting entitled *Martedi Grasso*, completed in 1982 by **Franco Allessandrini.** While its style and subject matter are contemporary, it relies on some of the same procedures that Sypher attributes to Cubists. The result is a literal *dazzle.* Courtesy the artist.

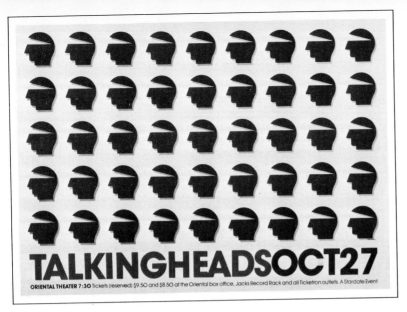

FIGURE 1–30 Esthetic patterns are a mixture of unity and variety, similarity and difference, or repetition and variation. But the most inventive art of any particular culture or time will fall toward one extreme or the other. That is, it will attempt to be as unified as possible while still maintaining some surprising variety, or it will attempt to be as variegated as possible with the most daring and subtle unifying factors. Extreme repetition is used in this poster for the Talking Heads, a contemporary music group that frequently works in a region between esthetics and anesthetics, because of its stress on invention. Designed by **Ken Hanson.** Courtesy of the artist.

Aesthetic experience is the vividly apprehended sum of a viewer's perceptions of visual form on any given occasion.

Edmund Burke Feldman, *Art as Image and Idea.*

The designer's aim is to achieve unity, but a unity that branches out into variations that relieve boredom.

David Lauer, *Design Basics.*

FIGURE 1–31 Stripelike shapes are rampant in this complex gouache design by student artist **Emilie Burnham.** It was developed (but not used) for a short story about a man who was excessively concerned with the upkeep of his lawn. He is, as depicted here, an illusion of a man, a body without substance that casts an opaque shadow. The space between the fence slats rhymes with the width of the hose, the band on the hat, the stripes on the socks, and the donut shapes that dot the shirt. Notice too the precarious way in which shapes that appear to be figure are tucked behind at times as ground. Courtesy the artist, 1984.

Esthetics and Visual Art

When we are anesthetized, we become oblivious to things and events outside of ourselves. Things that are anesthetic, whatever their virtues in other regards, are the direct opposite of things that are esthetic.

The term *esthetic* is derived from a Greek word that refers to things that are "perceivable." Before 1735 (when it was used in an essay by Alexander Baumgarten), the word did not refer to art, and it had little or nothing to do with visually pleasing things. Contrary to popular usage, things that are esthetic are not necessarily pretty. They need not be pleasant or simple to view. The role of art, as Otto Baensch so aptly said, "is not to give us pleasure, but rather to present us with something which we did not know before."

Patterns that are anesthetic tend toward either of two extremes. At one extreme, as John Dewey tried to show (in *Art as Experience*), we find such mal-adapted forms as "rigid abstinence, coerced submission, and tightness." At the other we confront "dissipation, incoherence, and aimless indulgence." Joseph Kupfer, a contemporary philosopher, calls them "constriction" and "petering out," in his book *Experience as Art*. Both philosophers have proposed that not just art should be designed, but all of life should be composed. Esthetic lives are wholesome lives, and esthetics is just as essential to health as it is to works of art.

One of the oldest canons of art, one of the most enduring maxims of design, is that it should mediate between two diametrically opposite tendencies: **unity with variety.** Unity arises from the perception of similarities, while variety is produced by contrasts. Thus, as Dewey proposed, anesthetic patterns fall at either of two extremes: (1) they lack variety—that is, they consist of extreme similarity (which he described as "tightness"), or (2) they lack unity—that is, they consist of extreme diversity (which he described as "looseness"). In this they reflect the two extremes of camouflage (blending and dazzle) and the two extremes of trance (meditation and ecstasy).

It is a fashion to assume that people who make art should be impractical, inarticulate, quixotic, and disorganized. But as Dewey clearly saw, "the enemies of the esthetic are neither the practical nor the intellectual." Instead, the foes of esthetics consist of rigidity on the one hand and slackness on the other, or *humdrum* and *hodgepodge*—that is, extreme similarity and extreme diversity, or monotony and chaos.

"Complexity without order produces confusion," Rudolf Arnheim has written, and "order without complexity produces boredom." Compare that with the demand of Sir E. H. Gombrich that if we are to fathom art, we must be able to explain "the most basic fact of aesthetic experience, the fact that delight lies somewhere between boredom and confusion."

. . . the nonesthetic lies within two limits. At one pole is the loose succession that does not begin at any particular place and that ends—in the sense of ceasing—at no particular place. At the other pole is arrest, constriction, proceeding from parts having only a mechanical connection with one another. . . .

John Dewey, *Art as Experience* (New York: Capricorn, 1958).

Too much order in a photograph or a design deprives a person of the creative act of participation. Some variation is needed to engage a person. . . .

Richard Zakia, *Perception and Photography.*

UNITY WITH VARIETY The paramount characteristic of things that are esthetic. Unity is brought about by the perception of similarity, variety by difference. Patterns that fail as esthetic designs (however else they might succeed) are characterized by either too much repetition (that is, they are *humdrum*) or too much variation (that is, they are *hodgepodge*). Esthetic patterns may be created in any style of visual art, within any medium.

Organization in art consists of developing a unified whole out of diverse units. . . . Rhythm and repetition act as agents for creating order out of forces that are otherwise in opposition.

O.C. Ovcirk, et al., *Art Fundamentals* (Dubuque, Iowa: William C. Brown, 1981).

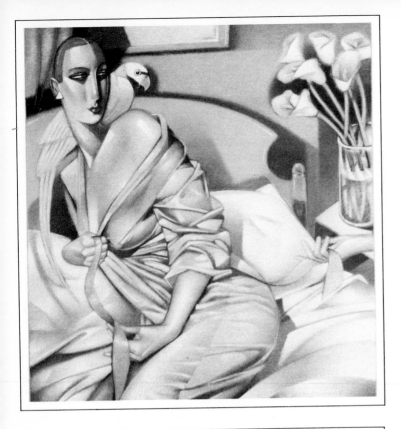

FIGURE 1–32 Repetitions of structural traits, or **underlying visual rhymes,** are not necessarily consciously planned. Such decisions are sometimes made on an intuitive level, so that the artist might only appraise whether or not the shapes "look right," just as a poet might consciously ask if a certain group of words feels or sounds appropriate, without extensively wondering why. However unconscious the process, the resulting work of art can be extremely logical and astoundingly complex, as in the deceptively innocent rhyme:

> Hey diddle diddle,
> The cat and the fiddle,
> The cow jumped over the moon;
> The little dog laughed
> To see such sport,
> And the dish ran away with the spoon.

Was the poet completely aware of the ingenious echoes that occur throughout these lines? For example, did the poet consciously think about the fact that violin strings are made from catgut, that cheese is made from cow's milk, that the Moon is made of cheese, that "moon" is a vocal reminder of "moo," that the crescent moon is shaped like a cow's horn, that there are alliterative links between c̲at and c̲ow and l̲ittle and l̲aughed and s̲ee and s̲uch and s̲port and s̲poon, that there is a rhyme among "diddle," "fiddle," and "little," and between "moon" and "spoon"? . . . I have recited this "nonsense" since I was a child, and yet I had thought about few of these links until I was alerted to them by Robley Wilson, Jr., This is but the beginning, since we could decipher the meter as well (the pattern of stressed and unstressed syllables), but maybe this is sufficient to show that it is the varied recurrence of traits (the repetition with variation) that determines the degree to which a design is *esthetic.* This is as true of visual art as it is of verbal art. No wonder Whistler thought of art as "the poetry of sight." All this is wonderfully evidenced in this pastel drawing by the American illustrator **Gary Kelley,** published in 1983. As the accompanying diagram shows, a commalike shape is repeated in the parrot's beak (1), the space to the left of the bedpost (2), the woman's head (3), the parrot's chest (4), the woman's exposed shoulder (5), her breast (6), and her buttocks (7). The eyes of the woman as well as the bird direct our focus to the right. There, the petals of the calla lilies (8) reflect the folds of the robe (9), while the phallic spadices (10) mimic the nearly identical shape, size, position, and color of the visually severed finger tips that come out from under the tie of the robe (11). The setting was inspired by a quotation from the humorist Will Rogers, who advised that you should "Lead your life so you won't be ashamed to sell the family parrot to the town gossip." The resulting artwork is, in Gary Kelley's words, "a nonpartisan comment on today's morality." The pictorial content is purposely puzzling, unresolved, and ambiguous. Who is the woman in the work? Is she the subject of the quote or the town gossip? To whom does the hand on the right belong? Regarding the work's pictorial sense, Kelley has observed that "actually, the situation which is illustrated (an affair?) is not so shocking by today's standards. That's why I have added the suggestive concept of a hand untying the robe, so that the viewer is left to decide whether the hand on the right belongs to a man or a woman. It is a deliberately genderless hand." Courtesy the artist. A detail of this work is reproduced on the front cover of this volume.

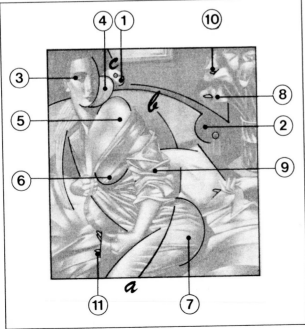

FIGURE 1–33   This colored pencil drawing, made in 1980 by **Bill Nelson,** is a brilliant reminder that art is artifice. The four embedded circles, which may or may not have been consciously planned, serve as implied visual rhymes. They are of three different sizes. The largest (1) forms the edge of the puppeteer's chin, the second (2) draws us to his hand (which is missing), while two others (3 and 5) are smaller and the same in size. As proven in the diagram, the figure's posture fits within an underlying triangle, *ABC.* Ingeniously, the background gridwork has been extended to cover the coat, yet omitted from the heads of the puppet and the man.

This highly complex work could be analyzed at length. To the right of the puppeteer's elbow, for example, the folds of the coat seem to echo the puppet's face. Ellipses in the hat (4) may be reminders of circles. The fly in the upper right corner is an example of *trompe l'oeil,* or "fool-the-eye," technique. An illustration thus becomes the mouthpiece of the illustrator, in much the same way that puppets are artificial forms through which puppeteers perform. Courtesy the artist.

UNDERLYING VISUAL RHYMES   Implied esthetic recurrences of the elements of design—for example, when a shape is partially repeated or somehow echoed in diverse regions of a work. In looking at an artwork, we may not be fully aware of these repetitions, and yet they can contribute to the coherence of the work. In the same sense, although we are not conscious of the measured rhythm of a poem (for example, any limerick), its use of internal rhyme, alliteration, and so on, we may still sense how well it works.

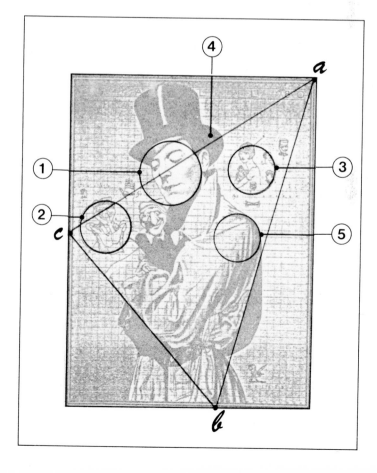

From another man I learned that constructing a business organization could be a creative activity. From a young athlete, I learned that a perfect tackle could be as esthetic a product as a sonnet and could be approached in the same creative spirit.

Abraham Maslow, *Toward a Psychology of Being* (New York: Van Nostrand, 1968).

A basketball game is more enjoyable when appreciated as an aesthetic whole, with its changing rhythms, its sudden grace, and its dramatic tensions finally, decisively resolved.

Joseph H. Kupfer, *Experience as Art* (Albany: State University of New York Press, 1983).

FIGURE 1–34 This illustration for an interview with an anonymous woman was originally published in *Oui*. The contemporary Dutch-born illustrator **Braldt Bralds** has constructed a web of resemblance by making objects that call to mind other, quite different classes of things. Thus, the seashell is displayed in such a way that it recalls (whether consciously or not) the folds of female genitals. So do the folds of the armpit. The shell shape is also embedded in the very large negative space (beneath the arm) in the lower left side of the picture. The swirling pattern of hair on the left rhymes with the swirling design on the shells. Nor is the hair so different from the features we observe in the lace or in the curled telephone cord. This chorus of esthetic traits is strengthened by the link between the thin black shoulder straps and a similar thickness of line on the shells. Much of this painting's power derives from what it purposely omits, such as the calculated way in which the torso is skillfully cropped. Notice that Bralds has avoided the corners as stages for major distracting events, since corners are themselves events (changes in direction). By that he increases the number of points that the viewer is likely to scan. The art director was Michael Brock. Courtesy the artist.

FIGURE 1–35 This charcoal drawing was published as an illustration for "Mal," a short story by Henry H. Roth in *The North American Review* (March 1984). The subject of the story was a middle-aged suburban man who devoted too much of his focus to grooming his lawn and defending his grass. In this work by **David Lenz,** the face of the man is omitted, as is the scene behind the tree. The man is observed from a point on the ground. The underlying visual rhymes were undoubtedly consciously planned. The artist has admitted that the trunk of the tree was intended to resemble the leg of the trousers, and in the top left corner, a handlike shape is embedded in the tree. There are several other, less evident rhymes. Courtesy the artist and the publisher.

FIGURE 1–36 In this conspicuous poster by Canadian illustrator **Heather Cooper,** layers of richness are amply supplied by the tacit congruence of shapes that call to mind adjacent forms. The earlike shells mimic the open mouth, the shapes around the eyes echo the singer's horns, and so on. The poster was developed to advertise the 1977 season of the Canadian Opera Company. Courtesy the artist.

There are two basic morphological archetypes—expression of order, coherence, discipline, stability on the one hand; expression of chaos, movement, vitality, change on the other.

Gyorgy Kepes, *The New Landscape in Art and Science* (Chicago: Paul Theobald, 1956).

The aesthetic sense makes possible the perception of opposites so that the organism does not move too far in one direction or become monotonous, thus providing stability and liveliness.

Frances Wilson, "Human Nature and Aesthetic Growth," in C. E. Moustakas, ed., *The Self* (New York: Harper & Row, Pub., 1956).

FIGURE 1–37 The sixteenth-century portraits of Henry VIII by his German court painter, Hans Holbein the Younger, were the immediate models for this poster illustration for the Iowa Shakespeare Festival in 1983. The advertised theme of the festival was *Public Faces, Private Fears.* The illustrator **Gary Kelley** recalls, "The idea of the mask is twofold. It suggests a public face contrasting with a private face, while it also suggests theater in general." The ambiguity of the eyes of the face and the mask is especially disturbing. An intended confusion results when the left eye of the mask is mistakenly perceived as a central third eye. As an esthetic arrangement, the work is held together by cryptic repetitions of fingerlike elliptical shapes. These occur in the fingers of the actor, in the texture of the arms, in the pattern of white diagonal shapes on the bodice of the shirt, within the moustaches of both the actor and the mask, and even in the eyes themselves. A second important repetitive trait is the impressionistic zigzag stroke (compare the edging of the collar with the edging of the mask) that is used throughout the work. The art director was Dick Blazek. Courtesy the artist.

FIGURE 1–38 No doubt the pictorial motive for this cover illustration had to do with railroad trains. But the implied formal themes, the structural characteristics that give it its visual logic, are patterns of circles and vertical lines. The lines are so predominant that even the computerized purchasing code (in the lower left corner) seems to belong. This work was made with collage, ink, and line tape by student artist **Jon Cisler** for *The North American Review* (June 1982). Courtesy the artist and the publisher.

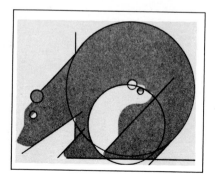

FIGURE 1–39 Elegant logos and trademarks virtually always use underlying visual rhymes, as does this one, which was designed by **Michael Vanderbyl** in 1976, proposed for but not used by the California Conservation Corps. As shown by the diagram, the curve of the backs of both bears is formed by an incomplete circular form. The same half-circle is then used to indicate the eyes and ears. Courtesy the California Conservation Corps.

Using the aesthetic sense seems to produce a feeling of being more intensely alive, of feeling significant, of knowing what is liked or disliked, wanted or not wanted by the person, and what is possible or impossible for him. Using it results in greater sensitivity, clearer perception, clearer memory, and a more effective selection of what is needed for growth.

Frances Wilson, "Human Nature and Aesthetic Growth."

. . . what I really thought of becoming, and wanted to become, was a commercial artist. I had, and continue to have, a great regard for commercial artists.

Wayne Thiebaud, artist, in Mark Strand, ed., *The Art of the Real* (New York: Potter, 1983).

Generally speaking, illustration is a business of give-and-take between artist and client, one of compromise. It's that compromise, the challenge of creating a painting to solve someone else's visual problem without sacrificing your integrity, that gets me excited.

Gary Kelley, illustrator, to the author, 1984.

The main trouble [with the field of illustration] I find . . . is in order to make enough money to live on, we have to take on far too much work, and the standard of most of the work produced, no matter how good the artist, is well below what it could and should be . . .

Anne Yvonne Gilbert, British illustrator, to the author, 1983.

FIGURE 1–40   By coincidence, this work may remind you of the preceding symbol design, not just because it's a picture of bears. It uses a similar scheme in its visual rhymes. The eye of the bear in the foreground is an echo of its ear. That same shape recurs two or three more times, as do shapes that look like claws. This is a pastel drawing, completed by student artist **David Lenz** in 1984. Courtesy the artist.

FIGURE 1–41   This portrait of George Rogers Clark by **Mark English** uses **broken continuity lines,** or implied structural axes. These are virtually always employed, essentially as a skeletal plan, in the layout of pages in graphic design, in which they are referred to as **grid systems.** Because they align in space, broken continuity lines make separate parts of a surface appear to be continuous. At the same time, the incompleteness of the lines allows for closure. This device is often used in art, at times strictly and rigorously, at others casually. In this painting, as shown in the diagram, the line that forms the back of the neck also forms the back of the collar and the edge of the lapel. Above the neck, the line disappears very briefly and then recurs within the ear. It is a broken continuity line. There are many other examples of such lines within this work. For example, the line of the top edge of the flag goes on to become the top of the collar and then the edge beneath the chin. This work was commissioned by the National Park Service for use on a commemorative poster in 1975. Courtesy the artist.

BROKEN CONTINUITY LINES   Embedded structural lines, or implied marginal axes (like margins in a page of type), that contribute to the logic of a visual arrangement. These lines are usually broken or partially concealed in some way so that complicity (by way of the process of *closure*) will result whenever the viewer encounters the work.

GRID SYSTEMS   When broken continuity lines are used in a graphic design layout, they are referred to as *grids*. Grids are not necessarily formed by straight, perpendicular axes at ninety-degree angles. They can be erratic, diagonal, and even curved. Almost every printed book, magazine, or newspaper (this book is no exception) is based on an embedded grid.

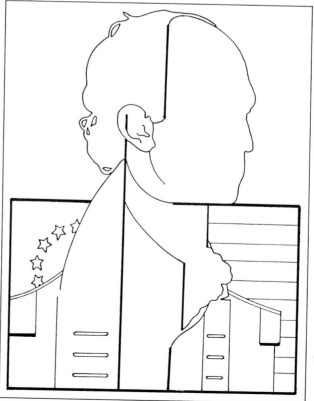

ACCENT When two things are juxtaposed, their differences are heightened, as when twins stand side by side. In color theory, this is known as the principle of *simultaneous contrast,* by which it is predicted, for example, that any hue of red will appear more vivid when juxtaposed with green (a radically different color) than when juxtaposed with orange (a highly similar color). Accents are small amounts of difference that heighten or accentuate the features of any design.

Very few illustrators' work interests me . . . most of it is junk. We live in a junk culture and it's just as true in illustration as in movies and television and everything else.

Robert Weaver, illustrator, in an interview in *Print,* 1978.

FIGURE 1–42 Incidental-looking words ("BLADE", graffiti on the wall, the number on the locker door) play an indispensable role in this composition by Canadian illustrator **Blair Drawson.** In concert with the checkered tiles, the jacket studs, and the garbage on the floor, the purposely extraneous words function as compositional gnats (disturbing little differences) or **accents,** giving the work its persistence and bite. The illustration was originally published in *New York Magazine* for an essay on life in New York City public high schools. Courtesy the artist.

FIGURE 1–43 The most famous American tea party is the Boston Tea Party. But in England it is the Mad Hatter's tea party, from *Alice's Adventures in Wonderland* by Lewis Carroll, published in 1865. The pen and ink drawings, from which the final engravings were made, were the work of **Sir John Tenniel,** a highly respected cartoonist for *Punch,* England's weekly humor magazine. In this particular cut from the book, the Mad Hatter and the March Hare are dunking the Dormouse headfirst in the tea. Carroll's remarkably durable text and Tenniel's illustrations are almost inseparable now, but that was not initially so. When Carroll suggested that Alice be drawn from a picture that he had provided, Tenniel protested that he no more needed a model than Carroll (a mathematical genius) would need a multiplication table to solve a simplistic example in math. Notice how levels of darkness are created by sets of intersecting parallel lines, or *crosshatching.*

FIGURE 1–45 These ancient Egyptian hieroglyphs, dating from the thirteenth to the first century B.C., are the pictographic names of King Ramses II (left) and Queen Cleopatra. Because they designate royalty, the names are enclosed in a linear ring, or cartouche, which was initially drawn as a rope. From *Symbols, Signs, and Signets* by Ernst Lehner (New York: Dover Publications, 1969), from the Dover Pictoral Archives.

FIGURE 1–44 In the very remote past, a text and its illustration were one and the same. Written words, in fact, evolved from images called hieroglyphs and pictographs. These are drawings of Mayan hieroglyphs that were carved on altar stones in the Temple of Inscriptions in Palenque, Mexico, sometime between 300 and 600 A.D. More than 800 different Mayan hieroglyphic characters have been identified, but few are clearly understood. From *Symbols, Signs, and Signets* by Ernst Lehner (New York: Dover Publications, 1969), from the Dover Pictoral Archives.

FIGURE 1–46 The world's oldest illustrations are found on the walls of prehistoric caves. Among the most magnificent is the cave at Lascaux in southern France. It was discovered on September 12, 1940, by a fourteen-year-old boy and his friends, when his dog Robot dashed into a hole in the side of a hill. As the boys pursued the dog, they entered a large cavern with 20,000-year-old paintings of horses, bison, deer, and bulls on the walls. One account of this find is "Robot," a story by the American writer and scholar, **Guy Davenport,** which was published in his book *Tatlin!* (Baltimore: Johns Hopkins University Press, 1979). Unlike most writers, Davenport illustrates his own stories. This is his drawing of "the Chinese horse" in the Lascaux cave, so named because it resembles a style of Chinese brushwork. When asked about this drawing, Professor Davenport replied: "This drawing [in India ink and crow-quill on Bristol board] is the first sentence of a story about the discovery of the painted cave at Lascaux. That is, I wanted the reader to encounter this neolithic animal at the beginning of the text. Other prehistoric drawings like this one are distributed throughout the story, and I consider them part of the writing, much like the diagrams in detective stories or examples of printing in a book about typography. What can be shown need not be described." Courtesy the author and the publisher.

FIGURE 1–47 Some of the oldest surviving illustrations are in the Egyptian Book of the Dead, which is not a single book but a collection of funeral scrolls that deal with the afterlife. In 1977, **James Buckels** was commissioned to illustrate the cover of a book of poetry by Richard Rackstraw, a popular teacher of writing who had died three years before. Buckels proposed a disquieting face in which the darkest areas contain hieroglyphic excerpts from the Book of the Dead. Reproduced from *Learning to Speak* by Richard Rackstraw (Cedar Falls: The North American Review, University of Northern Iowa, 1977). Courtesy the publisher.

FIGURE 1–48 The hieroglyphs in this lithographic print are not authentic. They are the fabrication of **Beauvais Lyons,** a contemporary American artist who calls himself a "mock-archaeologist" and classifies his artwork as "archaeological fiction." Lyons pretends to have discovered the clay tablets, pottery, and other remains of cultures that he has imagined. He invents scholarly experts (from the Université de Lyons, for example,) who reassemble the detritus and present their conclusions in ponderous monographs. Lyons is responsible for every stage of this process: he makes the clay tablets, breaks and reconstructs them (conveniently losing some pieces), researches and writes the spurious commentaries, prints the lithographic plates, and publishes the catalog of archaeological findings. His lithographs are parodies of scientific illustrations from the nineteen and early twentieth centuries. Plate XII from *The Excavation of the Apasht* by Beauvais Lyons, 1983. Private collection. Courtesy the artist.

FIGURE 1–49 A memento is a souvenir, a scrap that helps us recall a highly significant thing or event. A *memento mori* (Latin for "remember death") is something that reminds us that we are only mortal. This specific reminder of death is a calligraphic illustration by **Francesco Pisani,** dated 1640. From *Devils, Demons, Death, and Damnation* by Ernst and Johanna Lehner (New York: Dover Publications, 1971) from the Dover Pictorial Archives.

FIGURE 1–50 Until the middle of this century, women were rarely encouraged to study to be artists, much less illustrators. A highly accomplished exception was the German printmaker and sculptor, **Käthe Kollwitz,** who was first acclaimed as an illustrator of books by Gerhart Hauptmann and Émile Zola. Kollwitz was a passionate socialist and pacifist, whose teaching career was brought to an end with the rise of the Nazi party in 1933. This particular print is an etching and sandpaper aquatint and was completed in 1910. Entitled *Women and Death,* it is a superb attempt to show the horrifying futility with which a human faces death. Reproduced from *Medicine and the Artist* by Carl Zigrosser (New York: Dover Publications, 1970) by permission of the Philadelphia Museum of Art, from the Dover Pictorial Archives.

FIGURE 1–51 Omar Khayyam was a prominent eleventh-century Persian mathematician and astronomer. Despite his scientific achievements, his fame depends chiefly on *The Rubaiyat,* a collection of four-line rhymes, or quatrains. This is **Edmund Sullivan's** illustration for Quatrain XXXV of the English translation by Edward Fitzgerald, published in 1859. The poet refers to the pleasures of drinking and wonders when that may be halted by the "cold Lip" kiss of death. Compare this macabre depiction of death with the preceding by Käthe Kollwitz. Reproduced from *Devils, Demons, Death, and Damnation* by Ernst and Johanna Lehner (New York: Dover Publications, 1971) from the Dover Pictorial Archives.

38

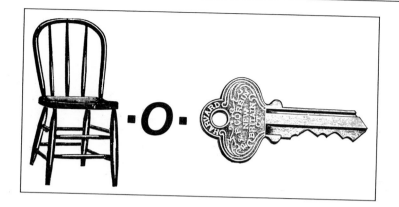

FIGURE 1–52 Words and pictures are the same in the pictographic game called a *rebus*. Entire texts can be transcribed by the substitution of pictures for sounds, as in this version of *Cherokee*.

FIGURE 1–53 New York is a cultural mecca, of course, but every coin has its flip side. As this unkindly cut reveals, big roaches are fond of big apples. Typographic illustration by **Chad Draper.** Copyright © 1980 by Sketchpad Studio. Courtesy the artist.

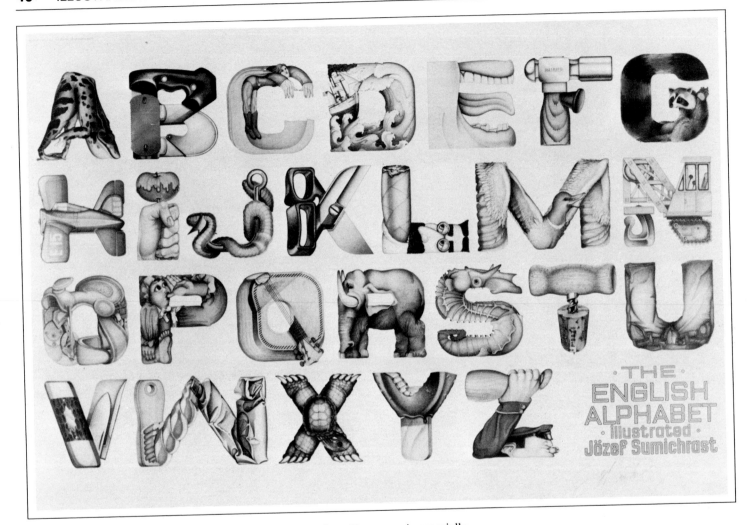

FIGURE 1–54 Jözef Sumichrast, a contemporary American illustrator, is especially adept at inventing *pictorial alphabets* (this is his version of the English alphabet), typographic illustrations in which the letters are derived from pictorial shapes. He usually works with concentrated transparent watercolors. He stretches his paper like canvas, and the watercolor dyes are put down over a sepia underpainting, in much the way that oils are used. Courtesy the artist.

FIGURE 1–55 Illustrations are pictures of pictures sometimes. The watercolor paintings of **Warren Taylor** often depict comic strips as if they were landscapes. In this artwork, entitled *Mint Garrison* (1980), a combative context has been given to the cartoon's words of CRRAASHH and I'M ANGRY! Throughout the history of art, artists and illustrators have frequently borrowed and quoted (in both verbal and visual ways) from the works of other artists. For a superb overview of artistic allusions and takeoffs, see *Art about Art* by Jean Lipman and Richard Marshall (New York: E. P. Dutton, 1978). Courtesy the artist.

FIGURE 1–56 In this composite media work (much of which has been collaged), **Fred Otnes** alludes to a famous face in the history of art, the *Portrait of the Infanta Maria Theresa,* painted about 1651 by the Spanish master, Diego Velázquez. Here, she is hauntingly juxtaposed with a storehouse of intricate visual delights, from antique cards to drawn facades to fragments of typography. The work has been composed over an underlying grid system (some of the vertical pencil lines are still visible at the top), and implied marginal axes (or broken continuity lines) occur throughout. This collage was developed for Artists Associates in 1980. Courtesy the artist.

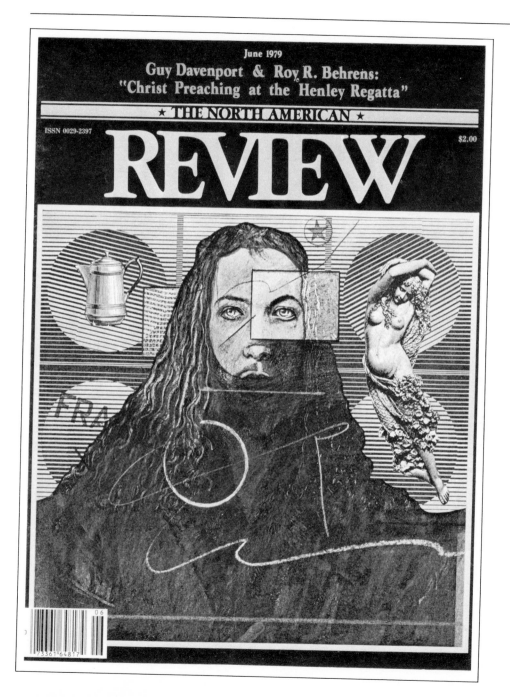

FIGURE 1–57 In 1979 the American fiction writer **Guy Davenport** (who often illustrates his own stories) agreed to collaborate with the author of this book on the text and images for an innovative short story. With Behrens' style of art in mind, Davenport invented a story entitled "Christ Preaching at the Henley Regatta," an allusion to a painting by the twentieth-century British eccentric, Stanley Spencer, called *Christ Preaching at the Cookham Regatta*. The short story by Davenport, accompanied by eight black and white illustrations and this cover by Behrens, was published in *The North American Review* (June 1979). Christ is not mentioned in the story, only in the title. Likewise, the image of Christ does not appear in the story illustrations, only on the cover. The portrait of Christ on the cover is derived from a self-portrait by Albrecht Dürer (dated 1500) in which he portrayed himself as Christlike. The cover was accomplished with Xerox collage, combined with colored pencil, rubber stamps, ad marker, watercolor, and pencil. The short story and its black and white illustrations, without the full-color cover, have since been reprinted in *Eclogues* by Guy Davenport (San Francisco: North Point Press, 1981), and in *The Pushcart Prize VII: Best of the Small Presses,* edited by Bill Henderson (Wainscott, New York: The Pushcart Press, 1982). Courtesy the publisher.

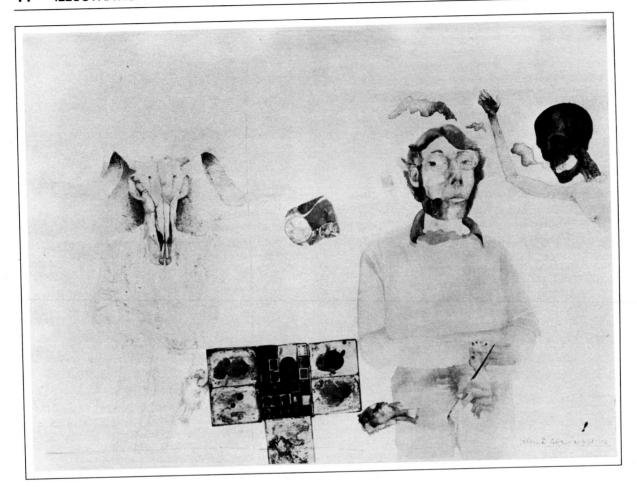

FIGURE 1–58 *Accoutrements* are the equipment other than weapons and clothing that soldiers are supplied with when they first enter the army. This painting by **Alan E. Cober** is called *Self-Portrait with Accoutrements,* as if it were an official guide to the artist and his basic gear, including the tools that he prefers, and the things he loves to paint ("I was really trying to see if I could render the crushed Coke can," he said when asked about this work, "I could!"). The original artwork was 41 by 29 inches. The image of the watercolor palette was made by color Xerox, while the rest of the work was produced with watercolor, pencil, and ink. It was commissioned as a poster by the Art Directors' Club of Phoenix in 1982. Suzanne Nelson was the art director. Courtesy the artist.

The term "commercial art" has a very mercenary ring to it, fueling that nasty rumor that we "applied artists" are in it mostly for the money. Some are, I'm sure. But the successful, respected ones are not. It's a good living, but my philosophy, attitudes, methods, et cetera, wouldn't change one bit if I were earning half my present income or twice my present income. The keyword for me is "integrity." I try to inject that into each piece I do.

Gary Kelley, illustrator, to the author, 1984.

I don't think there's any way a student can learn to be an illustrator. The only way to learn is to be one.

Anne Yvonne Gilbert, British illustrator, to the author, 1983.

FIGURE 1–59 Although he is not employed as an illustrator, the paintings of **Dennis Bayuzick** have occasionally been used as illustrations for short stories, in part because his cryptic works portray such an uncommonly diverse range of things, including, for example, smoking volcanoes, bleeding hearts, floating fish, pneumatic humanoids, barbed wire fences, toy tanks, melting crosses, and impenetrable walls. This particular oil painting (dated 1976) is entitled *Self-Portrait with Volcano and Cat.* In addition to being an active painter, Bayuzick is also a professor of art. In his artworks, he incorporates the mysterious items and situations found in dreams, reverie, and imaginative reflection. From these and other sources, as he has described it, "I have developed over the years a complex repertoire of enigmatic visual symbols and forms in my work, and altogether they comprise a kind of hybrid personal mythology of recurrent narrative images that function as psychological autobiography." Courtesy the artist.

FIGURE 1–60   This drawing is entitled *Lenny's Silver Bowling Shoes Used for Dancing*, dated 1981. The last in a series of self-portraits, it was produced by **Lenny Long** while he was in graduate school, in response to a request to portray the concept of *metamorphosis*. Asked about the work, Long said, "I did [self-portraits] regularly to document the changes I was going through mentally and physically. . . . I tried getting closer to myself, looking from different angles, and adding objects that were meaningful to me. The final drawing in the series became this particular one, *Lenny's Silver Bowling Shoes*. . . . It incorporated all the previous self-portraits plus my debris. The small first oil painting of my sister. My long hair braid, plus my Yoga books and incense from my hippie days. The bowling shoes that I had used when I took tap dancing lessons at Utah State University (I was horrible). . . . I did the drawing on a rather poor grade of paper. Which I regret. It had to be sent to the conservators within six months of completion. I used the full range of drawing pencils from 6B to 8H. I set up my studio with all the objects and drawings. I made a line drawing first. I'm left handed so I started shading in from the upper right-hand corner. I used gouache highlights for the whites. I matched the paper color, then added a touch of blue for the cool whites and a touch of yellow for the warm whites. It took 236 hours to complete." Courtesy the artist.

Chapter 2

Illustration as Invention

Feats of Association

Robert Williams Wood was an American physicist who was born in 1868, three years after the first publication of *Alice's Adventures in Wonderland*. Wood survived for ninety years and died in the year that *Lolita* came out. Like the authors of those two books, Lewis Carroll and Vladimir Nabokov, he was a scientist in part, but one who was famous for writing. Carroll (the author of *Alice*) was an accomplished mathematician, while *Lolita's* Nabokov was internationally known as an entymologist, a specialist in butterflies.

Wood's writings consisted of jokes. Aside from his textbooks on physics, he wrote a brief and curious book, *How to Tell the Birds from the Flowers,* in which, through drawings and amateur rhymes, he pretended that we might be apt to confuse such normally separate classes of things as pansies and chimpanzees, carrots and parrots, or cows and cowries.

We should stress the word "pretend," since Wood was a prominent member of the American scientific community, and it is highly unlikely that he would try to teach carrots to talk, or cook up parrots mixed with peas. He was trying

Man likes to bring two things together into one. . . . He lives by making associations, and he is doing well by himself and in himself when he thinks of something in connection with something else that no one ever put with it before. That's what we call a metaphor.

Robert Frost.

Look for points in common which are not points of similarity. It is thus that the poet can say, "A swallow stabs the sky," and turns the swallow into a dagger.

Georges Braque.

Wit may be considered a combination of dissimilar images, or a discovery of occult resemblances in things apparently unlike.

Samuel Johnson, *Lives of the Poets* (1780).

The greatest thing by far is to be a master of metaphor. . . It is a sign of genius, because a good metaphor implies an intuitive perception of the similarity between dissimilar things.

Aristotle, The Poetics.

When an individual steps across the traditionally accepted boundaries of sameness and treats two different things as the same, he is displaying originality.

H. G. Barnett, Innovation: The Basis of Cultural Change (New York: McGraw-Hill, 1953).

Man is a classifying animal: in one sense it may be said that the whole process of speaking is nothing but distributing phenomena, of which no two are alike in every respect, into different classes on the strength of perceived similarities and dissimilarities.

Otto Jespersen, Language (New York: Norton, 1964).

AMBIGUITY   The term evolved from *ambi*, a Latin root that indicates "around" or "on both sides." When people are ambidextrous, they have equal facility with both hands. When they are ambivalent, they are able to maintain contradictory feelings or thoughts. Ambitious people *go around*. An ambiance is all around. In the same spirit, things that are ambiguous are not devoid of meaning. Rather, they have the potential of being interpreted in several distinctly different ways. Ambiguous forms are of especial value in art because they facilitate *closure*.

I learned from her and others like her that a first-rate soup is more creative than a second-rate painting, and that, generally, cooking or parenthood or making a home could be creative while poetry need not be; it could be uncreative.

Abraham Maslow, Toward a Psychology of Being (New York: Van Nostrand, 1968).

to amuse, and the key to amusement, said Anna Louise de Staël, "lies in the likeness of things which are different, and in the difference of things which are similar." Wood was teasingly trying to show that things that are normally separate can also be seen as connected at times, that shapes that are normally different can also be seen as being alike.

This is not a radical thought. About six centuries before Christ (close to the time of Homer), the Chinese philosopher Lao-tze said: "Beyond mountains there are more mountains, and although they seem to be separate things, they are as well a mountain range. Beyond trees there are other trees, and although they look like woods, they are as well just single trees."

What Lao-tze was cryptically saying (as William James would also write) is that under certain circumstances it is extremely difficult to perceive similarity in a field of diversities (to see two mountains as a range), while under other circumstances, it is extremely difficult to perceive diversity in a field of similarities (to see each tree despite the woods).

Recall from Chapter 1 the embedded-figure diagrams and the dazzled and blended camouflage shapes. They exemplify the effort required to interpret ambiguous figures, to see a chopped-up shape as whole, or to see a single part within a larger complex whole.

One thing that we can learn from Wood (who should not be confused with woods) is that jokes can be designed by playing with alternate patterns—uprooting a plant from the vegetable garden and tossing it in with a parrot, or using a carrot to parrot a bird, as if a parrot and a plant were birds of a feather that wanted to flock.

All humor consists of intended mistakes. Wood is full of them. Wit is an embedded shape within that larger, complex whole that artists and others are likely to call "creativity." "Creativity," however, is a misleading term, since it conveys the impression that ideas come from nowhere, that they are created out of nothing. But that is not the case at all. Ideas are invented (from the Latin verb *invenire*, "to come upon"). We "come upon" them in the sense that they are alternative patterns. We select them from the permutations of the things we have at hand, or the things that are within our reach. Ideas are the hybrid offspring of the union of distant relations. A person invents an idea (including a visual idea, of course), as Francis A. Cartier has said, "by the combination or association of two or more ideas he already has into a new juxtaposition in such a manner as to discover a relationship among them of which he was not previously aware." An invention comes about by a "feat of association."

FIGURE 2–1 **Robert Williams Wood** was a professor of physics at Johns Hopkins University who was known for his work in optics and spectroscopy. In 1917 he published an illustrated children's book in which normally separate classes of things (for example, parrots and carrots) are made to look and sound alike. These are pen and ink drawings, but Wood could not help labeling them Wood-cuts. From *How to Tell the Birds from the Flowers*, by Robert W. Wood (New York: Dover Publications, 1959). Courtesy the publisher.

AMBIGUOUS FIGURES Forms in which two or more meanings have been implied within one space. For example, some figure-ground patterns are reversible, so that the figure can be ground, and the ground can be seen as a meaningful shape. Some patterns appear to be one thing when close up, another when viewed from a distance, while still others seem to switch when they are looked at upside down.

FIGURE 2–2 There are few better examples of purposeful visual invention than the collage novel *What a Life!*, by **E. V. Lucas** and **George Morrow**, published in 1911. Lucas was a well-known British writer and an editor of *Punch*. The authors cut out steel engravings from a British mail-order catalog, arranged them in a halfway reasonable way, and then wrote a story that does and does not fit the plates. This is a two-page spread from the book in which the Crystal Palace (site of the great design exposition held in 1851) is talked about as if it were a bird cage, while an animal at the zoo is represented by an electric iron, and the game of leapfrog is illustrated by a coat hanger. These are intentional confusions, in which two different kinds of things are treated or regarded as if they were a single type. From *What a Life!* by E. V. Lucas and George Morrow (London: Methuen & Co., 1911; unabridged republication, with introduction by John Ashbery, New York: Dover Publications, 1975). Courtesy the publisher.

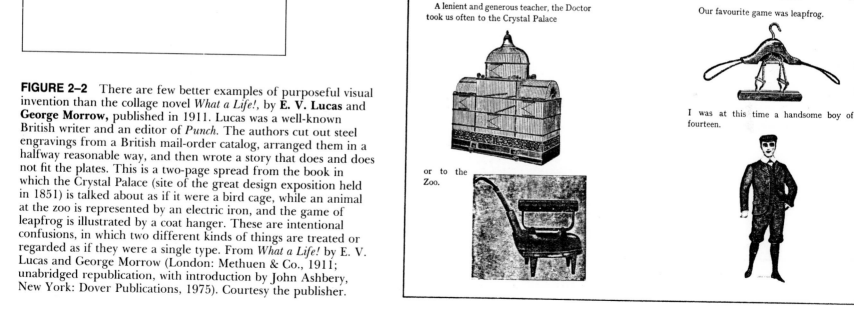

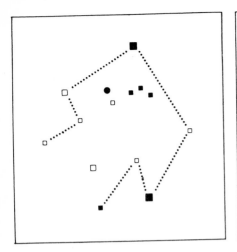

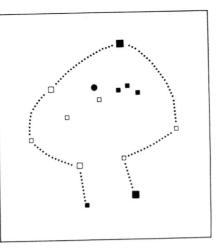

FIGURE 2–3 Perception is not an impartial absorption of facts. It is an interpretive process in which we pay attention to only a part (the *figure*) of what we are physically able to see, while we disregard those parts (the *ground*) that we anticipate to be of little or no significance. As a consequence, two people may witness the same event but perceive it in vastly different ways. In the diagrams shown here, the same data have been used to produce two different hypotheses, depending on which facts are stressed and how they are connected. For an instructive discussion of the interpretive nature of perception, see "The Confounded Eye" by R. L. Gregory, in *Illusion in Nature and Art,* edited by R. L. Gregory and E. H. Gombrich (New York: Charles Scribner's Sons, 1973).

SHIFT OF EMPHASIS Most inventions, perhaps all, seem to have come about as a result of a shift of emphasis, a displacement of attention, or a surprising distraction, in which importance is ascribed to things that were ignored before. It is not easy to make this occur because we tend to focus in ways governed by habit. As a consequence, shifts of emphasis may result from seemingly purposeless fooling around (*play*), from times of rest and idleness (*incubation*), or from accidents or mistakes that occur in the quest for extraneous goals (*serendipity*).

FIGURE 2–4 Ironically, in order to see we have to be blind. We cannot perceive a thing without ignoring other things. In **ambiguous figures,** both figure and ground are significant shapes. Thus, in a set of American stamps (**a**), we can disregard the quilted shapes and switch our attention to the central white diagonal shape. Or, in another American stamp (**b**), we can perceive the central star, in which case we ignore the stripes, or vice versa. In the maple leaf on the Canadian flag (**c**), two men with pointed noses appear to be butting their foreheads. And in the flag of the American General of the Army (**d**), a group of pentagons is formed by the shapes between the stars. All these figures work because of a **shift of emphasis** (or displacement of attention), which is the main technique employed by pickpockets, sleight-of-hand magicians, and gifted sleuths like Sherlock Holmes. The genius of Holmes, as Arthur Koestler once observed (in *The Act of Creation*), "manifested itself in shifting his attention to minute clues which poor Watson found too obvious to be relevant, and so easy to ignore." The Danish theologian Søren Kierkegaard referred to the same device as the "rotation" of attention (just as farmers rotate crops) in "The Rotation Method" in his book *Either/Or.*

a

b

c

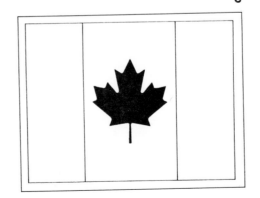

d

FIGURE 2–5 According to its title, this eighteenth-century engraving is an illustration of *Puzzle-Brain Mountain*. In fact, it is an ambiguous figure, or "puzzle picture," in which two pictures are contained within one array of shapes. When the print is turned clockwise, and the right side is placed at the bottom, the mountain's shape becomes transformed into the head of a bearded man. Reproduced from a book of engravings originally published around 1790 by Bowles and Carver entitled *Catchpenny Prints* (New York: Dover Publications, 1970) from the Dover Pictorial Archives.

There must, it seems to me, be some human activity which serves to break up orientations, to weaken and frustrate the tyrannous drive to order, to prepare the individual to observe what the orientation tells him is irrelevant, but what very well may be highly relevant. That activity, I believe, is the activity of artistic perception.

Morse Peckham, *Man's Rage for Chaos* (New York: Schocken, 1967).

FIGURE 2–6 This ambiguous painting is almost overwhelming in its repeated use of reversible figure and ground. For example, in the lower left corner, there is a stack of storklike heads in which the background of one bird can be seen as the beak of another, and so on. Near the center and toward the right, it is not difficult to find the image of a vulture, with an embedded human face emerging from its foremost wing. Other hidden shapes appear when looking at the painting upside down or on its sides, in somewhat the same way that we see shapes in trees or clouds. Gouache by student artist **Mary Jane Bergmann,** 1981. Courtesy the artist.

The prerequisite of originality is the art of forgetting, at the proper moment, what we know.

Arthur Koestler, *The Act of Creation* (New York: Macmillan, 1964).

My advice, in the midst of the seriousness, is to keep an eye out for the tinker shuffle, the flying of kites, and kindred sources of surprised amusement.

Jerome Bruner, *On Knowing: Essays for the Left Hand* (New York: Atheneum, 1966).

Many if not all scientific discoveries are made by a kind of inspiration fastening on an accident.

David Pye, *The Nature of Design* (New York: Reinhold, 1964).

. . . if you strive hard enough to get to India you are bound to get to some America or other. . . . The history of discovery is full of such arrivals at unexpected destinations, and arrivals at the right destination by the wrong boat.

Arthur Koestler, *The Act of Creation.*

SERENDIPITY Inventions that occur by chance. However, as Pasteur observed, "Chance only favors invention by minds that are prepared for discoveries by patient study and persevering efforts." Most of us dismiss mistakes. Inventors take a second look. The term was coined by the British writer Horace Walpole in homage to the characters in the fairy tale of *The Three Princes of Serendip*, who found what they did not expect by methods that were "incorrect."

52

FIGURE 2–7 (*Opposite page, top.*) Categorizing means thinking of things and addressing them not as individuals but as members of classes or groups. We categorize when we sort playing cards into suits. However, categories (like constellations) are just patterns that we choose to see in preference to others. They are not permanent, unchangeable facts, and indeed they are constantly shifting from time to time and place to place. In much the same way, the two of hearts does not necessarily group with the three of hearts. As shown here, it could as easily be paired with the five of diamonds and the ace of hearts, because all three cards are red. Prejudice and narrow-mindedness (to which all of us are prone) are characterized by inflexible categorization. Humor and inventiveness are based on surprising but logical grouping shifts that come about when our attention is displaced to traits that we did not stress before. The process of categorization should be of paramount concern to illustrators, since every work they produce (regardless of whether they know it or not) is colored by a point of view. All illustrations are caricatures to the extent that they result from the selective *inclusion* of only certain features of the things portrayed, and the *omission* of other traits.

FIGURE 2–8 (*Opposite page, first from top.*) All human beings, states Edmund Leach (in *Culture and Communication*) "have a deep psychological need for the sense of security which comes from knowing where you are." Our category systems are like the maps in shopping malls that indicate that "you are here" in relation to everything else in the world. If our categories are threatened, we are threatened. We are constantly exposed to new patterns that contradict our customary categories. These can pose a serious threat to our mental and emotional stability. If we are inventive and flexible, we respond by changing our expectations of life. At other times we may react by simply ignoring the attributes that contradict the way we expect things to look. If you had not been forewarned, would you have at first perceived the strange "mistakes" in almost all these playing cards?

FIGURE 2–9 (*Opposite page, second from top.*) Different cultures select different aspects of reality; as a result, they arrive at different "hypotheses" of what things should be paired or grouped. As Kenneth Burke has written (in *Permanence and Change*), "The universe would appear to be something like a cheese; it can be sliced in an infinite number of ways—and when one has chosen his own pattern of slicing, he finds that other men's cuts fall at the wrong places." This diagram shows three different ways of categorizing the color spectrum, as evidenced by language. At the top, European speech communities point out six distinctive colors. The Shona people customarily speak of three, while the Bassa use just two. See *Word Play* by Peter Farb (New York: Knopf, 1974).

FIGURE 2–10 (*Opposite page, bottom.*) To different cultures, the world is comprised of surprisingly different patterns. Language is a clue to these constellations, since words are tags assigned to sets. Some cultures categorize humans separately from animals and plants. Others assume that humans are an inseparable part of a larger range of natural forms, and that they are no higher or lower than the other life forms. As these drawings illustrate, young Native American males of the Osage and Omaha nations wore haircuts showing the plant or animal species (or clan) with which they identified. For example, *a* was meant to indicate the head and tail of an elk, while *b* was the emblem of the head, tail, and horns of a buffalo. The others were as follows: *c*, outline of a buffalo's back as observed against the sky; *d*, head, tail, and body of a small bird; *e*, head, wings, and tail of an eagle; *f*, head, feet, tail, and shell of a turtle; *g*, head of a bear; *h*, the four compass directions; *i*, shaggy side of the wolf; *j*, horns and tail of a buffalo; *k*, head and tail of a deer; *l*, head, tail, and growing horns of a buffalo calf; *m*, teeth of a reptile; and *n*, horns of a buffalo. In the context of these categories, it is no joke to say that parrots and carrots belong together in a set. See "The Osage Tribe. Child-Naming Rite," by F. La Flesche, in *43rd Annual Report, Bureau of American Ethnology* (1925–1926) (Washington, D.C. 1928); and "Anthropological Aspects of Language: Animal Categories and Verbal Abuse," by Edmund Leach, in *New Directions in the Study of Language*, edited by E. H. Lenneberg (Cambridge, Mass.: MIT, 1964).

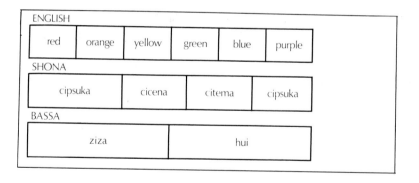

ENGLISH					
red	orange	yellow	green	blue	purple

SHONA			
cipsuka	cicena	citema	cipsuka

BASSA	
ziza	hui

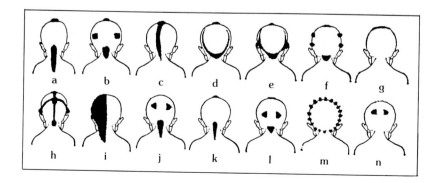

INCUBATION A part of the act of invention that seems to be a time of wasteful idleness, a time that may go on for hours or years. However, it is a period of rumination, in which (while the person is taking a bath, as in the case of Archimedes, or taking a walk or mowing the lawn) the mind continues to mull the problem over on a less than conscious plane.

BRAINSTORMING A technique in which play is used to produce unusual ideas. Members of a group are asked to *free associate* in response to a question or problem. The participants must be guaranteed immunity from criticism of anything they say. A faithful listing is maintained of all comments, uncensored and unevaluated. Without exception, all contributions are encouraged and accepted. Later, when the storm has passed, the items are discussed and judged.

One sometimes finds what one is not looking for. For instance, the technician who set out to find a way to synchronize the rate of fire of a machine gun with the revolutions of an air screw discovered an excellent way of imitating the lowing of a cow.

Arthur Fleming.

53

All the really good ideas I ever had came to me while I was milking a cow.

Grant Wood.

I do not seek, I find.

Pablo Picasso.

FIGURE 2–11 Within any one cultural group, considerable variance exists in the ways people classify and categorize, especially from region to region, and from time to time. It was not so long ago that Europeans classified bats as birds and whales as fish. People who sort things in unusual ways are often assumed to be comic, poetic, inventive, eccentric, naive, or mentally deranged. Such people seem to mistake one thing for another, to call things by the wrong names. When they do so on purpose (as poets and humorists frequently do), we say that they are speaking "metaphorically." Miguel de Cervantes was speaking that way throughout *Don Quixote de la Mancha*, the famous novel he wrote in the early seventeenth century about a mad Spanish squire who thought he was a knight-errant. Throughout the book, Don Quixote continually mistakes commonplace things for other, more exotic things. For example, he attacks a windmill because he believes it to be a giant. At a country inn (which he believes to be a castle), he stabs a row of wineskins because they appear to be giants, and is only further convinced when "blood" (red wine) flows out of the skins. This is one of 120 full-page wood engravings drawn by **Gustave Doré,** and engraved by H. Pisan for a French translation of the book in 1863. Reproduced from *Doré's Illustrations for Don Quixote* (New York: Dover Publications, 1982) from the Dover Pictorial Archives.

Cabbages and Kings

There are few better examples of a feat of association than a famous passage in Lewis Carroll's second book, *Through the Looking Glass and What Alice Found There*. I mean of course those memorable lines from the poem that Tweedledee recites about the story of "The Walrus and the Carpenter":

> *"The time has come," the Walrus said,*
> *"To talk of many things:*
> *Of shoes—and ships—and sealing wax—*
> *Of cabbages—and kings—*
> *And why the sea is boiling hot—*
> *And whether pigs have wings."*

In a tribute to this verse, Arthur Koestler once defined what he described as a feat of *bisociation* (so as to distinguish it from routine associative thought) as an "unlikely marriage of cabbages and kings—of previously unrelated frames of reference or universes of discourse—whose union will solve the previously unsoluable problem."

Koestler may have been aware of a satirical portrait of King Louis Philippe of France, as rendered by the caricaturist Charles Philipon in 1834. The sequence of four drawings derides the physiognomic evolution diagrams of Johann Caspar Lavater (in which, for example, a man was portrayed evolving from a frog), as well as making fun of the king, whose head gradually takes the shape of a disgustingly corpulent pear. The cartoon is almost a literal view of the process that Koestler describes. It is a betrothal of alien species, a marriage of pears and kings.

Inventions in science or humor or art are often the result of arduous efforts because, as William James and Lao-tze said, it is not a simple task to perceive similarity in a field of diversities (to see the forest in spite of the trees) and to see diversities in a field of similarities (to see each tree despite the woods).

Particular phrases are often applied to these two ways of looking at things (seeing two things as if they were one, and seeing one thing as if it were two), phrases that show that these ways are substantially different from those we ascribe to noninventive, routine thought. The first way of seeing is sometimes called **elopement,** or "making the strange familiar," while the second is called **estrangement,** or "making the familiar strange." The former is accomplished by

Wit is the sudden marriage of ideas which before their union were not perceived to have any relation.
H. L. Mencken.

A favorite definition of joking has long been the ability to find similarity between dissimilar things—that is, hidden similarities.
Sigmund Freud, *Jokes and Their Relation to the Unconscious* (New York: Norton, 1963).

Joking is the disguised priest who weds every couple.
Jean Paul Richter, *Vorschule der Aesthetik*, 1804.

INVENTIVE THINKING Any style of thinking, perceiving, or behaving characterized by the intentional violation of customary categories, resulting in unconventional sets. It has been called all sorts of names, including *bisociation* (Arthur Koestler), *productive thinking* (Max Wertheimer), *divergent thinking* (J. P. Guilford), *lateral thinking* (Edward de Bono), *planned incongruity* (Kenneth Burke), *sort-crossing* (C. M. Turbayne), *translogical thinking* (Gregory Bateson), and *metaphorical thinking* or *synectics* (William J. J. Gordon). It is synonymous with creativity.

ELOPEMENT A method of inventing, derived from the principle of *similarity grouping,* in which one watches carefully for unexpected likenesses between two normally disparate things; also called *making the strange familiar.* It is related to blending camouflage and mimicry.

ESTRANGEMENT A method of inventing, derived from the principle of *similarity grouping,* in which one heavily emphasizes the differences between members of a pair and splits the set; also called *making the familiar strange.* It is similar to dazzle camouflage.

[Joking] likes best to wed couples whose union their relatives frown upon.

F. T. Vischer, *Aesthetik*, 1846–1857.

When innovation takes place, there is an intimate linkage or fusion of two or more elements that have not been previously joined in just this fashion, so that the result is a qualitatively different whole.

H. G. Barnett, *Innovation: The Basis of Cultural Change.*

A person, asked in what way wood and alcohol are alike, is given a zero score if he answers: "Both knock you out." No doubt, this answer testifies to a bright intellect. It comes from a person capable of finding at the spur of the moment a striking common feature in two things not obviously alike.

Rudolf Arnheim, *Visual Thinking* (Berkeley: University of California Press, 1969).

. . . an innovation is like a genetic cross or hybrid; it is totally different from either of its parents, but it resembles both of them in some respects.

H. G. Barnett, *Innovation: The Basis of Cultural Change.*

ARRANGED MARRIAGE   In some cultures, marriage contracts are arranged by the families of the couple (sometimes when the pair are still children), regardless of whether they like it or not, and with little if any concern for the compatibility of the pair. By analogy, the term also refers to a method of inventing, derived from the principle of *proximity grouping,* in which things are juxtaposed with little if any concern for their similarities or differences. The customary name for this procedure is *radical juxtaposition.*

FIGURE 2–12   To talk about invention as if it were a marriage is not a new idea. Wit, in H. L. Mencken's words, is "the sudden marriage of ideas which before their union were not perceived to have any relation." The writer Jean Paul Richter said that humor is a "disguised priest" who always weds incompatible pairs. In this exquisite *caricature*, the pair is only half a pear. The cartoon was entitled *Les Poires* ("The Pears"), which in French slang means "fatheads." It was published first in France in 1834, at which time the king was Louis Philippe, *Le Roi Bourgeois*. The artist was **Charles Philipon,** who was as well the editor of the paper in which the drawing appeared, *Le Charivari* (the original spelling of "chivaree," a noisy wedding serenade). His portraits of the king as *poire* led to his indictment, and he was fined 6,000 francs. In his defense, he tried to show (with tongue in cheek), in this sequence of four steps, that the king was a pearhead by natural fact, not by any sleight of art. Of course the artist lost his case, but in the end his prank bore fruit, since henceforth no one could look at the king without thinking of a pear.

being especially vigilant of unforeseen resemblances between two normally alien things (for example, attending to the rhyme between "carrot" and "parrot"). The latter results from the opposite tack, by watching for hidden distinguishing traits between two things that no one doubts are perfectly consonant partners (for example, proposing that carrots are less like plants than like birds that talk). These are two purposeful methods by which illustrators (as well as all artists and everyone else) come up with astounding portrayals of life.

However, as Koestler once noted, self-conscious, deliberate thinking is not always the best cocktail shaker. And so a third means has evolved, and that is to willfully leave things to change. It has come to be called a radical juxtaposition, or **arranged marriage,** in which the partners are wedded in space, regardless of whether they like it or not. It is, said Comte de Lautréamont, "the fortuitous encounter of a sewing machine and an umbrella on a dissecting table." It is the principle of collage, as in the work of Joan Miró, who, in 1936, assembled a curious sculpture (which he entitled *Poetic Object*) in which we find connected a parrot, a derby, a ball on a string, the leg of a doll, and an antique map.

But the arranged marriage method is really much older than Miró's artwork (see Figure 2–17). It was used in the nineteenth century by Lewis Carroll when he wrote "The Walrus and the Carpenter." Carroll, it seems, left the carpenter out. He instructed Sir John Tenniel, the book's illustrator, that he, Tenniel, could decide if the poem would be about a carpenter, a butterfly, or a baronet (since all three comply with the meter), depending on what he was eager to draw. The carpenter was selected by chance. He was placed next to the walrus, and there they have happily lived ever since.

To reiterate, there are at least three methods by which we can purposely invent. "To make the strange familiar" is roughly the same as elopement. "To make the familiar strange" is equivalent to estrangement (see Figures 2–13, 2–14). And "radical juxtaposition" (in which the partners' compatible traits are not considered in the match) is like the blind alliance of an arranged marriage.

Whenever I think of the third, I am reminded of that quote from Christian Zervos's interview with the middle-aged Pablo Picasso, two years before Miró combined the parrot, hat, and antique map. "To my distress and perhaps to my delight, I order things in accordance with my passions," Picasso said to Zervos, "I put in my pictures everything I like. So much the worse for the things—they have to get along with one another."

Finally, we should add a fourth procedure by which unusual groupings are predictably produced. It is most commonly employed in "behavioral conditioning." It is based on the principle of *contiguity grouping* (that things will tend to be confused if they recur together in time, regardless of their appearances), and it is best thought of as a kind of **common-law bond.**

In order to think new thoughts or to say new things, we have to break up all our ready-made ideas and shuffle the pieces.

Gregory Bateson, *Steps to an Ecology of Mind* (New York: Ballantine, 1972).

COMMON-LAW BOND In a common-law marriage, a couple can claim to be legally wed (without actually being married) if they have lived together for a certain length of time. By analogy, things that are customarily unrelated become paired if they coincide repeatedly over a period of time. This method of invention (most commonly associated with "behavioral conditioning") is based on the principle of *contiguity grouping.*

FIGURE 2–13 In this page from his children's book, the American physicist **Robert Williams Wood** is emphasizing the unexpected visual rhyme between the mouth of a cow and a cowry. His drawings are blatantly fudged of course, but they are superb examples of two of the primary methods by which inventive ideas (visual, verbal, or otherwise) can be deliberately produced—by *elopement* and *estrangement,* or "making the strange familiar" and "making the familiar strange," respectively. From *How to Tell the Birds from the Flowers,* by Robert W. Wood (New York: Dover Publications, 1959). Courtesy the publisher.

The Cow.   The Cowry.

The Cowry seems to be, somehow,
A sort of mouth-piece for the Cow:
A speaking likeness one might say,
Which I've endeavored to portray.

46.

*New things are made familiar, and familiar
things are made new.*

Samuel Johnson, *Lives of the Poets* (1780).

*Genius, in truth, means little more than the
faculty of perceiving in an unhabitual way.*

William James, *Principles of Psychology* (New York: Dover,
1950).

*The whole secret lies in arbitrariness. . . . You
go to see the middle of a play, you read the
third part of a book. By this means you insure
yourself a very different kind of enjoyment from
that which the author has been so kind as to
plan for you. You enjoy something entirely
accidental; you consider the whole of
existence from this standpoint. . . .*

Søren Kierkegaard, "The Rotation Method," in *Either/Or*
(Garden City, N.Y.: Doubleday, 1959).

FIGURE 2–14   This inventive confusion of a
building with a horn was developed by **Mark
Hess** for CBS Records to illustrate the jazz
saxophone music of Arthur Blythe. The
illustrator had been told that "Upper Harlem
was a place with which Blythe could be
comfortably associated, so my first job was to
research the types of buildings that are common
to that area. The brownstones and other brick
buildings constructed at the turn of the century
seemed to be perfectly suited to the scale and
weight of a saxophone." It was essential, Hess
recalls, *not* "to make the saxophone
architecturally accurate, but to suggest that it
might be possible. . . . It was important to work
in a primitive or naive style, and not to be photo-
realistic, so that the viewer is allowed to 'believe'
the illusion." Hess is depicting a building *as if* it
were a saxophone and/or he is depicting a
saxophone *as if* it were a building. He is using
the techniques that are described in this book as
elopement and estrangement, or what could as
well be called a *visual metaphor*. The art director
was Gene Greif. Acrylic on canvas. Courtesy the
artist.

FIGURE 2–15 In this pen and ink portrayal of General George Armstrong Custer, the illustrator **R. J. Shay** has stressed the similarity between a button and a skull. By that shift of emphasis, he has constructed a visual metaphor, or pun, between the brass buttons of Custer's cavalry jacket and the skull and crossbones sign, the traditional symbol for death. By this seemingly simple act of *substituting one thing for another* (putting the skulls where the buttons belong), Shay suggests two salient characteristics of this controversial man: his legendary flamboyance (which was expressed by flashy clothes) and his foolhardy defiance of death, which led to the slaughter in 1876 of 200 men at the Battle of Little Bighorn. Shay is both an illustrator and a university professor. Courtesy the artist.

FIGURE 2–16 The ability to pretend is the quintessential trait of the ability to invent. Because inventions are fabrications, we should not be surprised to find that *Wishes, Lies, and Dreams* is the title of a book by the poet Kenneth Koch (New York: Vintage Books, 1971) in which he describes his ways of teaching children to write poetry. As some critics would contend, all poetry is metaphor. And in metaphorical thinking, something is thought of or treated *as if* it were some other kind of thing. We can do this to ourselves, as indeed we always do (to one degree or another) whenever we portray ourselves. This is one of a series of contemporary photographs by **Leslie Bellavance** (who is not a nurse) called *Self-Portraits as a Nurse*, in which she depicts herself within the cloak of a fictional role. Courtesy the artist, 1984.

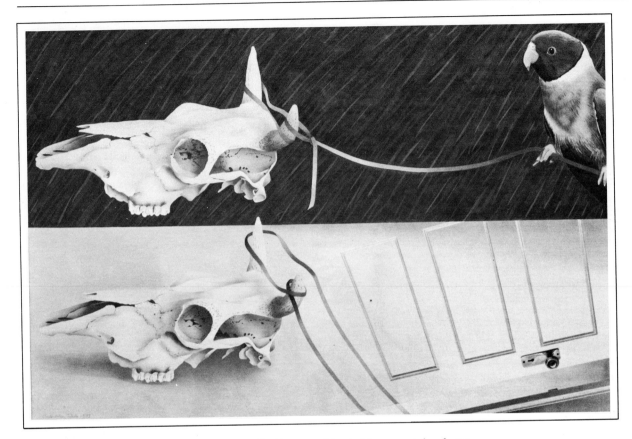

FIGURE 2–17 In an *arranged marriage* (or radical juxtaposition), things must simply get along, whether they are compatible or not. There need not be any good reason for a particular mixture of things. There need not be any resemblance between any of the items; objects may be picked by chance or by whim. The artist is not expected to interpret the work, only to construct it, in somewhat the same sense that dreamers are only required to dream, not to interpret their products. If the combination is sufficiently provocative, viewers will try to interpret the work; they will attempt to decide what it means, albeit in ways that are varied. Thus in this acrylic work by **Christel-Anthony Tucholke** (1983), entitled *Desert Echoes, Double Harmony*, the range of interpretation is purposely extremely wide. A strange wedding has occurred between two skulls, a parrot, and a ribbon that changes its meaning (at one point it seems to be part of a door, at another it looks like a lasso). How shall we react to this? What are *we* to make of it? Works of this kind are disturbing in part because we are asked to resolve them ourselves. Courtesy the artist.

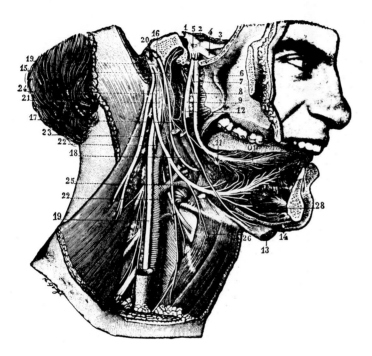

THE NERVOUS SYSTEM.

Pathways of Afferent and Efferent Impulses

FIG. 322.

Tentative identification of current nerve pains causing patient's nervous condition (as of May 3, 1973) 1. C.r.p. root of current trouble. 2. Ganglion of Dean. 3, 4, 5. Branches of Hunt, LaRue and Liddy. 6, 7, 9, 01, 12. Suspected pain center of McGovern, Muskie, Woodward, Bernstein and Mollenhoff. 11. Ganglion of Mitchell. 13. Muscle of Ehrlichman. 14. Muscle of Haldeman. 15. Ziegler nerve. 16. Ganglion of Magruder. 17, 18. Branches of Petersen and Colson. 19, 20, 21. Pneumogastric of Gray. 23. Segretti nerve. 24. Chapin nerve. 25. Collector of Stans. 26. Vesco branch of Mardian. 28. Branches of Krogh and Young.

What is a double petunia? A petunia is a flower like a begonia. A begonia is a meat like a sausage. A sausage-and-battery is a crime. Monkeys crime trees. Tree's a crowd. A crow crowd in the morning and made a noise. A noise is on your face between your eyes. Eyes is the opposite of nays. A colt nays. You go to bed with a colt, and wake up in the morning with a case of double petunia.

Alex Osborn, *Applied Imagination* (New York: Scribner's, 1963).

Then fill up the glasses with treacle and ink, or anything else that is pleasant to drink: Mix sand with the cider and wool with the wine— and welcome Queen Alice with ninety-times-nine.

Lewis Carroll, *Through the Looking-Glass* (1871).

FIGURE 2–18 The infamous Watergate affair during Richard Nixon's presidency began in the summer of 1972, when police arrested five men who were attempting to wiretap the national headquarters of the Democratic party at the Watergate Apartment Complex in Washington, D.C. By May of 1973 (when this derisive work was made), there seemed to be plenty of reasons for the president to be nervous. This is a fictitious chart of President Nixon's "nervous system," including such supposed parts as the "ganglion of Dean" and the "pneumogastric of Gray." This collage by the American artist and educator **Ken Gogel** was originally published in *The North American Review* (Fall 1973). Courtesy the artist and the publisher.

FIGURE 2–19   As evidenced by this painting by the American illustrator **Carol Wald,** *radical juxtaposition* can be an effective way to arrive at a powerful image. When asked to comment on her work (not just this particular piece), the artist said, "I have never tired of the excitement of creating a new image, although I have been creating images incessantly since the age of six. The collage medium offers me the opportunity to arrange and rearrange tones and forms until the most satisfying solution emerges. It sometimes takes days before the image is complete. . . sometimes only hours. . . but when the final juxtaposition of elements is properly balanced in a beautiful environment, I always feel the thrill of accomplishment. After the concept is finally settled in the medium of collage, I may progress to a painting, using the collage study as my solution and inspiration." This particular painting, an oil on canvas entitled *Memory with Architecture,* was interpreted from a collage. It was published in 1982 in a promotional booklet for Jacqueline Dedell, Inc., in New York City. Courtesy the artist.

Categorical Patterns

A parrot is a kind of bird. A carrot is a kind of plant. It is not efficient to think of any particular thing as if it were completely unique. Indeed, perhaps we never do. Rather, we almost always respond to people, objects, and events as if they were members of classes or sets. If we did not respond this way, if birds of a feather did not flock together, if everything were grouped apart, we could not use a coffee cup unless it was specifically a cup that we had used before. We could not start or drive a car unless it was one we had driven before.

The act of grouping is so essential that if we did not categorize in one way or another—if only to separate figure from ground—we would not be able to function at all. "All thinking is sorting," as I. A. Richards once observed, and so is all perceiving.

We tend to see things as a group to the extent that they are similar. We see things as separate to the extent that they are dissimilar. Recall the general rule that hedgehogs live among the thorns because they too are prickly—the rule known as *similarity grouping*. Things also tend to group (regardless of appearance) when they are simply paired in space—the rule known as *proximity grouping*. Later, we shall discuss *contiguity grouping*, the fact that things will tend to group when they recur together in time.

But all of this is more complex than it first appears. For example, it is not strictly true that hedgehogs live among the thorns because they too are prickly. Instead, we might point out that hedgehogs' thorns are spines, *not* thorns; that a hedgehog has as little to do with hedges as it has with hogs. Hedgehogs and hedges are alike only if we stress the fact that both are prickly, or that the lives of both are bound up in English hedgerows.

In order to perceive two things as belonging together, we must stress certain likenesses and ignore certain differences. In order to see them as separate types, we must emphasize their differences and disregard their likenesses. This is an especially critical point because inventions come about (elopements and estrangements, especially) by means of a *shift of emphasis* or a *displacement of attention*. We will pursue that momentarily, but for now, things will group to the extent that they are *perceived* as sharing significant features—"perceived" because, under certain circumstances, virtually any two items can be seen as being alike or distinct (see Figure 2–20).

Things do not *fall* into categories. We *push* them. Members of categories are somewhat like the stars at night. Yes, the stars are in the sky, but they do

Even one of the classical methods of psychoanalysis, free association, can be interpreted as another working-out of the Surrealist principle of radical juxtaposition.
Susan Sontag, *Against Interpretation* (New York: Dell, 1969).

You watch Apollo taking off on a TV in a bar in San Francisco, then go around the corner to have your shoes shined by a topless shoe-shine girl. These kinds of ironical juxtapositions happen in life all the time.
Eduardo Paolozzi, artist, in an interview in *Studio International* (1971).

. . . some people are far more sensitive to resemblances, and far more ready to point out wherein they consist, than others are. They are the wits, the poets, the inventors, the scientific men, the practical geniuses. A native talent for perceiving analogies is reckoned . . . as the leading fact in genius of every order.
William James, *Principles of Psychology*.

The progress of science is the discovery at each step of a new order which gives unity to what had long seemed unlike.
Jacob Bronowski, *Science and Human Values* (London: Hutchinson, 1961).

Metaphoric combination leaps beyond systematic placement, explores connections that before were unsuspected.
Jerome Bruner, *On Knowing*.

Every like is not the same.
William Shakespeare, *Julius Caesar*.

We go through the world . . . discovering differences in the like, and likenesses in the different. . . .

William James, *Principles of Psychology.*

Nature does not create genera and species, she creates individua, and it is our shortsightedness which makes us look for resemblances, so that we should be able to retain in our minds many things at once.

Georg Christoph Lichtenberg.

PLAY Pretending or make-believe behavior that can be pursued with no fear of doing wrong or making a mistake. In playful activity, there is little pressure to behave in ways considered to be correct or true. Instead, a person at play can be absurd, deceitful, inept, irresponsible, and mistaken. A frequent consequence of play (when the harvest has been appraised) is serendipitous invention.

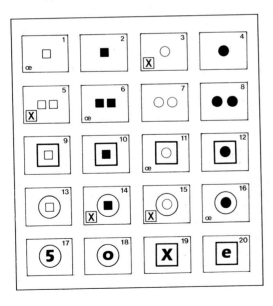

not connect themselves. It is in the act of perceiving that constellations are produced. It is the mind that links the dots, that looks at six adjoining stars and sees them as a larger shape, which in turn connects with a shape beyond the sky (for example, a bear or a dipper).

We can easily perceive a similarity between the words "parrot" and "carrot." If we decide to stress that fact (as Wood did), we may indeed confuse the two. At the same time, there are radical differences between a parrot (the actual bird) and a carrot (the actual plant). If we decide to stress those differences (which Wood ignored), as solemn adults are expected to do, we will not confuse the two. But Wood was not addressing adults. He was talking to children, and the paramount pleasure of being a child is that we are granted the freedom to **play.**

All categories, therefore, are constructions or inventions. They are like constellations. They are patterns that result from the ways in which we see. This includes, as Jerome Bruner and others described in *A Study of Thinking,* "the class of prime numbers, animal species, the huge range of colors dumped into the category *blue,* squares and circles: all these are inventions and not 'discoveries.' They do not 'exist' in the environment." We could have opted for others instead. We could have grouped parrots with carrots. "The objects of the environment," as Bruner observed, "provide the cues or features on which our groupings may be based, but they provide cues that could serve for many groupings other than the ones we make. We select and utilize certain cues rather than others."

FIGURE 2–20 As William James and Lao-tze observed, it is difficult at times to perceive similarity in a field of diversity, or to perceive diversity in a field of similarity. This diagram is meant to show just how difficult it is (as Carolus Linnaeus proposed) "to join the similar to the similar, and to separate the dissimilar from the dissimilar." Which of these are similar and which are dissimilar? To paraphrase a children's show, which of these things belong together? After a moment of study, it should become apparent that there are innumerable answers to that. Under certain circumstances, depending on what we attend to, any and all of these items could be perceived as being alike; or, if we shift our emphasis, any two can be perceived as being distinct. There are no absolute groupings. See *A Study of Thinking* by Jerome Bruner et al. (New York: Wiley, 1956); and *The Nature of Prejudice* by Gordon W. Allport (Garden City, N.Y: Doubleday Anchor Books, 1958).

RIPENESS There are several hundred known cases of *simultaneous inventions* by two or more people who were working independently and were unacquainted with the efforts of the others. Thus there are times when it is highly probable that inventions will occur, a kind of cultural "ripeness" perhaps. Among the most striking examples of this are the discovery of natural selection by both Darwin and Wallace (1858), the invention of photography by Talbot and Daguerre (1839), the invention of the telephone by Bell and Gray (1876), and the invention of the airplane by Dumont and the Wright brothers (1903).

The environment is not a natural thing, it is a set of interrelated percepts, a product of culture. It yields food to the aborigine but none to the white traveller because the former perceives food where the latter sees only inedible insects.

Edmund Leach, "Culture and Social Cohesion," in Gerald Holton, ed., *Science and Culture* (Boston: Beacon Press, 1967).

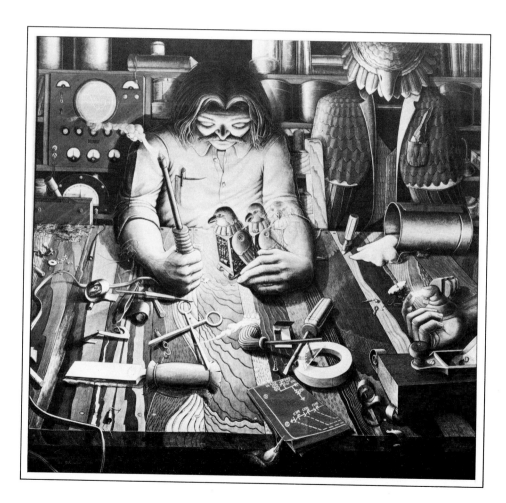

FIGURE 2–21   Moments of insight in science and art, according to Jacob Bronowski (in *Science and Human Values*), "are explorations—more, are explosions, of a hidden likeness." This painting by **Paul Pratchenko** is entitled *Inventor at the Moment of Invention* and was completed in 1976. It refers, in the artist's words, "to a two-year period when I was employed as mold maker and micro-parts fabricator for an inventor working on roto-craft. The 'spark of invention' appears in the hand at the right of the painting. It was our goal to create a flying machine as efficient as a bird. . ." Pratchenko has discussed his work in "Painting and Drawing as Manifestations of Visual Perception" in *Leonardo* 16 (4)(1983): 273–79. Acrylic on canvas, 137 × 130 cm. Collection of Ulrich Schreier, Inc., San Francisco. Courtesy the artist.

CONVERGENT AND DIVERGENT THINKING   Terms employed by J. P. Guilford to indicate the two opposite processes by which productive ideas result. In convergent strategies, a specified problem is expediently pursued with little if any distraction. In divergent thinking, the process is purposely fluent but lax, in the hope that a wealth of ideas will result. Each of us tends to prefer one strategy or the other, but we should try to be masters of both, since different problems call for different approaches. The prototypical divergent thinker is Rube Goldberg, who devised absurd cartoons in which, for example, a man pulls his own tooth in the following way: He ties himself to a chair, then wiggles his foot, which tickles a duck. The giggling duck shakes an alcoholic drink tied to its back, then falls forward, spilling the cocktail on a squirrel in a revolving circular cage. The cocktail makes the squirrel drunk, which turns the cage, which turns the crank on a record player, which then plays a record. The music enrages a dwarf, who gets hot under the collar. Flames from the dwarf's collar ignite a fuse, which causes a cannon to fire. The cannonball is attached to a string, and the string is attached to the man's tooth. At last, the man extracts his tooth. See also *bricolage.*

BRICOLAGE   The term was initially introduced by the French anthropologist Claude Lévi-Strauss (*The Savage Mind,* 1966). The *bricoleur* (a cobbler or handyman) works without the proper tools and employs improper procedures. The result is *bricolage,* a structure contrived out of reassembled detritus and "whatever is at hand." It often produces unusual results. It employs no given technique and is the antithesis of something engineered.

FIGURE 2–22   It is not easy to invent. We are most often rewarded for thinking in *convergent* ways, and we are frequently punished for acting in ways that are especially *divergent* or odd. All inventive behavior is more or less divergent, but divergent acts are not always inventive. In Greek mythology, invention is personified by the sculptor and architect Daedalus, who escaped from the wrath of King Minos by making wings from feathers and wax for his son Icarus and himself. Despite a warning, Icarus flew too close to the sun, the wax melted, and he plummeted to his death. **Albrecht Dürer** recounted that tale in this woodcut version of "The Fall of Icarus" in 1493. Reproduced from *The Complete Woodcuts of Albrecht Dürer,* edited by Willi Kurth (New York: Dover Publications, 1963) from the Dover Pictorial Archives.

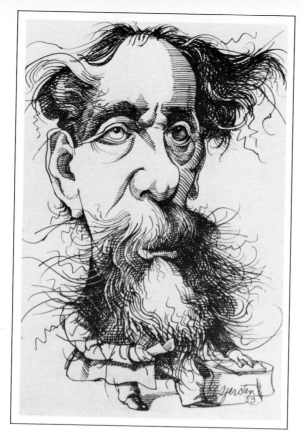

FREE ASSOCIATION   A psychoanalytic ploy in which the patient is impelled to spurt out whatever comes to mind. The tactic is analogous to *brainstorming, play,* and *divergent thinking* in that the only immediate goal is a flood of uncensored ideas. These odds and ends are then sifted for clues about the patient's drives.

FIGURE 2–23   One of the most common examples of intentional distortion by inclusion and omission is the practice of caricature. A caricature might best be termed a "charged" or "loaded" portrait (from the Italian *caricare*, meaning "to load"). A good caricature selects and exaggerates as few features as possible to capture "the essence" of someone, whether flattering or insulting, from the artist's point of view. Part of caricature's charm is due to the economy with which it convincingly represents complex persons. **Gerry Gersten,** a prominent contemporary caricaturist, prefers to work in pen and ink. This is his portrait of the author Charles Dickens, commissioned by the Quality Paperback Book Club. Courtesy the artist.

FIGURE 2–24   Invention is often referred to as *metaphorical thinking.* A metaphor is an intentional deviation. It is a violation of a standard category or definition. Since different cultures classify in different ways, and since these systems change in time, what is metaphorical in one time and place may be regarded as literal fact in another. In Western culture, we often make rigid distinctions between the categories of "human" and "animal." However, as Edmund Leach has shown (in *Culture and Communication*), whenever a boundary is firmly defined, the nature of trespass is also defined, so that, throughout all cultures, boundaries are sources of conflict and stress. This concept is confirmed by the prevalence of hybrid humanoid animal shapes as personifications of humor and horror. Offhand it is easy to think of Dr. Jekyl and Mr. Hyde, Mickey Mouse, Batman, the Green Hornet, King Kong, Kafka's *Metamorphosis*, Tarzan, vampires, werewolves, and so on. That is the kind of invention that **James Buckels** used in this illustration for "Pinter's Main Course" by Andrew Clark, a satirical comment on the plays of Harold Pinter, originally published in *The North American Review* (Spring 1976). A line in Clark's burlesque no doubt inspired this drawing. He begins by describing Lucilla as a woman who is dressed in a "tight, short, black leather skirt, black fishnet stockings, and black, very high-heeled shoes." The key observation is that she sits down opposite Jake (the male character) on the settee, "exposing a considerable expanse of thigh." Under Buckel's pen, the exposed thigh has become the thigh of a chicken. Reproduced courtesy the artist and the publisher.

EMPATHY The capacity to feel as if we are in the place of someone or something other than ourselves. When artworks invoke closure, a sense of empathy results from the viewer's participation in the completion of the work.

The universe would appear to be something like a cheese; it can be sliced in an infinite number of ways—and when one has chosen his own pattern of slicing, he finds that other men's cuts fall at the wrong places.

Kenneth Burke, *Permanence and Change* (Indianapolis, Ind.: Bobbs-Merrill, 1965).

The whole drift of my education goes to persuade me that the world of our present consciousness is only one out of many worlds of consciousness that exist.

William James, *Varieties of Religious Experience* (New York: Collier, 1961).

FIGURE 2–25 A subtle confusion exists between the categories of human and animal in this story illustration, a link that is not at all funny. The woman in the foreground seems to feel **empathy** in response to the chicken's confinement. The cage is drawn in such a way that we are left to wonder whether she or the bird is caged. But the most conspicuous link is the mimicry between the gesture of the woman's hand and the foot of the bird as it clutches the line. The cage is a convenient way to cloak an underlying grid. Broken continuity lines are employed throughout the work, as the diagram makes clear, but the strongest occurs in the center. It is an implied vertical that acts as the right edge of the cage door, disappears momentarily, then reappears at the bottom, where it becomes the chicken's leg and then (slightly shifted) the edge of the woman's left arm. This painting by **Mark English** was originally published in *Redbook*. Courtesy the artist.

FIGURE 2–26 Do we become what we behold? Do we unknowingly adopt the characteristics of our own contraptions? Have we grown to deal with life as if it were a TV show? Or, do we regard TV as if it were the core of life? Those may be some of the questions we face when we are confronted by this bizarre carved wood sculpture by **Tom Uebelherr** entitled *The Station Break.* The customary boundary between a person (the seated man) and an inanimate object (the television set) is disturbingly obscured by the anthropomorphic features of the television and the robotomorphic characteristics of the man. Courtesy the artist, 1984.

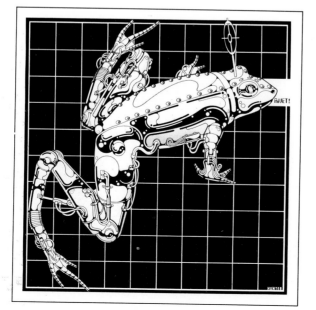

FIGURE 2–27 Despite our dependence on gadgets, we are quick to insist on a boundary between the categories of the "living" and the "mechanical." Accordingly, an invention may result when a living thing is seen as if it were mechanical, or conversely, when a mechanical form is perceived as if it were a living thing. This drawing of a robot frog was produced by **Stephen Hunter** in 1977 to illustrate an extract from Mark Twain: "I don't see no p'ints about that frog that's any better'n any other frog." The work was drawn with pen and ink and shaded with adhesive screens. Courtesy the artist.

FIGURE 2–28 In a nontechnical way, a *genus* is a general group, while a *species* is a specific group. Milwaukee is a species of the genus Wisconsin, while Wisconsin is a species of the genus U.S.A. Of course the terms are relative to the "level of magnification." In this kind of categorization, treelike shapes are convenient to use because distinctions can be made within two main dimensions, horizontal (the spread of the branches) and vertical (the upward growth). This is a familiar example of that. It is the genealogical tree, the tree of evolution, from **Ernst Haeckel's** famous book, *The Evolution of Man* (1874).

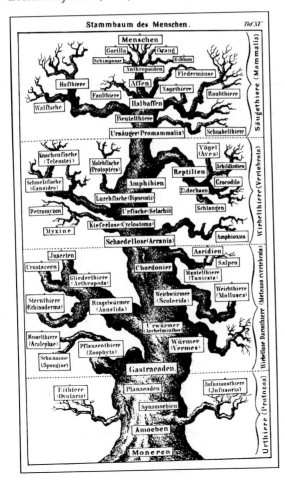

Species and Genera

When we make categories, whatever features we stress and whatever aspects we ignore, in general we incline to group within two dimensions, horizontal and vertical—that is, across and up-and-down.

In binomial grouping schemes, we designate general groups by the term *genera*, while specific groups are referred to as a *species*. The taxonomic name for a human being is *Homo sapiens,* in which the genus, or general group, is *Homo* (Latin for "human"), while the species, or particular group, is *sapiens* (Latin for "wise"). In the same sense, the taxonomic label for the Turquoise-Fronted parrot from South America is *Amazona aestiva.*

Less rigorously, I use a binomial grouping scheme when I designate my home as the species *Milwaukee* in the genus *Wisconsin,* or (by turning the knob on the focus control) when I designate my home as the species *Wisconsin* in the genus *U.S.A.* Even when I write my name (generally *Hancock,* specifically *John*), I am essentially trying to show where I can be found within the system of assigning names to indicate relationships (somewhat like the maps in malls that tell the shoppers "you are here"). Thus, if a carrot signed its name, it might put down the Latin term *Daucus carota sativa.* The third term is its middle name, which is the *subspecies* to which it belongs.

A grouping scheme is often referred to as a kind of tree. Thus we often hear about the tree of knowledge, the tree of evolution, and, of course, each person's family tree (see Figure 2–28). In the model of a tree (unlike the models of ladders or chains), there is an equal emphasis on both dimensions of the scheme, since trees spread out sideways and up-and-down.

Parts of the body, constituents of the cosmos, military organizations, academic institutions, and almost all public and private concerns are systems that can be perceived as vertical layers of lateral groups. Indeed, the same is true of books, which are the modulation of a chain of increasingly generalized parts, from words to phrases to clauses to sentences to paragraphs to sections to chapters, and so on.

In treelike systems (or more accurately, systems perceived to be treelike), each whole is comprised of a cluster of parts, while parts are also wholes themselves. Pausing at any one vertical tier, we find that every species is a part of the genus from which it derives, while it, in turn, is the genus for the species that derives from it. I am the son of my father, but I am father to my son.

There is no absolute linkage of things. To this degree or that extent, our groupings are constantly changing. "We are," in the words of Morse Peckham, "forever engaged in constructing around us an architecture of categories as fluid and yielding to our interests as the air. There is nothing that man has not sacrificed, including millions of his fellow human beings, in the vain effort to fix that architecture, to stabilize his categories."

METAPHOR Narrowly defined, a verbal expression that speaks of a thing *as if* it were the same as some other thing that it is customarily different from. Broadly defined, any action is metaphorical when it treats a thing as if it were some other thing. Metaphors are not mistakes, since they are intentional trespasses.

FIGURE 2–29 Two years before Ernst Haeckel's book, this German satirical drawing was distributed in Berlin. It was intended to make fun of Charles Darwin's theory of evolution as set out in *The Descent of Man,* published the year before. If humans could evolve from apes, would it not make sense to say that the parlor piano descended from the lion? Ironically, there is a touch of literal truth in this pretended confusion of remotely different species, because the legs of Victorian furniture were often designed to resemble the legs and feet of lions and other animals.

Metaphor joins dissimilar experiences by finding the image or symbol that unites them at some deeper emotional level of meaning.

Jerome Bruner, *On Knowing.*

FIGURE 2–30   The greatest thing by far, said Aristotle, is to be a master of **metaphor.** It is a sign of genius, "since a good metaphor implies an intuitive perception of the similarity in dissimilars." In *The Poetics* he defines what a metaphor is in relation to genus and species. A metaphor consists, he says, "in giving the thing a name that belongs to something else." Here the term is used in a loose and general sense to refer to an action—any action (not just the act of naming things)—in which a thing is treated as if it were some other thing. It is a type of planned confusion. And how might that confusion occur? In Aristotle's words, it is most likely to occur "either from genus to species, or from species to genus, or from species to species, or on ground of analogy." In this superbly composed piece by **Dean Bressler,** a visual metaphor is implied (there is an intended confusion) between two different genera, "living" and "mechanical." The intuitive link between the two, the bond between the disparates, is that both can cut the grass. This work was developed as a cover illustration for the *Indiana Review* in 1984. The medium is pen and ink in combination with collage. Courtesy the artist.

FIGURE 2–31   In this visual metaphor, there is no confusion between two genera in the sense that boys and birds can both be classed as "living" things. Instead, the pretended mistake is produced by a gradual blending of species, in which "boy" and "bird" converge. Artist unknown (nineteenth century).

FIGURE 2–32 *Figurative* phrases and *literal* phrases are kinds, or species, of statements. An invention may result if those species are confused. Thus, in this illustration, a cliché analogy ("the cat's eyes were bigger than saucers") is purposely misunderstood, as if it were a literal phrase, and thus taken to extremes. Artist unknown (nineteenth century).

The Factor of Attention

The key to inventing resides in the fact that (in the words of Alan Watts) "we think by ignoring"—that is, we attend to certain features of our surroundings (those that "make a difference") while we blindly disregard features that might have been equally stressed.

Attention is the main concern of pickpocket teams. When someone steals a wallet, the victim is distracted by a coinciding disturbance created by a decoy thief. It is the prime component in the tack of "misdirection," which is frequently employed by sleight-of-hand magicians. It is the essence of Sherlock Holmes, who discloses in one of his stories that the substance of his means is "the observation of trifles," which is to say that he attends to features that others are prone to ignore.

Some of the most vivid examples of attentive behavior occur in a field as supposedly unlike art as comparative ethology, a branch of modern biology that studies how humans and animals act. The founder of ethology was Konrad Lorenz, who was especially known for his studies of the greylag goose. In 1973, Lorenz shared the Nobel Prize with Karl von Frisch, who cracked the code of the honeybees' dance, and Niko Tinbergen, the versatile Dutch zoologist who tested a curious freshwater fish, the three-spined stickleback.

Tinbergen studied the stickleback male, which mates with several females and which is in charge of hatching the eggs and guarding the young. Among its other characteristics, when the male is ripe to mate, its underbelly turns bright red. In this prenuptial costume, the fish is hypersensitive to the territorial in-

ATTENTION Often called *selective attention.* A filtering or screening that enables us, at any one time, to focus on specific portions of our environment and to delay or neglect the remainder. In one experiment, for example, people were instructed to watch a videotape of a basketball game. Those who were assigned the task of observing all the fouls rarely were aware of a woman who walked past the court, carrying a multicolored umbrella. We are especially attentive to change (to differences that make a difference), but we are also predisposed by past experience, physiological factors, and the nature of the thing perceived.

We think by ignoring—or by attending to one term of a relationship (the figure) and neglecting the other (the ground).

Alan Watts, *The Two Hands of God* (New York: Collier, 1969).

In one of Sherlock Holmes' cases there was a large dog. Dr. Watson dismissed the dog as being of no importance because it had done nothing on the night of the crime. Sherlock Holmes pointed out the great significance of the dog was precisely that it had done nothing. He shifted attention from the significance of what the dog might have done to the significance of the fact that it had done nothing. This meant that the criminal must have been known to the dog.

Edward de Bono, *Lateral Thinking* (New York: Harper & Row, Pub., 1970).

. . . an animal does not react to all the changes in the environment which its sense organs receive, but only to a small part of them.

Niko Tinbergen, *The Study of Instinct* (New York: Oxford, 1951).

Needs make for perceptual selection. . . . Uninteresting things cast their images on the retina, but as a rule are not perceived.

Rudolf Arnheim, "Gestalt Psychology and Artistic Form," in L. L. Whyte, ed., *Aspects of Form* (Bloomington: Indiana University Press, 1951).

The occurrence of such "errors" or "mistakes" is one of the most conspicuous characteristics of innate behavior. It is caused by the fact that an animal responds "blindly" to only part of the total environmental situation and neglects other parts, although its sense organs are perfectly able to receive them. . . .

Niko Tinbergen, *The Study of Instinct* (New York: Oxford, 1951).

vasions of competing sticklebacks. It will pugnaciously attack any other mating male that comes too close to where it nests.

The problem that Tinbergen posed might be simply phrased like this: Which features of invading males allow a nesting stickleback to know which targets to attack? To ask that question of the fish, Tinbergen constructed a series of dummies that were like sticklebacks in some ways while remarkably different in others.

Some of the models were fairly "realistic" representations of fish, except that they left out one trait—they did not have red stomachs. At the same time, Tinbergen developed other shapes that were emphatically distorted. These shapes looked like pizzas (or green beans or midget eels) more than they looked like stickleback fish—for example, they had no fins and gills. Yet each of them had a bright red underside. When these two types of dummies (those with red markings and those without) were placed in front of the actual fish, the male sticklebacks were "fooled" by the distorted models and they attacked them as if they were invading males, while they ignored those that were "realistic" but lacked the red beneath.

The predilection of the fish to challenge anything that had a red stomach was so overwhelming that when an aquarium in which they were housed was placed beside a window, they even reacted to a red British mailtruck when it drove by as if it were a stickleback. As if by some genetic pun, they mistook the *mail* for *male*, in much the way that Wood confused (by purposely stressing a feature which others are highly unlikely to stress) a parrot with a carrot, a pansy with a chimpanzee, or a cowry with a cow.

The features that we focus on are in part determined by the conspicuousness and novelty of things within our visual field. We are also guided by specific goals or urgent needs, such as the need for companionship or food. The sticklebacks focused on red markings because their physiological state (that is, their readiness to mate) caused them to be open to certain visual traits and to be oblivious to a host of others—for example, fins and gills.

Tinbergen's dummies show that fish will respond to distorted models as if they were "the thing itself." That may come as some surprise if you are inclined to think that representations that deceive the eye are simplistically similar to the objects they represent. Indeed, even Leonardo said that "that painting is most praiseworthy which is most like the thing represented."

It is puzzling, then, that sticklebacks would not respond to models that had fins and gills and yet be taken in by the most absurd cartoons, as long as they had red beneath. How could they be deceived by such distorted, "unreal" models?

Sir E. H. Gombrich has observed, referring to Tinbergen's dummies, that "the scientist's laboratory has turned into the artist's workshop." Gombrich did not mean to say that ethology is art. But he did intend to stress that a kinship might be drawn between the models that artists construct and those that scientists invent.

Artists are makers of models, whether those models are "pictures" or not. Like Tinbergen's stickleback dummies, the representations that artists contrive may incorporate some of the features of the things that they depict, but they *always* leave out other features. Judging from Tinbergen's dummies, we might now begin to ask if the works that feel so "real" to us are always the ones that are "most like" the feeling, thought, or thing conveyed.

It is not just that good works of art possess properties worth attending to; the attending itself must be worthwhile. Great works of art are so rich and complex that they lend themselves to unending discussion and analysis.

Marcia Eaton, *Art and Nonart* (East Brunswick, N.J.: Associated University Presses, 1983).

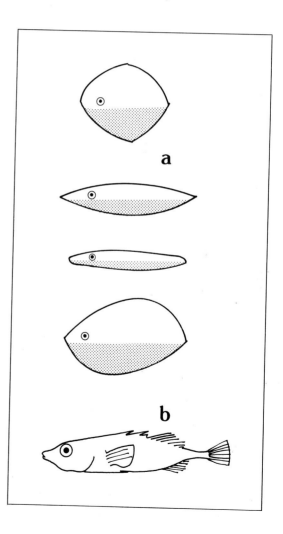

FIGURE 2–33 These drawings are similar to the two types of stickleback dummies devised by the Dutch ethologist Niko Tinbergen to identify the attributes that enable a male stickleback to recognize another male. To the scientist's surprise, the fish responded most actively to simple, abstract nonfish shapes (as shown in *a*), each of which had red beneath. They were not misled by conventional looking fishlike shapes (*b*) that were not marked with red. This and similar tests with animals, insects, and humans confirm the assumption that no organism can ever attend to all of the things that take place within its field of vision. Whenever we perceive the world, we pay attention to some features and ignore others. Further, when we record what we have seen (as artists, scientists, or historians), the best we can do is to make a symbol (a painting, a theory, a statement of fact) that incorporates some of the features we have seen and omits others. Tinbergen's work is more fully described and illustrated in *The Study of Instinct* (New York: Oxford University Press, 1951).

FIGURE 2–34 Each and every time we see, we attend to certain features of our environment, while we disregard the rest (such as the ticking of the clock and other so-called "background noise"). This factor has an enormous effect on how we represent the world, since we are likely to omit the traits that we did not perceive and to overemphasize the features that we focused on. This process can be eavesdropped on in this series of successive copies by twelve different people. Each drawing (labeled *a* through *l*) was made by a person who was asked to reproduce the preceding drawing as accurately as possible. The participants were allowed to look at the preceding drawing while they copied it. In other words, drawing *b* is a replica of *a*, while *c* is a copy of *b*, and so on. None of the participants was aware of the purpose of the experiment. No one saw any drawing other than the one he or she was asked to copy. The original drawing is shown on the left. Its major features have been numbered so that they can be followed through the series. As we might anticipate, some features are omitted in the copies. Most shapes are simplified or particularized, and errors are often emphasized and strengthened and become permanent parts of the work. Thus, in stages *c*, *h*, and *j*, three drawing errors (*8*, *9*, and *10*) become major aspects of later copies of the work.

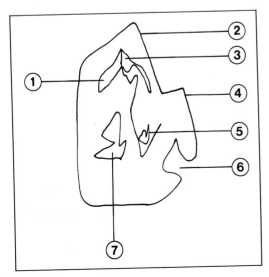

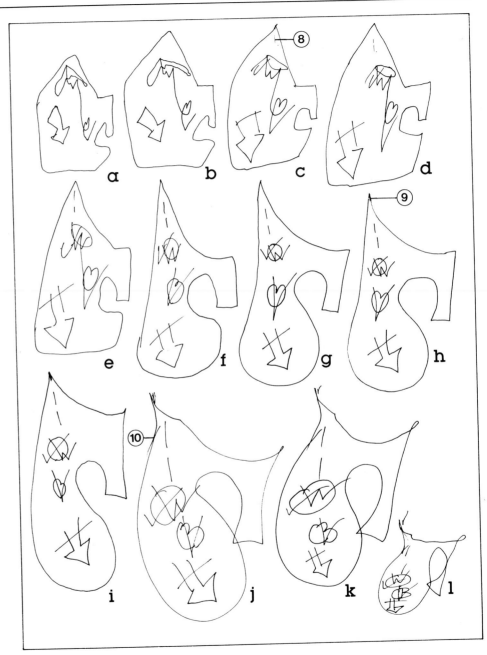

FIGURE 2–35 In *The Evolution of Designs* (Cambridge, Eng.: Cambridge University Press, 1979), Philip Steadman talks about the fact that whenever successive copies are made, a surprising amount of distortion occurs, even when these experiments are done "with fairly skilled copyists instructed to make as exact reproductions as they are capable of . . . ." What may be occurring, as Steadman suggests, is that mistakes and accidents "are being picked on and developed, perhaps subconsciously, or expanded into new features, while others are being omitted." This curious procedure of inadvertent invention, which some contend is analogous to *natural selection*, was discussed and illustrated in 1875 in a paper by John Evans, entitled "On the Coinage of the Ancient Britons and Natural Selection" (*Proceedings of the Royal Institution*, volume 7, pp. 476–87), in which he included a sequence of twenty-nine stages in the evolution of copies of a coin design. Shown here are the first four stages (heads above, tails below), beginning on the left with the Greek original and moving toward the right as copies were made of the copies.

FIGURE 2–36 In this chronological sequence of seven steps, we can observe the changes that were deliberately introduced in the evolution of a trademark from 1898 to 1973. Courtesy of PepsiCo, Inc., owner of the registered trademarks "Pepsi" and "Pepsi-Cola."

. . . *my influences in illustration come more from the great masters (and a few obscure masters) than from other illustrators, with the notable exception of N. C. Wyeth.*

Gary Kelley, illustrator, to the author, 1984.

I try to maintain a sense of mystery in much of my work. I want to provide enough seduction and enough clues for someone to want to spend the time looking for them, but no solutions. I prefer to raise questions or to provoke them, not to answer them. I have no answers.

Martin Krohne, designer, to the author, 1983.

Or in the night, imagining some fear,
How easy is a bush supposed a bear!

William Shakespeare, *A Midsummer Night's Dream.*

FIGURE 2–37 One of the most reliable ways to see things in an original way (to cause them to "evolve" into something else) is to turn them upside down. It was by this simple device that the sewing machine was invented. The needle was placed upside down, and the eye was displaced to the pointed end. These are two reproductions of the same drawing, derived from a comic strip by **Gustave Verbeek,** *circa* 1905. Viewed from one orientation (left), it is a drawing of an owl, but when viewed the other way, it is a drawing of two men sleeping under a haystack.

Do you see yonder cloud that's almost in shape of a camel?

William Shakespeare, *Hamlet.*

FIGURE 2–38 Two pictures are within one space in this nineteenth-century American version of an antique image from India. From a distance, it is a conventional rendition of an elephant, but when viewed more closely, it is comprised of human shapes. It plays on one of the oldest methods of visual invention, the construction of a shape from parts that one would not expect.

FIGURE 2–39 Double images were a popular advertising gimmick in the nineteenth century, just as they are in our own time. These are the puzzling profiles of two merchants, the shoe salesman on the right and the hatter on the left. Reproduced from Clarence P. Hornung, *Handbook of Early Advertising Art: Pictorial Volume* (New York: Dover Publications, 1956) from the Dover Pictorial Archives.

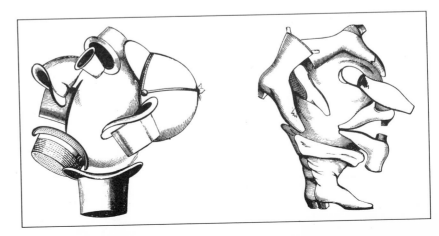

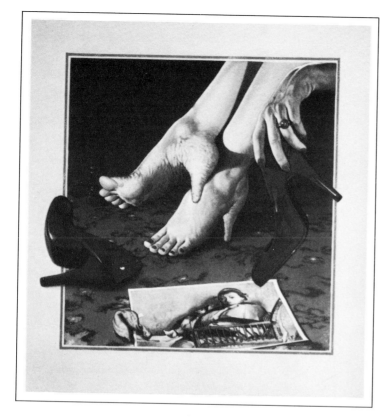

FIGURE 2–40 This is an illustration for a book with the curious title, *A Visit from the Footbinder,* published in 1982. Until the beginning of this century, it was a custom in China to bind the feet of upper-class women, starting at an early age, so that their feet were abnormally shaped, with the toes pressed toward the heels. It was believed at that time that this increased the sexual attractiveness of a woman, but at the cost of crippling her. In the lower center of this acrylic painting by **Frank K. Morris,** there is a copy of an antique photograph of a Chinese woman with one of her bound feet unwrapped. To the left of the photograph, the artist has inserted a Chinese fortune cookie; the surprising resemblance between the cookie and the foot in the photograph is jolting and somewhat repulsive. But no doubt the paramount pun in this work is the disturbing confusion between the Chinese practice of footbinding (crippling a woman by binding her feet) and the modern method of footbinding (crippling a woman by teaching her to wear high heels). Courtesy the artist.

Next, when you are describing
A shape, or sound, or tint;
Don't state the matter plainly,
But put it in a hint;
And learn to look at things
With a sort of mental squint.

Lewis Carroll, "Poeta Fit, Non Nascitur."

The artist's aim is to turn his audience into accomplices.

Arthur Koestler, *The Act of Creation.*

A good drawing involves the decision to leave things out, finding out what is essential and putting that in.

Robert Weaver, illustrator, in an inverview in *Print* (1978).

FIGURE 2–41 "The Loved One," a short story by Adrienne Wolfert, told of the innermost feelings and thoughts of a desperate foster child who wanted to remain with (to become a loved one with) the old farm couple to whom she had been assigned. The story was first published in *The North American Review* (June 1984), with this illustration by student artist **David Lenz.** In his charcoal rendering, the artist has elected not to portray the central people in the work (the figures) but to shift attention to the peripheral tokens of permanent homes (the background or surroundings). Courtesy the artist and the publisher.

FIGURE 2–42 Idi Amin, the deposed president of Uganda, had a knack for murdering his countrymen, while Henry VIII, king of England in the sixteenth century, had a gift for killing his wives. Both were as tyrannical as they were rotund in shape. When Amin was still in power (he fled the country during a coup in 1979), the illustrator **Gary Kelley** developed this portrait of the Magne Pater (approximate Latin for "Big Daddy") as one interpretation of a phrase from the writings of Mark Twain: "All kings is mostly rapscallions." Kelley's painting is a *parody*, or takeoff, of the portraits of Henry VIII by his magnificent court painter, Hans Holbein the Younger. This work was accomplished with acrylic, colored inks, ball-point pen, and tissue paper collage. Courtesy the artist.

FIGURE 2–43 Like the earlier portrait of Idi Amin, this illustration by **Marvin Mattelson** is also purposely derived from the sixteenth-century portraits of Henry VIII by Holbein. It is in addition a clear use of the technique of radical juxtaposition. Why is the king of England eating with foreign utensils? The chopsticks are perfectly appropriate in this case, since the artwork was commissioned to support an article entitled "Confronting Cultural Stereotypes" in *Psychology Today*. The work is acrylic on canvas. Courtesy the artist.

FIGURE 2–44   Underlying visual rhymes are rampant and yet rather subtle in this work by **Norman Walker,** rendered with ink and gouache on board. The painting was commissioned by Polygram Records for an album called *Fear of the Unknown.* Regarding this work, the artist recalled, "I worked directly with the musicians and attended many of the recording sessions in New York. This gave me a better insight as to the mood and feeling the musicians wanted to convey on the cover. The music had a very surreal quality, much like a Magritte painting. That feeling I tried to capture in the painting." Notice the recurrence of square and rectangular shapes in the window, the frame, and the molding. The wallpaper echoes the floorboards, and the muscular stance of the man on the wall is mimicked by the fireplace. Courtesy the artist.

Boredom is a major opponent for the illustrator, since most of the time all we are doing is drawing other people's pictures.

Anne Yvonne Gilbert, British illustrator, to the author, 1983.

I don't mind working with a certain amount of restrictions, as long as they're intelligent and reasonable. A well-art-directed project is just as enjoyable as a non-art-directed one.

Gary Kelley, illustrator, to the author, 1984.

Our problem with advertising is that we're given a concept that has already been established, and we've little chance to add our thoughts because the client has already seen what the Art Director has done. . . . For us, advertising means rendering an Art Director's ideas. What the agency buys is only a style, and I prefer to tack my thinking to an assignment.

Seymour Chwast, illustrator, in an interview in *U&lc* (September 1981).

. . . it's becoming more difficult for me to work with clients who have a too-clear idea of the aesthetic solution. Frequently clients want performance based on previous solutions; my own tendency is to become less receptive to repeating what I've already done.

Milton Glaser, *Graphic Design* (Woodstock, N.Y.: Overlook Press, 1981).

Chapter 3

Illustration as Representation

Fooling the Eye

In his essays, "On the Wonders of Painting," a seventeenth-century painter named Pierre Lebrun called attention to a certain kind of artist who, when he tries to draw an ass, ends up with a picture of a horse. To make up for his lack of skill, he writes beneath the picture, in large letters, GENTLEMEN, THIS IS AN ASS. And yet, the snide Lebrun laments, even then he lies to us, for really he shows us two asses. The ass he drew is one, but the artist who drew it is the other.

Lebrun required of excellent art that "the eye must be deceived, or the picture is worth nothing." Thus, the most accomplished art deserves the tag *res ipsa*, which is Latin for "it's the real thing" or "this object is *the thing itself*, not a representation." In Lebrun's time (and even today), many people believed (as Leonardo had advised) that the best artworks are the most similar to the things they are models of.

And what is the test of a good likeness? Lebrun implies that one can apply methods that are parallel to Tinbergen's for fooling fish. The artist merely

The artist notoriously selects his items, rejecting all tones, colors, shapes, which do not harmonize with each other and with the main purpose of his work. . . . Any natural subject will do, if the artist has wit enough to pounce upon some one feature of it as characteristic, and suppress all merely accidental items which do not harmonize with this.

William James, *Principles of Psychology* (New York: Dover Publications, 1950).

82

exhibits the work and if (for only a moment) the viewer errs in thinking that the work of art is actually the thing portrayed, then the artist has done what an artist should do. The practice of attempting this, at least within a certain range, is formally known as ***trompe l'oeil,*** which is French for "fool the eye."

One wonders what Lebrun would say if he were alive today, since in their field experiments ethologists have reached what Lebrun recommended as the highest goal of art. If Tinbergen's fish could speak, perhaps they would also say (judging from how they reacted), "It's the real thing," or "This object is the thing itself, not a representation." And yet Lebrun would be surprised to find sticklebacks deceived by models so vastly different from the things they are models of.

As it is, Lebrun's paintings are of interest mostly to historians. His essays, however, should be studied by illustrators because they record certain misguided ideas that he assumed to be common sense and that he had inherited from writers long before his time. Indeed, there is a long tradition (one that goes back to ancient Greece and still survives today) of fascinating anecdotes of feats of *trompe l'oeil,* of moments when people responded to works of art as if the works themselves were the things portrayed (see Figures 3–1, 3–2, and 3–3).

TROMPE L'OEIL   French phrase meaning "fool the eye." The term refers to works of art or nonart that prompt the viewer to respond (if only for a moment) as if the representation were the thing it represents. Pronounced "tromploy."

This selective factor manifests itself in pictorial representation. It determines subject-matter and form. It tells what the artist—or his patron—considers important or safe.

Rudolf Arnheim, "Gestalt Psychology and Artistic Form," in L. L. Whyte, ed., *Aspects of Form* (Bloomington: Indiana University Press, 1951).

FIGURE 3–1   Gentlemen, this is an ass. Or is it two asses? It is the work of **Gustave Doré,** the nineteenth-century French illustrator, who was in his twenties when he decided to embark on the monumental task of illustrating the great classics of literature, including both testaments of the Bible, Milton's *Paradise Lost,* Dante's *Divine Comedy,* the *Fairy Tales* of Perrault, Coleridge's *The Rime of the Ancient Mariner,* and more than a hundred other books. At first Doré developed all the wood engravings himself, but eventually he produced only the drawings, which were then translated into wood by a skilled and loyal engraver, often Helidore Pisan. Thus, in this portrait of Sancho Panza from *Don Quixote* (1863), there are two signatures on the plate, those of Pisan and Doré. Reproduced from *Doré's Illustrations for Don Quixote* (New York: Dover Publications, 1982), from the Dover Pictorial Archives.

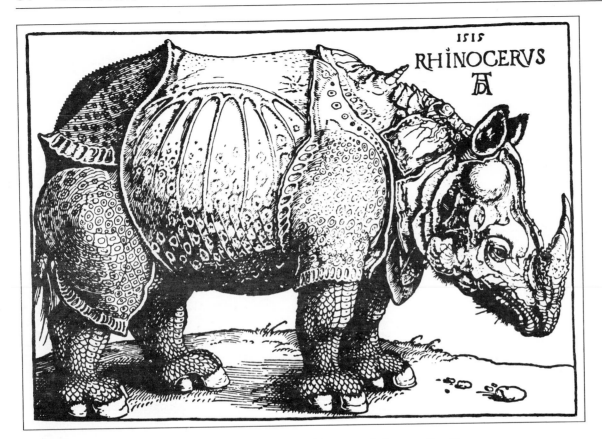

FIGURE 3–2   This is **Albrecht Dürer's** woodcut of a rhinoceros. It is a peculiar if beautiful beast, since it appears to be a rhino disguised as a dragon, with its magnificent excess of armor and a unicorn's spiraling horn on the top. Perhaps it proves, as Heinrich Wölfflin said, that art owes more to other art than it does to things out there; or, in E. H. Gombrich's words, "The familiar will always remain the likely starting point for the rendering of the unfamiliar. . . ." Dürer was familiar with unicorns and dragons (at least with representations of them), and he tried to render something he had not seen, based on a sketch and a written report. In spite of its fanciful details (or perhaps because of them), the print has such a factual air that it served as the model for all scientific depictions of rhinoceroses until the nineteenth century, long after most Europeans had become familiar with the real thing. Reproduced from *The Complete Woodcuts of Albrecht Dürer,* edited by Willi Kurth (New York: Dover Publications, 1963) from the Dover Pictorial Archives.

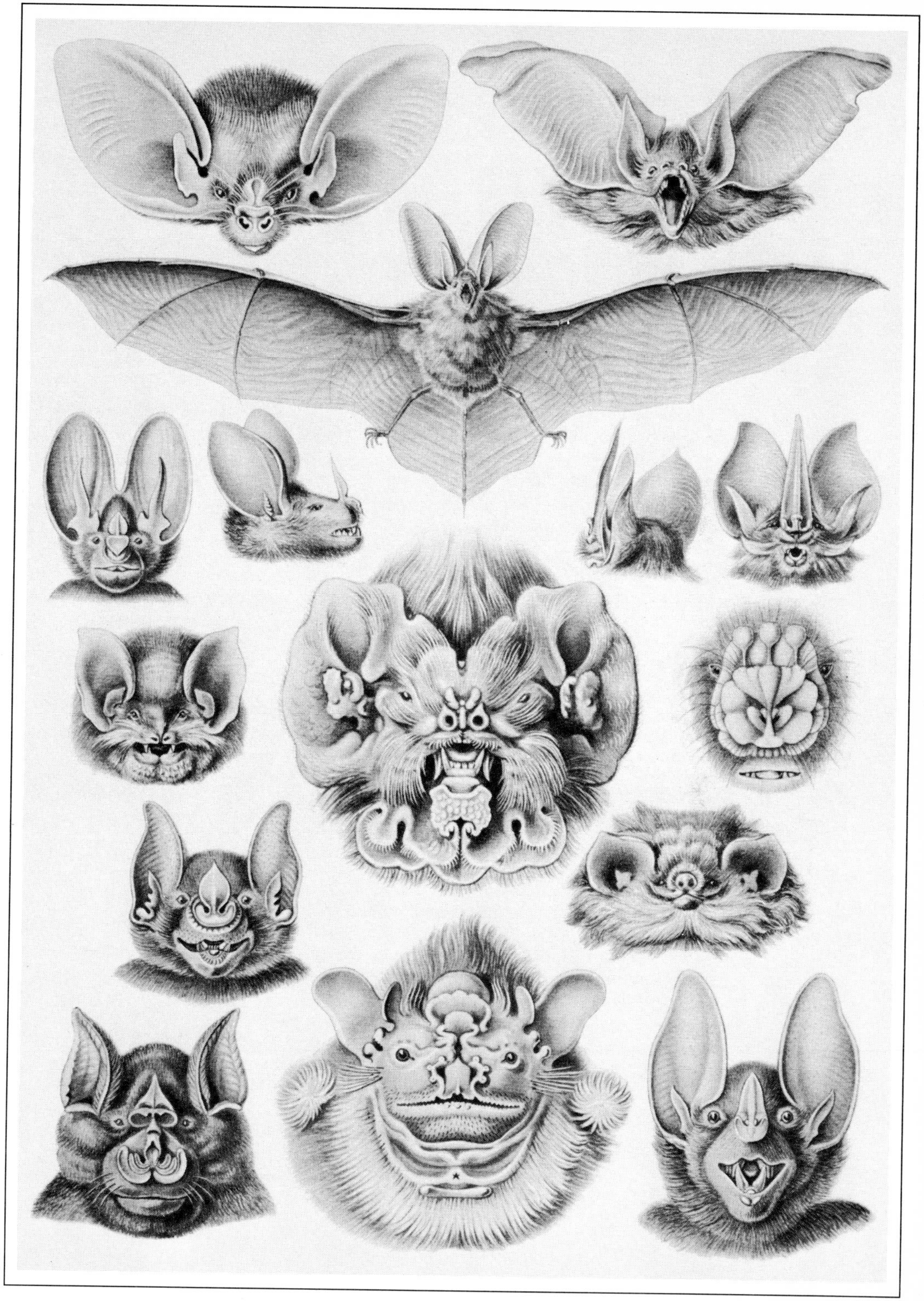

FIGURE 3–3 Some of the most exquisite examples of scientific illustration are the drawings of the nineteenth-century German philosopher and biologist, **Ernst Heinrich Haeckel.** Throughout his years of research, Haeckel made intricate drawings of a wide variety of natural forms. In 1899, at age 65, he collaborated with an artist named Adolf Giltsch in the refinement of his drawings and then their translation into lithographic reproductions. Over a period of five years, they published ten portfolios, each containing ten pages like the page of bats shown here. Reproduced from *Art Forms in Nature* by Ernst Haeckel (New York: Dover Publications, 1974) from the Dover Pictorial Archives.

Have we not seen pictures which bear so close a resemblance to the actual thing that they have deceived both men and beasts?

Leonardo da Vinci, quoted in Robert Goldwater and Marco Treves, eds., *Artists on Art* (New York: Pantheon, 1945).

It's the real thing.

Advertising slogan for *Coca-Cola.*

His master's voice.

Advertising slogan for *RCA Victor* phonographs; after the title of a painting by Francis Barraud, which shows a dog named Nipper listening to a human voice on a phonographic talking machine, *ca.* 1900.

Is it real, or is it Memorex?

Advertising slogan for *Memorex* recording tapes.

Paintings can never directly reproduce the taste or smell of fruit, the touch and texture of yielding flesh, or the note in an infant's voice that makes the milk begin to flow in a mother's breasts. Yet both language and painting symbolize such things, sometimes so effectively that they elicit responses close to those evoked by the original stimuli.

Edward T. Hall, *The Hidden Dimension* (Garden City, N.Y.: Doubleday, 1969).

Zeuxis and Parrhasius

Perhaps the oldest *trompe l'oeil* tale is that of a competition between Zeuxis and Parrhasius, two famous painters of ancient Greece. Zeuxis had become renowned for painting such convincing images that they were often mistaken for actual things. Presumably jealous of Zeuxis' fame, Parrhasius proposed a public contest; and, on a legendary day in the late fifth century B.C., they met at a public gathering spot to unveil the paintings they had prepared.

Zeuxis presented a painting of grapes that was so naturalistic that a flock of birds flew down and tried to eat them. Zeuxis was so excited by this (what better proof of fooling the eye?) that he momentarily forgot the painting by Parrhasius, which had yet to be unveiled.

When Zeuxis finally asked that the veil be lifted from his opponent's work, he was astonished to see that there was in fact no veil, that Parrhasius had brought a *trompe l'oeil* painting of a veil. Zeuxis conceded his defeat since, as he admitted, it was a greater accomplishment to trick the eyes of an artist than to fool a flock of birds.

Whether this story is truthful or not (it was reported by Pliny 500 years after it happened), at least it summons up several curious thoughts.

First, whether or not it is greater, it is at least a different feat to fool a human being than it is to fool a bird. Birds are deceived by scarecrows, which nowadays are made by tying shiny shapes on strings or suspending plastic strips. Ethologists would be aghast (remembering the sticklebacks) if Zeuxis proclaimed today that his artistic worth was proved because his painting fooled a bird.

As ethologists have shown, and as hunters and anglers have long known, birds and fish can be deceived by the most outlandish concoctions of shapes—forms blatantly unlike the natural things they represent. It has been found, for example, that an English robin will readily defend itself against a bundle of red feathers (attached to a wire and fixed to a perch), while it will ignore an actual mounted intruder lacking red feathers on its breast. In fact, experiments have shown that animals are more likely to be deceived by so-called *supernormal* forms, models larger in size or greater in number than the actual things themselves.

Second, assuming the story of Zeuxis is true, it seems improbable today that we would be deceived by the paintings of Zeuxis and Parrhasius. None of their paintings exists anymore, but there is reason to believe that all of Zeuxis' works (at least) were probably colored in monochrome gray, or what is technically known as grisaille. We might wonder, then, if what could fool the ancient Greeks was a style that widely differed from what we would find convincing now (see Figures 3–4, 3–5, and 3–6).

REALISM The word is commonly used in six or seven different ways, depending on whether it is used in opposition to *naturalism, stylization, abstraction, idealization, illusionism,* and so on. It is often naively assumed that there is a single, simple look that constitutes absolute realism, but the range of styles of art (including photographic styles) that are considered realistic is very broad.

FIGURE 3–4 When Zeuxis unveiled his painting of fruit, a flock of birds flew at the grapes. Would they be even more deceived by this contemporary rendition of grapes? It is difficult to say, since birds are deceived by utterly simple forms. Regardless of that, this painting does a superb job of using those familiar means by which pictures were judged to be "realistic" by members of the European speech community, beginning with the Renaissance. Still, in this unpublished oil, the principal meal is the color, as the strange suspended fruit bobs and wafts above the squares in the austere paintings of Josef Albers, who taught at the Bauhaus and later at Yale. This is one of a series of works by student artist **David Lenz.** Courtesy the artist, 1984.

FIGURE 3–5 This is an early landmark in the history of medical illustration. It is the portrait of one of the greatest figures in the history of Western medicine, the Belgian physician and anatomist **Andreas Vesalius.** His book on human anatomy, *De Humani Corporis Fabrica* (1543), in which this woodcut first appeared, was so exceptionally accurate in its illustrations that it is sometimes said to mark the beginning of modern science. This portrait is perhaps less accurate (though no less powerful in its gaze), since some believe it indicates that Vesalius was a dwarf, which is apparently untrue. Why is his head outlandishly large in relation to his body? Why is his body so small in relation to the corpse he holds? Some historians contend that these and other "errors" prove that the woodcut is not the work of Jan Stephan von Kalcar, a student of Titian. It may even be a self-portrait of Vesalius. Reproduced from *The Illustrations from the Works of Andreas Vesalius of Brussels* by J. B. deC. M. Saunders and C. D. O'Malley (New York: Dover Publications, 1973) from the Dover Pictorial Archives.

The Company of Undertakers

Beareth Sable, an Urinal proper, between 12 Quack-Heads of the Second & 12 Cane Heads Or, Consultant. On a Chief Nebulæ, Ermine, One Compleat Doctor issuant, checkie Sustaining in his Right Hand a Baton of the Second. On his Dexter & Sinister sides two Demi-Doctors, issuant of the second, & two Cane Heads issuant of the third; She first having One Eye conchant, towards the Dexter Side of the Escocheon; the Second Faced per pale proper & Gules, Guardent.

With this Motto. ——— El Plurima Mortis Imago.

Price Six pence

FIGURE 3–6 In his autobiographical notes, the English engraver **William Hogarth** recalled that when he was a child, "I had a naturally good eye; shews of all sort gave me uncommon pleasure when an Infant; and Mimickry, common to all children, was remarkable in me." In 1736, the year this print was made, when he was thirty-nine years old, Hogarth was still imitating (or mimicking) the world around him by etching uncommonly caustic "shews" that were of great delight to all except the people he mocked. In this, "The Company of Undertakers," he unmercifully prescribes a coat of arms for the medical profession. In the upper background are three notorious "Quack-Heads," all of whom are suffering from the ills they pretend to cure. In the lower foreground are doctors, "Demi-Doctors" and "Cane Heads," most of whom appear content to sniff the handles of their canes, which in the eighteenth century contained a pungent pick-me-up that was in part ammonia. At the lower right, two doctors examine the color of a urine sample, while another dips his finger in the stuff. Their sardonic motto, *Et Plurima Mortis Imago,* reads "And Many Images of Death." Reproduced from *Medicine and the Artist* by Carl Zigrosser (New York: Dover Publications, 1970) by permission of the Philadelphia Museum of Art, from the Dover Pictorial Archives.

We do not always realize that the theory of perspective developed in the fifteenth century is a scientific convention; it is merely one way of describing space and has no absolute validity.

Sir Herbert Read.

PERSPECTIVE Any method of representation by which a three-dimensional thing is depicted by a visual means that has only two dimensions, as when, for example, the spherical surface of the earth is translated onto the flat surface of a map. Whatever the method one uses, some distortion must result.

LINEAR PERSPECTIVE A system of representation, first popularly used in fifteenth-century Italy, in which a progressive decrease in the size of an object is intended to depict a progressive increase in its distance from a single, stable point of view.

ISOMETRIC PERSPECTIVE A system of representation, usually associated with Far Eastern art, in which a greater distance is not indicated by a decrease in the size of things. An object's size remains the same whether it is far or near. Such methods are preferred today in engineers' and carpenters' plans, in which it is essential to know the actual sizes of objects.

AERIAL PERSPECTIVE A method of signifiying distance, invented by Leonardo da Vinci, in which nearer objects are sharply rendered while more distant objects are progressively indistinct. It is virtually the same as *atmospheric perspective,* in which increasingly distant things are obscured by zones of mist.

Differing Perspectives

Regarding the problem of fooling the eye, it is a further oddity to find that the ninth-century Chinese critic Chang Yen-Yuan complained (in much the way that Lebrun did) that artists were incompetent because "few can paint a fly looking so real as to be mistaken for a real one, and we see only those who end up by painting a tiger like a dog."

Horse for ass or tiger for dog, what Chang appears to ask for (like Leonardo and Lebrun) is works that are so similar to the things they represent that the two could be confused.

However, a problem arises because when we examine Chinese art from Chang's time and for centuries afterward, we rarely find a work that we would call "realistic," and we almost never find a work that we would call *trompe l'oeil.* How could Chang or anyone else have thought of these hopelessly stylized works as being like what they depict?

Shadows were excluded from almost all Chinese works. Chinese painters organized their landscapes within a vertical format, using a pattern of zigzags interlaced with zones of mist. They systematically employed **isometric perspective,** a method of depicting depth which, unlike European **linear perspective,** does not decrease the size of things as their distances increase. Instead, Chinese painters made important persons large and less important persons small, whether they are nearby or far away.

How could anyone be duped by misshapen representations as "primitive and barbaric" as these (as Westerners thought they were)? And thus we must also ask if Chinese art was founded on a style of sorting and seeing that differed radically from what we find convincing now.

To repeat, Leonardo said that "that painting is most praiseworthy which is most like the thing represented." If we simply listened to Chang and Leonardo (without looking at their art), we would conclude that they wanted more or less the same thing.

But if we were to ask these two artists to make realistic drawings of some common object, drawings that would fool the eye, they would produce two extremely different works. Suppose, for example, that we asked them to simply draw a table top. Using isometric means, Chang would produce a drawing in which the table's distant edge would be the same width as the front. Using Renaissance linear perspective, Leonardo's work would show the front edge largest while objects behind it would gradually shrink as their distance increased (as he did in *The Last Supper*). And so the troublesome question remains: Which picture is the more realistic?

Leonardo might respond that table tops and everything else appear to shrink as their distance from us increases, and that is simply an optical fact. But Chang would argue that while the table seems to shrink (because of **optical diminution,** which the Chinese knew about), the shrinkage is illusory, and the artist's primary goal is not to paint illusions but to show things as they *really* are—and table tops do not, in fact, shrink.

Again, we are left to wonder which drawing is most similar to the object it represents. Most Westerners would no doubt say that Leonardo is correct, providing they lived after 1400 or so, when linear perspective and shadows became traits of Western art (see Figures 3–7 through 3–10).

OPTICAL DIMINUTION The apparent shrinkage of objects as they become increasingly distant from the eye.

It will be shown that whatever the medium or method, every form of perspective representation has some innate falsity, but that most such forms offer an adequate makeshift; that rules of geometry often need to be bent; that labor-saving dodges and short cuts exist. Perspective drawing, like politics, is an art of the possible.

Lawrence Wright, *Perspective in Perspective* (London: Routledge and Kegan Paul, 1983).

FIGURE 3–7 The concept of *linear perspective* may have been invented innumerable times before the Renaissance. But it was in 1400 or so that it began to be embraced as an appropriate system for Western European painting. In linear perspective, the world is observed from a single fixed viewing point. Primary emphasis is assigned to the apparent shrinkage of objects (*optical diminution*) as they move farther from the eye. Thus (as shown on the left), a fifteenth-century European drawing of a table top would show the front edge as wider than the more distant rear edge. During the same time period, the preferred system in China was *isometric perspective,* in which (as shown on the right) the apparent shrinkage of objects did not symbolize an increase in distance. Instead, size was used to indicate the relative social magnitude of the subjects (for example, masters were drawn large and servants small), regardless of where they are standing in space. Chinese painters repeatedly rejected linear perspective when it was explained to them by Jesuit missionaries. They had no trouble understanding it apparently, but it seemed grossly inappropriate for clearly depicting the values they stressed. We have our own reasons for preferring isometric perspective systems, especially in cabinetmaking, technical drawing, and so on; linear perspective is less reliable, if not downright misleading, when one is trying to construct an actual table top. Finally, during this same time period, shadows were not usually shown in either Chinese or European representations. That omission must have seemed perfectly natural to them, as odd as it appears to us.

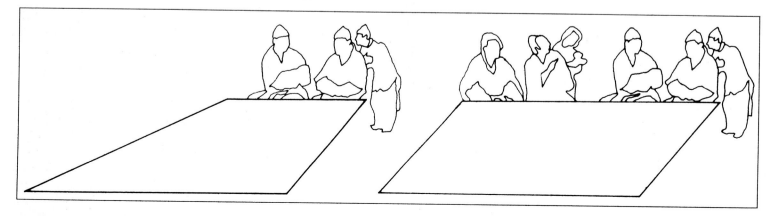

FIGURE 3–8 This diagram of alternating light and dark dominoes is drawn in *isometric perspective*, in that the height of the front block is the same as the height of the back block. Yet it does not look that way. The height of the blocks appears to increase as their distances increase, which is the inverse of linear perspective. Why are we deceived by this? Do we overcompensate when we look at isometric perspective because we have been trained to see in accordance with linear perspective? Some people have come to this conclusion and suggest that this drawing would not disturb a Chinese artist of the fifteenth century.

FIGURE 3–9 *Linear perspective*, or the "famous art of eyesight," as **Jan Vredeman de Vries** would say, was promulgated by his book, *Perspective*, which was published in The Hague and in Leiden in 1604–1605. The method was well known by then throughout Southern Europe, but Vredeman helped to spread the news throughout Holland and the North. This is one of seventy-three engraved demonstrations of how to build a picture for use by "all Painters, Engravers, Sculptors, Metalworkers, Architects, Designers, Masons, Cabinetmakers, Carpenters and all lovers of the arts who may wish to apply themselves to this art with greater pleasure and less pain." This particular plate is a demonstration of one-point perspective. The *vanishing point* (the point at which the lines converge) and the horizon line are easy to see in the background, where they meet within the arch. From this and Vredeman's other plates, it is evident that shadows had, by this time, become a trait of Western art. Reproduced from *Perspective* by Jan Vredeman de Vries (New York: Dover Publications, 1968) from the Dover Pictorial Archives.

FIGURE 3–10   This is one of thirteen Xerographic collages from an unpublished children's book, written and illustrated by the author and **Mary Snyder Behrens** in 1983. The background is directly derived from the preceding engraving of one-point perspective by Jan Vredeman de Vries. The engraving of the hen, the dog, the rabbit, and so on were all copied from collections of illustrations in the public domain.

Every portrait [in eighteenth-century China] had to be painted full face, not at an angle, and the eyes had to be looking at the spectator. Shadows had to be avoided; they looked to the Chinese like smudges on the face.

Cecile and Michel Beurdeley, *Giuseppe Castiglione: A Jesuit Painter at the Court of the Chinese Emperor* (Rutland, Ver.: Tuttle, 1971).

FIGURE 3–11 This ingenious (if crotchety) drawing machine was described and pictured by the German artist **Albrecht Dürer** in 1525. He was fascinated by the system of linear perspective, and this is one of his four attempts to devise an objective perspective machine, by which anyone could draw. It consisted of an upright frame bisected by moveable cross-hair threads, with a drawing board hinged to the side of the frame. A weighted cord (which represents a ray of light) was anchored to a pulley on the wall (which represented the human eye). The unweighted end of the cord was attached to a sticklike pointer, which was then passed through the frame and positioned on a point on the object being drawn (in this case, a lute). So positioned, a second person would adjust the cross-hair threads to mark the exact coordinates where the cord passed through the frame. The cord was then dropped, the drawing board (with paper attached) was closed upon the frame, and a single pencil dot was made at the intersection of the cross hairs. In theory (and perhaps in practice), if one were to repeat this innumerable times, adjusting the pointer each time, one would produce a dotted view of the object in flawless one-point perspective as seen from the site of the pulley. Reproduced from *The Complete Woodcuts of Albrecht Dürer* edited by Willi Kurth (New York: Dover Publications, 1963) from the Dover Pictorial Archives.

Realism and Attention

The Chinese hoped to paint pictures that were similar to actual things. But the essential characteristics they emphasized were vastly different from those Renaissance artists stressed.

Light casts shadows in China just as it does everywhere else, and the Chinese certainly saw them. But shadows are illusions. They are effects of biased light. They are properties of light, not of things, and thus Chinese painters chose to leave them out.

From a Western point of view, the Chinese were like the sticklebacks. Western art had fins and gills, but lacked a red underside. Chinese art had a red belly but no fins or gills. Which model is the more realistic? Within their own milieus, both were perceived as spitting images of the things they represented. As ethology has shown, depending on its *mental set*, any animal species, including humans, will respond to the oddest likenesses as if they were "the thing itself."

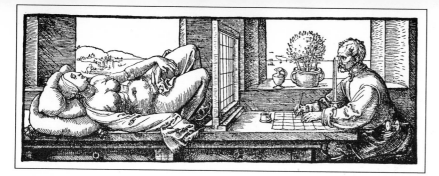

FIGURE 3–12 Like the preceding illustration, this and the next two woodcuts are from **Albrecht Dürer's** book *On the Art of Measurement*, published in 1525. They are depictions of drawing machines, devices he used to produce linear perspective. Each has a stable viewing point and a kind of window, often called the *picture plane*, which is meant to represent an intersection or vertical slice, of the cone of light rays that is reflected back to the artist's eye from the surface of the model. In this particular machine (virtually identical to one Leonardo da Vinci had used), the picture plane has been divided (using threads) into grids matching the set of penciled grids that the artist has drawn on his paper. Reproduced from Kurth, *op. cit.*, from the Dover Pictorial Archives.

FIGURE 3–13 In this variation of a drawing machine by **Albrecht Dürer,** the artist draws or paints on glass, which functions as the picture plane. Reproduced from Kurth, *op. cit.*, from the Dover Pictorial Archives.

PICTURE PLANE In linear perspective, it is assumed that a cone of vision, or conical bundle of light rays, reflects off objects and enters the eye. A drawing in linear perspective is said to be a slice of this, a window or pane of glass that intersects the rays of light. This window is the picture plane, the surface of the work of art.

FIGURE 3–14 This is a fourth variation on a perspective drawing machine by **Albrecht Dürer.** As in the preceding version, the artist draws directly on glass, but this one has a viewing point (a peephole) that can be shifted up and down so that an object can be drawn from slightly different views. The experience of using devices like this can easily be simulated by tracing the shapes of the landscape on a window from indoors, while maintaining a stable monocular view. Reproduced from Kurth, *op. cit.*, from the Dover Pictorial Archives. These devices are clearly discussed in relation to the history and theory of linear perspective in *Perspective in Perspective* by Lawrence Wright (London: Routledge and Kegan Paul, 1983).

The Emperor said that "the imperfections of the eye were no reason to represent the objects of nature as imperfect."
Ibid.

FIGURE 3–15 Art that is esthetic is not necessarily pleasant to view. This work deliberately conveys a sense of great discomfort. It was an illustration for "Exes," a short story by I. B. Singer, originally published in *Weekend Magazine.* The story concerned the feelings and perceptions of an estranged couple; in the illustration, the figures are estranged in space, in the sense that they are spread apart and pressed against the corners. The predominance of sharply drawn diagonal lines contributes to the air of stress, as do the contorted human figures and disproportionate heads and hands. The picture is also disturbing (at least to Westerners) because the isometric perspective makes the floor appear to rise (the distant tiles appear to be wider than the near ones), as if the space were inside out. The illustrator, **Blair Drawson,** is a contemporary Canadian artist. In one way or another, virtually all of his artworks are disturbing to some degree. When he was asked to comment on the significance of his works (not just on this single work), he offered the following statement:

"There are evidently two main tendencies in my work. One of them moves toward the light, the positive, the contemplative. The other, toward the dark, the negative, and the 'paranoid.' Both extremes take on a satiric flavor. One is typified by qualities of joy, amusement, exultation, humor. The other direction calls to mind those feelings reflective of loneliness and fear, and their spin-offs: anxiety, depression, small-mindedness. This direction is modified by wit—and there tends to be at least a bit of cruelty in that.

"There are extremes of the paradox, and both are equally 'real.'

"There is also a middle ground which is atmospherically somewhat neutral. It exists as a sort of ideal for me, secure as it is from the dangerous passions that permeate the two extremes. It is the place of harmony.

"Since Darwin and Freud and Marx and Einstein, the condition of modern man seems more and more unintelligible. Our situation is undefinable; the evidence is inconclusive. For every step we take forward in our proud march to an enlightened future, there is an accompanying rediscovery of our underlying savagery. Yet, for all the other things it might be, the human endeavor is a rich and spicy bouillabaisse—variously ingrediented, chock full of surprises, giving off flavors deliciously bitter and awesomely sweet. More than ever, it comes down to a matter of taste.

"Passion and paradox, metaphor and myth. For the artist, there is plenty to do."

For this particular illustration by Drawson, the art director was Robert Priest. Courtesy the artist.

Physiognomic Resemblance

We must not confuse Pierre Lebrun (who said that some artists were asses) with another Lebrun, a French painter of the seventeenth century whose first name was Charles. As the foremost artist in the court of Louis XIV, Charles Lebrun was largely responsible for the interior design of the palace at Versailles.

What is less known about Charles Lebrun is that he was also an author of sorts. He wrote two odd treatises on human expressions. In one of these, he juxtaposed drawings of animal heads with portraits of various people in order to show that animals share certain facial traits with humans.

Lebrun's odd essays were attempts at *physiognomy*, since he believed that he could readily discern people's personality traits by carefully studying facial features such as the shape of the nose, the height of the brow, and so on.

Lebrun also believed that animals and the humans who resemble them also tend to see and behave in the same ways. Thus, some people are "bullish," while others are "foxy," and so on. It is even possible (recalling the words of the other Lebrun) that certain artists look and act like asses.

Form is influenced by concern with, or neglect of, detail. Needs and mores make for distortion.

Rudolf Arnheim, "Gestalt Psychology and Artistic Form."

FIGURE 3–16 The seventeenth-century French artist **Charles Lebrun** began to work for Louis XIV in 1661. One year later, he was granted the rank of nobility and assigned the title of *premier peintre du roi*. And one year after that, he was placed in charge of the French Academy, where he lectured on the physiognomic resemblance between certain types of humans and animals. This is a plate from those lectures, originally published in 1806. For further information see "Understanding Man and Beast," by Timothy Foote in *Horizon,* (Autumn 1973); and *Resemblances, Amazing Faces,* by Charles Le Brun (New York: Harlan Quist Books, 1980).

ANTHROPOMORPHISM The perception or representation of nonhuman beings or things as if they were human.

Lebrun was very serious. His drawings were not meant as jokes. They are of course dismissed today, because we do not believe that a person's inner nature is reliably revealed by facial features. Further, we scoff at pseudo-scientific theories that certain animals look and behave like humans. That is the province of caricature, of Mickey Mouse and Donald Duck, not of science.

Nevertheless, these drawings are useful in a limited way. Even if they do not show the inner traits of humans and animals, they may still reveal to us why we tend to react to animals as if they did have human traits. Why are eagles regarded as proud, while foxes are thought to be crafty, horses impetuous, camels spleenful and snobbish, hawks vigilant, and doves peaceful and composed?

At least one ethologist, Irenaus Eibl-Eibesfeldt, believes that we react this way because (as with the sticklebacks) we have a built-in tendency to be fooled by certain traits. Eibl-Eibesfeldt suggests that when we see a model with half-closed eyes and a narrow mouth with turned-down corners (all eagle features), we automatically consider the person to be "justly proud."

FIGURE 3–17 An Old Testament passage (Isaiah 11:6) predicts that predators will reside peacefully with prey, that wolves will live aimiably with lambs, that leopards will lie down with goats, and so on. In one of his funniest verbal caricatures, the comic genius Woody Allen misinterprets the verse and concludes that "The lion and the calf shall lie down together but the calf won't get much sleep." Intended misrepresentation, or purposeful distortion, is a paramount element in visual caricature, as evidenced by this portrait of Woody Allen by the contemporary caricaturist **Gerry Gersten.** This drawing was developed for the Quality Paperback Book Club in 1983. Courtesy the artist.

FIGURE 3–18 An affinity is implied between a human and an animal in this pen and ink illustration by **Jack Unruh.** The drawing is a portrait of the "Red Fox of Kinderhook," the eighth president of the United States, Martin Van Buren. He was reputedly crafty, red-haired, small and a native of Kinderhook, New York. Unruh developed this artwork in 1976 for the Heritage Press. The art directors were Jack Summerford and Dan Ross. For the artist, this is a significant work, since it was (in his words) "the first example of what is now the way I work—brush and ink. In the years past it's been refined somewhat, but the circumstance of having to get an illustration done quickly led to this approach and it seemed to fit me. So I've been stuck with it." Courtesy the artist.

FIGURE 3–19 Color Xerox and adhesive line tapes were used by student artist **Ellen Homb-Nachreiner** to invent an artwork that picks up a lot of its power from the menace of the stare. The work is precisely constructed: There is a conceptual echo between the feline woman's eyes and the eyes of the cat in the center, and the shape of the eye is repeated throughout the top and bottom of the work. The artwork was originally used as an illustration for "The Funny Way She Winds Up," by Paula Newcomer, in *The North American Review* (December 1982). Courtesy the artist and the publisher.

INNATE RELEASING MECHANISMS   Inborn sensitivities in animals, and probably in humans too, in which specific stimuli (for example, certain shapes or color combinations) trigger certain acts on a less than conscious plane. There is research which seems to prove, for example, that a pair of circular shapes, aligned horizontally side by side, will produce an arousal response in human beings.

The history of modern art is the recurring story of making art resemble non-art.

Beauvais Lyons, contemporary American artist.

SUPERNORMAL STIMULI   Ethologists have found that certain counterfeit forms elicit a stronger response than does the original thing. For example, most males seem to respond strongly to images of women in which the legs have been abnormally lengthened, the buttocks and breasts greatly enlarged, and the waist reduced. This is the traditional bestselling shape that is commonly used in pin-up art, comic books, and low-brow science fiction art.

Realism will always be here. Realism sells. People are familiar with realism and they will always buy it.

David Plourde, illustrator, interview in *Print* (1978).

Innate Responses

Behavior in which an automatic act (like the stickleback's assault) is predictably "unlocked" by equally specific "keys" (for example, a red underside), is said to be the product of **innate releasing mechanisms** (or IRMs).

IRMs are additive. Features that contribute to the key (such as red bellies, or, in the case of humans, half-closed eyes and narrow mouths with turned-down corners) are added up in the mind. The more key features, the more vigorous the response.

Thus, in the male stickleback, the presence of the color red (whether above or below) will cause a minimum response (as happened with the mailtruck). When the red is placed below, the response increases, and the strongest reaction (the most convincing *trompe l'oeil*) occurs when a threatening posture is combined with red beneath.

This additive factor is further confirmed by the fact that one can make models that appear to be "more real"—that is, more convincing—than the things they represent. These are **supernormal forms,** models that exaggerate the features of the key. Since such models "total more," they elicit a stronger response than the thing itself would cause.

As proof of this, it has been shown that an oyster catcher, whose normal clutch of eggs is three, will be attracted to a dummy clutch that numbers five, while it also chooses eggs much larger than its own. Or, in the grayling butterfly, the male responds more actively to models of the female that are darker than in life, and responds most strongly to models that are painted black (radically different from what they depict) and markedly larger than actual size.

What bearing do these findings have on how we respond to illustrations? What connection might they have to how and why we are convinced that a mere array of lines, or so many splotches of pigment, deserve the term "realistic"— in that they prompt us to respond as if they were the thing itself?

Glance Aversion

We can all be deceived by certain basic shapes not because we are trained in a certain way, but because we possess innate tendencies, perhaps even IRMs. Certain phobias (for example, the fear of snakes) are behavioral vestiges of archaic defenses, which, when we first evolved, helped us survive. Such knee-jerk reactions helped us protect ourselves, just as we still protect ourselves by ducking when an object is tossed at our head.

Perhaps the most common example of this is the widespread human response to shapes that look like vertebrates' eyes. We all tend to avoid the direct stare of a stranger when we are walking down the street, or, even more disturbing, when standing in an elevator. In what is called *glance aversion*, we displace our line of sight to some detail on the ground, or pretend to watch the clouds.

Further, while the mouth and nose are equally prominent parts of the face, it is instead the eyes that are the locus of the phantom "person" housed inside. The eyes are the windows of the soul to such a degree that, in censored photographs, the identity of the person is effectively concealed by simply masking out the eyes. There is an eye on the reverse side of the U.S. dollar bill (the eye of Providence), and many shibboleths frequently mention the power of the "evil eye," which is the unaverted stare.

We respond innately to virtually anything that includes two concentric circles (close together and side by side), just as sticklebacks respond to virtually all objects that have the trait of red beneath. The objects on which these circles occur need not be like a vertebrate in any other manifest way. In fact, they can be absurdly *unlike* any known vertebrate species, and yet (because of the eyelike shapes) we will respond to some extent as if they were the thing itself.

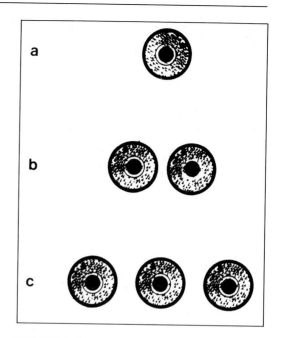

FIGURE 3–21 If certain experiments are valid, there may be general visual forms to which the human mind responds automatically. For example, in some experiments the pupil dilation reactions of human adults were found to be markedly greater in response to a pair of bilateral circles (comparable to that in *b*) than to arrangements of one or three circles. This and other experiments might be interpreted to mean that humans (and many other animals) are automatically aroused by shapes that resemble the eyes of vertebrates. In similar experiments with animals, chickens have been made to "freeze" simply by showing them eyelike shapes. For further information, see "Some Chickens I have Intimidated," by George G. Gallup, Jr., in *Psychology Today* (August 1972).

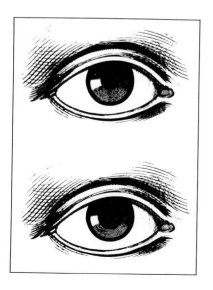

FIGURE 3–20 The pupil of the human eye will constrict or dilate in response to an increase or decrease in light. Pupil size is also changed by the injestion of various drugs such as caffeine and alcohol. Without drugs or altered light, the pupil will increase in size when people are aroused (either positively or negatively) by the form they are looking at. As a curious result, humans especially respond to faces or pictures of faces in which the pupils are dilated. For further information, see "The Role of Pupil Size in Communication," by E. Hess in *Scientific American* (November 1975); and "Rattlesnakes, French Fries, and Pupillometric Oversell," by B. Rice in *Psychology Today* (February 1974).

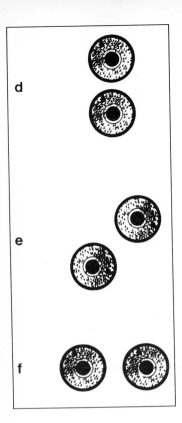

d

e

f

FIGURE 3–22 Human pupil dilation reactions to pairs of circles have been found to be much greater when the pair is positioned horizontally (as shown in *f*), and least when they are vertical (as shown in *d*). For further information, see "The Ethological Command in Art," by Richard G. Coss in *Leonardo* 2 (1968):273–287.

FIGURE 3–23 **James Buckels** developed this black and white airbrush illustration for Scott Sander's short story entitled "The Recovery of Vision," published in *The North American Review* in 1981. The story is concerned with a young man who is loosing his eyesight because of an infection, while, at the same time, he is beginning to conquer his fear of proposing to the woman he loves. Ironically, the story suggests, his physical blindness is also a symbol of a recovery of vision. Courtesy the artist and the publisher.

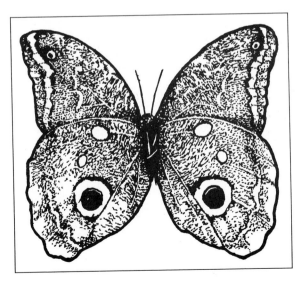

FIGURE 3–24 Eyelike shapes (eyespots or ocelli) are found throughout the natural world, but most commonly perhaps on the wings of butterflies and moths. The *caligo*, or owl, butterflies from Central and South America (as shown in this drawing) have as many as six such eyespots, the largest of which are highly meticulous "pictures" of eyes, complete with suggestions of volume, shadows, and white highlights. The circle, because it has no points of directional change, is said to be the simplest shape and probably the most conspicuous. Eyespot patterns are apparently protective. Small ones serve as decoy targets that displace the peck of a bird away from the butterfly's body. Large eyespots are probably intimidating because of their resemblance to the eyes of animals that prey on the butterfly's predators. From the author's collection.

FIGURE 3–25 This work is both optically and pictorially disturbing as a result of the incongruity of the union of two faces, which contradicts what we expect and yet in other ways makes sense. The ambiguity of the central eye is especially unsettling, and you may find that your own eyes are frequently switching their focus back and forth from face to face, in a fruitless effort to settle on a stable view of this mixed-media collage by **Constance Gage-Kivlin.** The work was originally published as an illustration for "The Novitiate," a short story by Erica Liederman in *The North American Review* (December 1982). Courtesy the artist and the publisher.

The Anatomy of Cuteness

In terms of illustration, the prime example of an innate human response to shapes is the **infant schema** that Konrad Lorenz described. It is Lorenz's hypothesis that we react to certain shapes (including drawings and cartoons) as if they were a human child. We say that these things are "cute," and we may feel an innate urge to cuddle and protect these forms. The perfect example is Bambi, the irresistable Disney deer.

INFANT SCHEMA Konrad Lorenz's hypothesis that humans respond automatically to virtually any object (including dolls and illustrations) that has attributes of infant physiognomy, including such specific traits as a large head in relation to the body, oversized eyes located at the middle of the skull or below, and so on.

103

Our response to infant characteristics and many other signals from the brood-tending or sexual field is . . . automatic, and "knowing better" makes no difference. If we want to guard against the abuse of these responses, for instance in advertising, we must intervene in the response after it has made its primary appeal to us, that is, not buy a product although the baby face on the package is very cute, not buy a car simply because truly attractive young ladies in the tiniest bikinis advertise it. . . .

Wolfgang Wickler, *The Sexual Code* (Garden City, N.Y.: Anchor Books, 1973).

FIGURE 3–26 This drawing was developed for an unpublished children's book. Much of the drama of the work derives from its angle of view and the way it is cropped. The artist is a gifted illustrator from England, **Anne Yvonne Gilbert.** Of the four drawings composed for the book, she remarked that they "were executed in colored pencils—almost all my work is—which gives a nice soft texture to the drawing, and usually very subtle coloring, just right for this kind of image. Most people prefer this drawing out of the four—the unusual viewpoint I expect. My drawings are not very dynamic, usually very statically posed, so I tend to look for an unusual angle when I set it up. I always use friends for models, as they look more human than pros. It appeals to my sense of humor to make them dress up in funny costumes and do ridiculous things. Costumes are made up from boxes and boxes of old clothes, curtains, and bits and pieces. It all adds to the fun. I really don't enjoy drawing contemporary people in ordinary situations—it's too boring, hence most of my work is in publishing as opposed to advertising. . . ." Courtesy the artist.

Not without significance, "bambi" is short for *bambino*, Italian slang for "baby." Disney's blameless little fawn has all the visual attributes of cuteness, just as Tinbergen's models of fish had the quintessential traits of intruders.

According to Lorenz, seven attributes make up the key that unlocks our inborn responses to babies. We need not list them all, but some cuteness cues include round and chubby cheeks, a cranium and forehead that are disproportionately large in relation to the face, and uncommonly enlarged eyes that are located as low as, or below, the middle axis of the skull.

Confronted by objects that bear these traits, we unthinkingly react as if they were the thing itself, regardless of how these objects are unlike a human child when judged for other traits.

If judged by Lorenz's list of traits, the Bambi image is undoubtedly cute, and it is only one of an endless list of dolls and cartoon surrogates (for example, Charlie Brown, Miss Piggy, and Barbie Doll) upon which people fawn. The economic yield from commercialized cuteness is enormous. To rephrase P. T. Barnum's quote, a stickleback is born every minute.

The Taxonomy of Style

Physiognomic comparisons of human and animal facial traits did not begin with Charles Lebrun. A similar system was proposed (including comparative drawings) by Giambattista della Porta, the Renaissance metaphysician, about a hundred years before. While Porta's ideas appear to be droll, he was no doubt a genius. At age six, he wrote a composition in Latin and Italian, completed three books on "natural magic" at age fifteen, and, within his adult life, added a lens to the camera obscura, which led to the birth of the camera.

Among his innumerable theories, Porta's writings recommend (although, as he admitted, he had never tried it) that if the afterbirth of mares is placed inside a lamp and burned (it has to be a new lamp), a person viewed within its light will seem to have a horse's head.

... the lapdogs kept by elderly spinsters in compensation for frustrated parental drives also display childlike attributes. One has only to think of Pekingese or pugs. And if one observes the relationship between the two, one will notice that the owners fondle their dogs and talk to them, just as if they were small children.

Irenaus Eibl-Eibesfeldt, *Love and Hate* (New York: Holt, Rinehart & Winston, 1972).

How useless is painting, which attracts admiration by the resemblance of things, the originals of which we do not admire!

Blaise Pascal, *Pensées*.

FIGURE 3–27 Within a single culture, categories tend to change with the passage of time. In the 1500s, the Renaissance mathematician Girolamo Cardano observed that "it is fairly widely known that plants have hatred between themselves. . . . It is said that the olive and the vine hate the cabbage, and the cucumber flies from the olive." At about that same time, Giambattista della Porta published this illustration (and the following one) as proof that there are likenesses between animals and plants (for example, the horns of the ram on the right are like the "horns" of the plant above it). For a superb though difficult account of the evolution of categories in Western culture, see *The Order of Things* by Michel Foucault (New York: Vintage Books, 1970).

FIGURE 3–28 In this illustration from *Physiognomonia,* Porta further attempted to show that there are affinities between human and animal types. This is his version of a man with a bovine nature. Today this grouping is funny, but it is very likely that much of what we now believe will seem equally absurd when viewed four hundred years from now, assuming that the world exists.

Porta's physiognomic scheme was more extensive than Lebrun's. The former's system tried to show (as did Lebrun's) that there are types of people who tend to look like cattle, rabbits, goats, and so on. However, Porta tried to show in his drawings that certain plants also feature "horns" and other shapes like those of certain animals which, in turn, can then be matched with certain groups of people. In other words, not only are there "sheepish" human beings, there are also "sheepish" plants.

These two taxonomic schemes are readily dismissed today as so much naive nonsense. They were effectively effaced by Carolus Linnaeus, the lone arranger of the eighteenth century. God had opened His cupboard to him, Linnaeus announced, and shown him the Natural Order of things.

"To him therefore," Linnaeus wrote, "vegetables are known who can join the similar to the similar, and can separate the dissimilar from the dissimilar." We must not believe, he said, that pigs and horses are the same just because they both have hoofs. Nor should we mistakenly think that the goat, the reindeer, and the elk belong to different genera simply because they have different horns. Rather, Linnaeus insisted, essential traits should be attended to while peripheral attributes (for example, hoofs and horns) should be ignored as background noise.

Despite their differing results, Linnaeus, Porta, and Lebrun were engaged in the process of categorization. They were attempting to classify things, to place them into logical groups (based on shared features), just as playing cards are grouped into suits.

It has long been understood that all thinking is sorting. But so is all perceiving and, to follow, so is art. The process of arranging suits is the key ingredient in every human mental act, from seeing to feeling to thinking. The logic of representation derives from this process of sorting.

The grouping of a deck of cards is no doubt an excellent model of this, providing that we keep in mind that every conceivable caucus of things (including models of stickleback fish, representations of vertebrates' eyes, and infant schema diagrams) can be sorted into suits.

Even those vaguely familiar with cards know that different suits result when we switch our focus to different features of the cards. Thus, if we should focus on *shape*, the five of diamonds will be grouped with all cards with diamond shapes. But then if we focus on *number*, the five of diamonds will now belong with cards that have the value of five. Or, if *color* is attended to (disregarding number and shape), diamonds and hearts will constitute one category, spades and clubs another.

We could go on with this, each time switching emphasis, and each time putting any card into a radically different suit, depending on the "facial traits" we might choose to focus on. Notice that each time we group, we do so by attending to certain similarities and ignoring certain differences among the cards within a group. Thus, when *number* is emphasized (so that all fives are in one group), we ignore the color and shape because, as Linnaeus would tell us, these are simply peripheral traits.

It is this same process in which the sticklebacks engage when they respond to that wide range of things that appear to be threatening males. As discussed in Chapter 2, they attend to certain similarities and ignore certain differences (differences that are blatant to us). Their suit does not stress fins or gills. Instead, it calls for red beneath.

FIGURE 3–29 During and after World War I, the American writer Ernest Hemingway lived in Paris, where he became a member of the circle of writers and artists who were friends of Gertrude Stein and Alice B. Toklas. Hemingway was preoccupied with his masculinity and Stein made fun of him by training her dog to "act like Hemingway," which meant to paw the ground and growl. This portrait of the writer is a *self-promotion piece* (a noncommissioned portfolio work, intended to show what an artist can do) by the illustrator **R. J. Shay,** who recalled that "it was first designed and lightly drawn for position, then masked and airbrushed for block colors. I then came back with prisma pencils and white acrylic for highlights." Shay has tried to capture the gritty brusqueness of the aging Hemingway. Courtesy the artist.

What is it that attracts and satisfies us in trompe l'oeil? When is it that it captures our attention and delights us? At the moment when, by a mere shift of our gaze, we are able to realize that the representation does not move with the gaze and that it is merely a trompe l'oeil. For it appears at that moment as something other than it seemed, or rather it now seems to be that something else.

Jacques Lacan, *The Four Fundamental Concepts of Psycho-Analysis.*

FIGURE 3–30 Most people believe that science is comprised of truths, while works of art are fabrications. Yet, as Sir Arthur Eddington said, the mathematical formulations with which a physicist invents new groupings "have as much resemblance to the real qualities of the material world . . . as a telephone number has to a subscriber." As Arthur Koestler once observed, "The scientist's discoveries impose his own order on chaos, as the composer or painter imposes his." All art and all science are systems of representation, each of which is subject to the insights and the blindnesses of its time. There are styles in science just as there are styles in art; as Koestler also said, "Einstein's space is no closer to reality than Van Gogh's sky." This is a portrait of Einstein as interpreted by **Mark English.** Is it closer to the actual man than, say, his fingerprint? There is an intended confusion (a visual metaphor) between the fluffy, hairlike background clouds and Einstein's fluffy, cloudlike hair. And both may suggest the considerably more ominous mushroom cloud with which he is historically linked. English has embedded two broken continuity lines that are fairly evident: The first comprises the top of the pipe as well as the horizon line, while the second forms the stem of the pipe as well as the edge of the finger. Courtesy the artist.

The Relativity of Realism

Porta, Lebrun, and Linnaeus began with a shuffled deck of things: the world of natural forms. Each man tried to sort those things. It was an astoundingly difficult task since each thing in the natural world features many more attributes (hoofs, horns, habitat, facial traits, body size, color, reproductive behavior, brain size, and so on) than does a simple deck of cards. They emphasized different attributes, so that it comes as no surprise that they arrived at different suits, at different constellations of things. Is there a Natural Order? Is there one "realistic" suit, while all other suits are wrong?

If two of us were sorting cards and we arrived at different suits, we are unlikely to insist that one way of sorting is always right while another is always wrong. Outside the rules of various games (for example, Whist or Bridge), they are simply different suits. Yet probably every cultural group (and every intracultural group) believes that the way it sorts the world is the *only* way to sort, since each intends to formulate arrangements they believe are *most like* the world they mean to represent.

All illustrations are made by this procedure, and it is in this sense that all illustrations are caricatures. Each and every one is made by including certain characteristics of things while omitting others. Depending on what we attend to, we will depict an alternate suit, arrive at a "different picture" of things, although the deck remains the same.

Probably every cultural group believes that its way of illustrating the world is more realistic than that of any other group. All other styles, it assumes, are absurd and distorted. Their authors are blind, inept, or simply misinformed.

When Leonardo sorted the world, he arrived at a sorting scheme radically different from the one used by the critic Chang Yen-Yuan. They sorted according to different games, in cultures that played by vastly different rules. Chang was playing Contract Bridge, while Leonardo was engaged in La Belle Lucie Solitaire. Was one correct, the other wrong?

Both began with a table in space. But Leonardo's scheme assumes that *size* and *distance* should be grouped (that these two things belong as one), that size should shrink as distance grows. Chang Yen-Yuan's scheme does not correlate size and distance. It attends to other similarities and ignores other differences. It places *size* within the same suit as *social importance;* as a person's role expands, so does his or her relative size.

Each culture subscribed to a logical game. Each artist arrived at a logical suit. And each believed that his was the Natural Order of things, that the model he made was most similar to the thing it represented.

OVERLAPPING A system of representation in which parts of background objects are omitted and foreground objects are completely rendered; in this way we can depict one thing in our line of sight as being behind another. Also called *masking.*

STACKING A system of representation in which an object is depicted as standing behind another object by placing the former above the latter.

TEXTURE GRADIENTS J. J. Gibson's term for the use of patterned planes in linear perspective. The recurrent use of the checkerboard floor in paintings since the Renaissance is a prime example. Gradual shrinkage of the squares supports the illusion of distance.

In every story, I search out the paintable part. Not necessarily the most significant, but the most paintable. . . .

Robert Weaver, illustrator, interview in *Print* (1974).

FIGURE 3–31 When an opaque object is placed in front of another object, a portion or all of the latter may be obscured by the former. This is called **overlapping.** It is a clue to where things are, since we usually conclude that the hidden object is more distant from the eye. But we can be deceived by shapes that only seem to overlap, as shown in this illusion, based on one devised by **Adelbert Ames, Jr.** In the left photograph, the eight of hearts appears to be nearer to the camera because it seems to overlap the back of another card. But as the second view reveals, the eight of hearts is not in front. A quarter of the other card has been carefully removed.

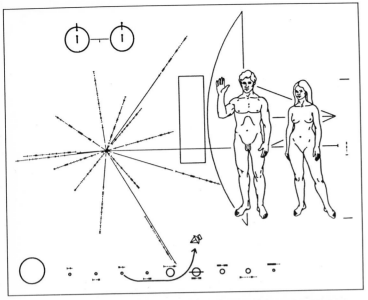

FIGURE 3–32 This picture was sent into space in 1972 by the National Aeronautics and Space Administration (NASA) as a plaque on the *Pioneer* spacecraft. It was intended to convey a message that might make some sense to extra-terrestrial creatures. The plaque designers were not so naive as to have written the message in words, since words are mere conventions that we can only understand if we speak the language used. What they did not realize apparently is that there are visual conventions that we unwarily employ whenever we use pictures. Outline drawing is one, the omission of shadows another, and the use of overlapping (in which opaque objects obscure the shapes behind them) is a third. This drawing, however, is really a medley of four different pictures, each one containing different assumptions. The pair of circles at the top is a symbol of binary thinking. At the bottom is a drawing of the Sun, the Earth, and other planets, showing their relative order and size, along with the path of the spacecraft. Above them is a web of lines indicating the fourteen pulsars of the Milky Way (the fifteenth line, the unbroken horizontal, is not to be confused with them, apparently). The humans have been drawn in proportion to the size of the spacecraft, which their opaque bodies hide. They appear to be naked Caucasians. The male is larger and more assertive than the female, as evidenced by his active stance, as well as his gesture of greeting (a gesture that is rare and not readily understood outside the European speech community). If this drawing confuses us, it would no doubt baffle most of the human beings who have occupied Earth throughout history, not to mention extra-terrestrials. Courtesy NASA.

FIGURE 3–33 In Renaissance representation, it is assumed that things are seen from a single point of view. One of the ways in which this work is intentionally disturbing (it makes us take a second look) is that the body faces us while the arm that holds the gun appears to be in profile. Some detachment is implied between the body and the arm, suggesting that the subject (or the viewer) is standing in two different places at once. This is a portrait of General George Armstrong Custer by the American illustrator **Mark English.** Attending to the work's design, it is apparent that the gun is a disguised repetition of the horizontal stripes, while the rounded band of stars is an echo of the hand. A broken continuity line forms the edge of the lapel (just to the left of the buttons), then reappears within the gun, and again as the edge of the collar. Courtesy the artist, 1975.

FIGURE 3–34 What is an appropriate way to illustrate a particular text? What kind of artwork might convey the message that the words express? The American illustrator **Alan E. Cober** was faced with that familiar problem in 1977 when *Skeptic Magazine* commissioned him to illustrate an article on the assassination of Martin Luther King, Jr. King was shot and killed on the balcony of the Lorraine Motel in Memphis in 1968. Later, a man named James Earl Ray was arrested and charged with the crime. "I was sent approximately 100 UPI and AP photos of King, James Earl Ray, the Lorraine Motel, and so on." the artist recalls. "In looking through the photographs, one stood out as being familiar and famous. It was King walking in Memphis with Ralph Abernathy during the garbagemen's strike." The photograph was taken on the day of the assassination while King participated in a protest march, arm in arm with Abernathy (a prominent American black leader) on one side and another leader on his other side. Cober's memory suddenly clicked: Two years before, he had developed an illustration for *The Trial* by Franz Kafka, in which the book's protagonist, Josef K., is shown being led away to his execution, with officials at his sides. Cober combined these two concepts (he pretended to confuse the two, and thus he made a *metaphor*) in an image in which Martin Luther King (as if he were Josef K.) is being led to his assassination by two unknown assassins. In Cober's words, "I reinterpreted the [Kafka] drawing and King in the photograph, leaving my assassins faceless. We did not (and still don't) know if Ray acted alone or in concert with others." Courtesy the artist.

Art does not reproduce the visible; it makes visible.

Paul Klee.

What we regard as the most realistic pictures are merely pictures of the sort that most of us, unfortunately, are brought up on. An African or a Japanese would make a quite different choice when asked to select the pictures that most closely depict what he sees.

Nelson Goodman, "The Way the World Is," in *Review of Metaphysics* 14 (September 1960): 48–56.

FIGURE 3–35 In linear perspective, an increase in distance is indicated by a decrease in the size of things. That system is not used in this work. The squares of the checkerboard floor are the same size throughout. The size of the people is always the same, whether they are far or near. The placement of objects in space is indicated by **stacking** (the nearest objects are at the bottom, and farther things are stacked in space above them) and by **overlapping** (in which opaque foreground objects block our view of background objects). In linear perspective, a scene is represented from a single point of view. In this illustration, however, several different points of view are simultaneously employed. Thus, we see the tables from above, while the wine bottle and the people are seen from the side. This painting by **Anita Kunz** was used to promote a dining periodical, the *Toronto Calendar Magazine.* Courtesy the artist.

Art as a Partisan Model

Three centuries after Pierre Lebrun proposed that art should copy life ("the eye must be deceived, or the picture is worth nothing"), Virginia Woolf erased her life. In 1941, the English novelist drowned herself, because she believed she was becoming insane. Before that, she had stated that art is not a copy of life because "one of the damned things is enough."

Woolf was right, Lebrun was wrong. Art is a partisan model of life. It is at best a half-truth. It is a selected assortment of signs in which only certain traits are included (for example, red beneath) while equally evident features of things (for example, fins and gills) are blurred, neglected, or left out.

In one way or another, to this degree or that extent, art is always *dissimilar* from the thing it is a model of. Art is able to function as "art" because it is distinct from "life." Art is artifice or pretense. It bears the tenuous link to life that actors have to the parts they play, that menus have to the food we eat, that words have to the things they mean. A map is not the land it charts, our food is not composed of ink, and words like "cat" do not meow.

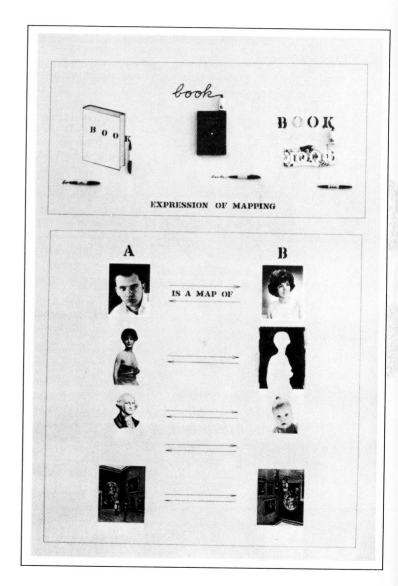

FIGURE 3–36 "No sign system has the same structure as the world," observed Morse Peckham in *Man's Rage for Chaos* (New York: Schocken, 1967). We should not mistake the menu for the stew. An illustration is not a full equivalent of the thing it illustrates. **Arakawa** is a contemporary artist who deals with the complex relationship between representations of things and the things they represent. This artwork, entitled "Mapping of Meaning," was published in *The Mechanism of Meaning*, by Arakawa and Madeline H. Gins (New York: Abrams, 1979). Reproduced courtesy Arakawa.

FIGURE 3–37 The representation of a thing is not the thing it represents. Or as Alfred Korzybski would say, "the map is not the territory," neither in illustration, nor in cartographic projection. The spherical surface of the Earth cannot be converted into two dimensions without some loss in fidelity. Here are five projections of the shape of the Americas, each quite distinct; and yet each is *like* the land when judged in terms of certain traits and just as certainly *unlike* when judged in terms of other traits.

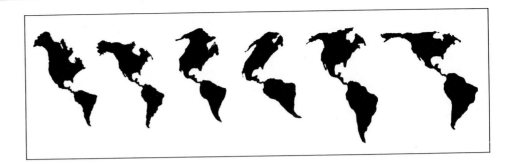

[The Japanese] could easily have adapted the Western scheme of representation which was offered and popularized in Dutch textbooks on perspective. They preferred to adhere to their own style because they felt it to be a true representation of reality. . . . They felt that perspective shortening depends on the accidental location of the viewer, while art is supposed to represent reality as such rather than a chance impression. For the same reason Japanese painters did not reproduce shadows. Of course they saw them, fled into the shade from a scorching sun, but they did not want to paint them. . . . They [the shadows] did not belong to the reality of things, being only changing phenomena.

Ludwig von Bertalanffy, *Perspective in General Systems Theory* (New York: Braziller, 1975).

Like all the other symbolic forms art is not the mere reproduction of a ready-made, given reality. . . . It is not an imitation but a discovery of reality.

Ernst Cassirer, *An Essay on Man.*

Picasso, you and I are the greatest painters of our time, you in the Egyptian style, I in the modern.

Henri Rousseau to Picasso, quoted in Man Ray, *Self Portrait* (Boston: Little, Brown, 1963).

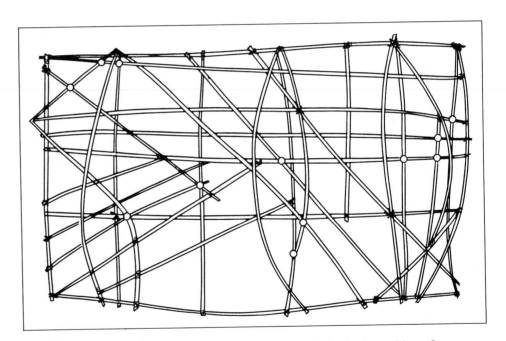

FIGURE 3–38 Cartographers are illustrators who specialize in the making of maps. But this map is not the work of a cartographer, at least not a Western one. This is a drawing of a sailing map constructed by the people of the Marshall Islands in the Western Pacific. Stones and seashells represent various islands while strips of cane are symbols of prevailing winds and currents. Could it be called realistic?

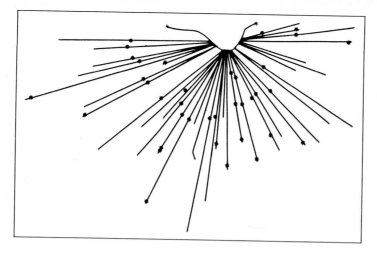

FIGURE 3–39 Is this a meaningful likeness of time? This diagram is derived from an ancient Peruvian *quipu*, which was made by knotting colored strings. It functioned like an abacus (a computing frame that uses beads) in that it was used to keep a record of accounts and to recall events. Using string and knots like this, we could represent our lives. Perhaps each string would be a year, each knot an important occurrence.

FIGURE 3–40 There is a famous fresco by the fourteenth-century Florentine painter Maso de Banco in which the artist illustrates the performance of a miracle by St. Sylvester. On the left side of the painting, St. Sylvester is portrayed as heroically binding the poisonous jaws of a ferocious dragon, which killed hundreds with its breath. On the right side, he reappears in a scene in which he is blessing four curious men, two of whom are lying down while the other two are kneeling. They look like two sets of identical twins. In fact, the scene is meant to show three different moments in time simultaneously within a single painted space. In the first, he binds up the jaws of the dragon; in the second, he blesses the bodies of two men who have been poisoned by the dragon's breath; and in the third, he addresses the same two men, who have revived and who kneel before him now. The fresco by Maso is relevant here because a somewhat similar scheme is being used in this mixed-media collage by **Constance Gage-Kivlin.** A simple story is implied which moves in steps from left to right. The sequence begins on the far left with a slingshot and a targeted bird. In the center, the bird is struck, and, on the right, it disappears. Three distinctly different times are simultaneously portrayed within a single time and space. Courtesy the artist, 1982.

FIGURE 3–41 A rich array of diverse parts has been skillfully combined in this *Portrait of a Young Girl,* a collage by **Carol Wald.** A section of the hair is from *The Birth of Venus* by Sandro Botticelli, the Renaissance Florentine painter. This has been subtly intertwined with fragments of a striped cloth, photographs of trees and sky, displaced scraps of mud or clay, and so on. The artist has said regarding her works that "My personal themes reside deep within my private psyche. They haunt me, inspire me and drive the machinery. Ideas seem to germinate for years before maturing, but once a series has begun, the form seems natural and predictable to me. My themes are often quite real people seen in unreal environments, or juxtapositions of ancient symbols in new unexpected places." The original artwork is in the collection of Hermann D. Tauchut in Detroit. It was published in 1982 by Hoechst-Roussel Pharmaceuticals, Inc. The art director was Richard Laurence Stevens. Courtesy the artist.

The value of representational art is that the object and the work are not the same. . . .

Stephen D. Ross, *A Theory of Art: Inexhaustibility by Contrast* (Albany: State University of New York, 1982).

This Is Not the Thing Itself

Illustrations are not to be confused with the things they portray. There is a prankish painting on this theme by the Belgian Surrealist René Magritte, a painting that depicts a pipe. Beneath the image of the pipe, the painter has carefully written in French, *"Ceci n'est pas une pipe,"* which means "This is not a pipe" (Figure 3–42).

Paintings of pipes are paintings of pipes. But pipes are pipes, and art is art. Magritte was a painter. He was not a pipemaker. His painting illustrates a pipe, but it is not a pipe per se, and thus his caption cautions us that we should not confuse the two. His label is the opposite of the label that Lebrun would use ("It's the real thing").

A pipe is a tangible, functional thing. It can be filled. It can be reamed and lit and smoked. Contrarily, Magritte's painting of a pipe cannot be filled nor reamed nor smoked. It is a space inscribed with paint. It would seem beyond dispute that his painting of a pipe is a remarkably disparate thing from objects known as "pipes." Indeed, *any painting is more like another painting than it is like any pipe.*

If we are to understand the possibilities and limitations of illustration (including its frequently harmful abuse), we must always keep in mind that the model of a thing can never be fully identical to the thing itself. Artists are not the makers of things. They are makers of representations of things.

The word "dog" does not bite.

William James.

My line wants to remind constantly that it's made of ink.

Saul Steinberg, quoted in H. Rosenberg, *Saul Steinberg* (New York: Knopf, 1978).

My beer cans have no beer in them.

Jasper Johns, quoted in Suzi Gablik, *Magritte* (Greenwich, Conn.: New York Graphic Society, 1973).

My rug is not to be walked on.

Tom Wesselmann, *ibid.*

This is not a pipe.

FIGURE 3–42 This is not a pipe, nor is it a painting of a pipe. It is instead a loose parody of a painting by **René Margritte,** the Belgian Surrealist, who painted a number of pictures of pipes (the first in 1926, the last in 1966) in which he also wrote the phrase *"Ceci n'est pas une pipe"* (French for "This is not a pipe"). And of course his paintings are *not* pipes; and, at least in relation to most of their traits, his paintings have little in common with pipes. Indeed, as Suzi Gablik notes, any painting is more like another painting than it is like any pipe. See *Magritte* by Suzi Gablik (Greenwich, Conn.: New York Graphic Society, 1973); and *This Is Not a Pipe* by Michel Foucault (Berkeley: University of California Press, 1983).

The Necessity of Difference

If a menu were the meal, it would be the same as food. A model is a model because it is not identical to the thought or thing it brings to mind.

The same applies to works of art. The people who gathered in ancient Greece to watch the *trompe l'oeil* contest between Zeuxis and Parrhasius were not in the least surprised that birds would peck at a cluster of grapes. But they were stupified to find that birds would peck at an *image* of grapes.

Nor would they have been amazed if Zeuxis had reached for an actual veil. But they were thrilled beyond belief when he perceived a painted veil (which is so *unlike* things called veils) as if it were the thing itself.

It is not just its link with life that causes us to gasp in awe when we confront an illustration. It is as much because we know that paint is not the same as pipes, that daubs are not the same as grapes. that lines are not the same as veils.

All this may bewilder you if you were taught (as most of us were) that it is the artist's task simply to arrange some shapes in such a way that they result in what a naive mind would term a "photographic view." Fortunately (and unfortunately), art is considerably harder than that.

If only art were as austere as Leonardo thought when he simplistically observed that "that painting is most praiseworthy which is most like the thing represented." In fact, as one can easily show (and as advertisements prove), resemblance is not required at all between the model and the thing to cause us to respond to signs as if they were the thing itself.

For the moment let us say that we agree to make a work that is profoundly similar to (*most like*, to use the earlier phrase) a pipe or veil or horse or ass, or virtually any observable thing. Where do we start? What shall we do? But before we can even begin to begin, two very troublesome questions arise: (1) What is the genuine nature of things? And (2), how can we construct a work that will be in essence equal to the thing that it will represent?

At the outset, it is an increasingly difficult task to say that things are this or that, to say for sure what life is like. Merely by posing the problem in words, we have employed a set of signs, and signs (as Ernst Cassirer knew) are far from identical to the things that they are models of.

We could restrict ourselves to sight, and thus refrain from using words. But meaningful seeing can only occur when we selectively attend to a limited number of traits. We cannot see unless we sort, and when we sort we must select and ignore. So even our signless perception of things is not an immaculate equal to the nature of the things we see.

. . . reality surpasses the fictions of even the wildest imaginations. Like a machine for milking a rat. Incredible, yet it actually exists. . . .

Eduardo Paolozzi, interview in *Studio International* (1971).

All the really good ideas I ever had came to me while I was milking a rat.

Anon.

As if these snares were not enough, we encounter another complication as soon as we become aware of the contextual or relative nature of life. There is reason to believe (in physics, perception, and certainly art) that the character, function, and meaning of things seem to change magically when they are extracted from one locale and radically shifted or juxtaposed. Thus, when we define a thing, we must also note the context in which we observed it. In other situations, or when perceived by other means, the nature of the thing may change.

The problem of specifying things has become much more complex within the past few hundred years. The invention and popular use of tools and systems for looking at things have enormously enlarged the range of ways in which things appear. The more familiar now include X-ray photography, microphotography, thermograms, laser holography, infrared devices, color coding, time-lapse photography, gamma-ray imaging, sonography, stroboscopic photography, and so on. Combined with the factor of context, these extensions of the eye have brought us to the stressful stage at which (in Siegfried Kracauer's words) "not one single object has retained a fixed, definitely recognizable appearance."

FIGURE 3–43 What is the genuine nature of things? In this pair of photographs, two people of virtually equal height are positioned in opposite corners of an Ames Distorted Room. It is one of approximately thirty unusual visual illusions (collectively referred to as the Ames Demonstrations in Perception) that were developed and discussed between 1935 and 1950 by an inventive American optical physiologist, Adelbert Ames, Jr. Look closely at the photographs. The height of the left wall is six feet, while (despite its deceptive appearance) the height of the right wall is only three feet. The floor and ceiling are inclined. From all but one position, the distorted nature of the room is obvious, but from this single point of view the room appears to be normal. We judge things by comparison and, in this case, a person might mistakenly think that the room is normal, that the people are radically different in size. This version of the Ames Room was constructed in 1973 by John Volker and the author as part of a children's exhibit at the Waterloo Arts Center in Waterloo, Iowa. Photographs by John Volker.

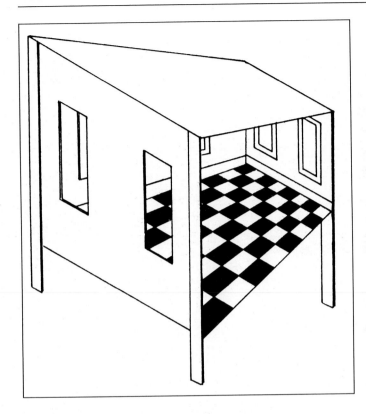

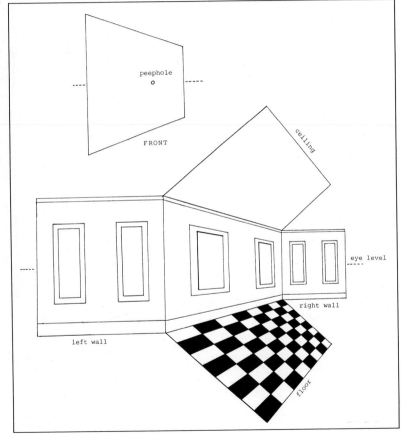

FIGURE 3–44 Drawing of a side view of an assembled Ames Distorted Room, with the peephole panel removed.

FIGURE 3–45 This is a simplified layout of an Ames Distorted Room, showing its flattened dimensions (as if it were an unfolded carton). Notice that the rear wall is a trapezoid. Ames had originally studied to become an artist, but he was apparently unaware that there was a long tradition of distorted rooms or peep shows in the history of art, all of which had been derived from variations on linear perspective. Considerably enlarged, cut out, and assembled, this diagram could be employed to make a model of the room.

FIGURE 3–46 Illusions of shrinking and growing associated with the Ames Distorted Room can be achieved without the room. In connection with part of her graduate work at the University of Wisconsin-Milwaukee, the artist **Amy Marein** developed a set of outdoor illusions that were in part inspired by the earlier work of Adelbert Ames, Jr. This photograph appears to show two people of differing sizes climbing a makeshift staircase. In fact, the people are the same size, and the staircase has been made by placing sticks of balsawood (of varying widths) in the ground or on the grass. Photograph by Amy Marein, 1981. Courtesy the artist.

FIGURE 3–47   In this pair of photographs, the same arrangement of objects is shown from two different positions. On the left, it would appear that shoes of different sizes are posed on top of a staircase. On the right, the illusion is revealed—the shoes are shown to be the same size, while the staircase is now seen as a deceptive arrangement of balsawood sticks. Illusions of this general kind (including the Ames Distorted Room) are made to work by playing with the relationship between size and distance. By increasing the distance of a thing (for example, the shoe in this photograph), it may appear to be smaller, if Renaissance rules of perspective are used. Photographs by **Amy Marein,** 1981. Courtesy the artist.

FIGURE 3–48 An **anamorphic** engraving of a skull, originally published in a book on linear perspective by **Lucas Brunn** (*circa* 1615), appears to be more or less normal when viewed obliquely from the top. It is reminiscent of the floating anamorphic skull that glides across the carpet, somewhat inexplicably, in *The Ambassadors*, a masterful double portrait by Hans Holbein the Younger in the National Gallery in London.

FIGURE 3–49 Anamorphic distortion was used in this acrylic painting by **John Martin** to represent executive stress. Regarding this particular work, Martin observed that "I have used distortion in my paintings a number of times, but I do not use it exclusively. Only when it is appropriate for conveying certain information to the observer do I attempt distortion." In a way, every illustration is a disguised depiction of its illustrator. This painting is especially autobiographical because, as Martin has explained, "I had just come through a very stressful period in my own life and so this painting became a self-portrait in which I had an opportunity to externalize the feelings I'd had during this period. Through my somber use of colors, side lighting, and distortion, I tried to show my isolation, body tension, the weight of external pressures and the distorted perception of my own body, which at times could seem so very far away." The painting was originally published in *Financial Post* in 1980. The art director was Jackie Young. Reproduced courtesy the artist. Those who are intrigued by the autobiographical content of artworks should see Leon Edel's *Stuff of Sleep and Dreams* (New York: Avon, 1982), in which he persuasively shows that there is no sharp division between "the dancer and the dance," between the artist and the art.

ANAMORPHOSIS A kind of elongated puzzle picture invented by Leonardo da Vinci (and, independently, by the ancient Chinese), and thereafter commonly used as a means of concealing erotic images. When viewed normally from the front, the image appears to be hopelessly stretched, but the picture is clear when observed from the side.

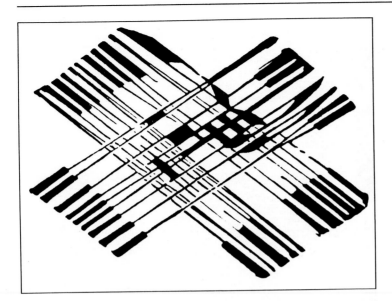

FIGURE 3–50 When viewed obliquely at eye level, this anamorphic message reads *A Happy New Year*.

Neither an artist nor a geometrician—not even a photographer—has ever produced a perspective wholly "true" in that it corresponded with the visual image received at the actual scene. This is not a mere philosophical quibble. The discrepancies are substantial and they have practical implications.

Lawrence Wright, *Perspective in Perspective*.

FIGURE 3–51 This anamorphic couple has been extracted from an engraving by **Grandville** (Jean Ignace Isidore Gérard), originally published in 1844 in his book *Une Autre Monde* ("Another World"). The distortion of the figures lessens when viewed obliquely from the top.

FIGURE 3–52 Jimmy Carter had just become the thirty-ninth president of the United States in 1977 when student artist **Kathryn Dyble Thompson** produced this watercolor portrait of him, in which he is anamorphically stretched. Courtesy the artist.

FIGURE 3–53 It is possible to produce an anamorphic image by simply drawing normally while viewing the page from the edge. A more formal method, described by **Jean-François Niceron** in 1646, is shown in the diagrams here. In this method, the drawing is first constructed as a normal drawing within a regular grid. The grid is then distorted, and the drawing is transferred within it.

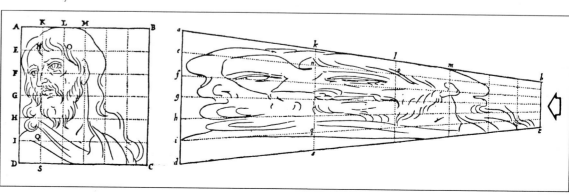

To those of us accustomed to the idiom of the realism of the photographic lens, the degree of conventionalization that inheres in even the clearest, most accurate photograph, is something of a shock. For, in truth, even the clearest photograph is a convention; a translation of a three-dimensional subject into two dimensions, with color transmuted into shades of black and white.

M. J. Herskovits, *Cultural Relativism* (New York: Vintage, 1972).

FIGURE 3–54 One of the most peculiar examples of anamorphosis occurs not in the visual arts but in perceptual psychology. It is the Ames Rotating Trapezoid Window, designed by **Adelbert Ames, Jr.,** inventor of the Distorted Room. In fact, the rear wall of the Distorted Room is the same shape as the Rotating Trapezoid Window. In the Rotating Window, an anamorphic image of a window, fake shadows, and a slow rotation movement are used to produce a wonderfully baffling effect. These are exact diagrams of the front and back sides of the window. It is supposed to be attached to a motorized vertical rod that rotates at a speed of 3 to 6 rpm's. However, when viewed at a distance of about 20 feet (or closer if you cover one eye), the window appears to sway back and forth rather than to rotate. Further, when an object is attached to it (for example, a ball or rod), the object appears to go around while the window continues to oscillate. A ball appears to float in midair around the window; a rod appears to bend in space or pass through the bars of the window. A small working model can easily be made from these drawings; they should be projected and traced to a width of about 6 inches, mounted to a piece of thin cardboard, and then cut out from it. In viewing the illusion, it is best to stare intently at the center of the horizontal bar. A black background or darkened room, and a low spotlight increase the illusion.

Models and Photography

Even if we do succeed in defining the genuine nature of things, we still have to construct a work equal to (or highly similar to) the thing that it will represent. However, a work that is entirely similar to a model is not necessarily a work of art. It may instead be the thing itself, or a clone of it.

Further, even if most of the work's features are irrefutably similar to the model's, they will still be dissimilar in their other traits. And thus another dilemma appears: What criterion do we use in deciding which features to include and which to omit or leave vague?

Most people would reply that we should emphasize those features that will best result in a "realistic" model of things. But what is realism if not the inclusion of genuine traits? And so again we have to ask: Which traits are we obliged to stress to produce a realistic representation of life?

Should they be the realistic traits of a photograph? But what kind of photograph? Taken with what kind of camera? With which filter? With which lens? Under what conditions of lighting? With what brand and type of film? With what film speed? With what aperture setting, what focus, what shutter speed? Printed on what kind of paper? Developed with what chemicals? Using which darkroom procedure?

All of these seemingly righteous techniques can vary much more than our culture admits. With each decision we insure that some features will be recorded, while others will not. Depending on which focus, filter, lighting, and lens we choose, we make it more likely that we will produce a comforting pattern of chemical stains, in which (like drawings and menus and maps) a preconceived fabric of features will be stressed, while equally visible features will be blurred, foreshortened, enshadowed, cropped, or just left out.

Of all the possible blotches and streaks that might be produced by placing a sensitive surface in light, we make only a miniscule percent (probably fewer than 5 percent); and most of those we disregard because they are *unlike* (we say) the nature of the things they show.

A camera does not "take" pictures of anything. It does not "capture" people's shapes. It does not "catch" the look of things, nor does it, by itself, even "record."

"You press the button. We do the rest." Indeed, we only point and press. But nature doesn't do the rest—Kodak does. The camera is a rigged machine, an intricate chemical staining device that can be somewhat reliably manipulated to fashion a partisan cluster of signs.

The camera is *not* an innocent eye.

FIGURE 3–55 Captain James Cook introduced the term "tattoo" to the English language in 1769, when he recorded in his log that the people of Tahiti "paint their Bodys, *Tattow,* as it is called in their Language. This is done by inlaying the Colour of Black under their skins, in such a manner as to be indelible." Thereafter, throughout Europe, there was a public interest in the freaklike exhibitions of the "illustrated" bodies of the heathen South Sea savages. Of particular interest were the inscribed visages of the Maori people of New Zealand, who preserved the embalmed heads of their enemies and their friends. No two tattoos were the same, and thus the pattern on the face was a unique emblem. As one Maori chief explained, a drawing of his tattoo (which he used on legal documents) was essentially the same as a Western signature—it was a genuine emblem of him. That same impression might also be reached by a comparison of these two drawings. The one on the top was done about 1800 by an Englishman, **John Sylvester.** It is the European way of portraying **Tupai Kupa,** a Maori chieftain. But the one on the bottom, done at the same time, is the chief's own drawing of how he should be portrayed. In comparing the two, it is apparent that both include some features of their subject, while ignoring others. Their focuses are distinctly separate. In the Maori drawing, everything contributes to the legibility of the tattoo. In the European version, the tattoo is no more important (indeed, it is partially hidden by shadow and the subject's pose) than the structure of the face, the details of the clothing, the direction of the light source, and the viewpoint of the artist. Reproduced from *The Childhood of Man* by Leo Frobenius (Philadelphia: Lippincott, 1909). Courtesy the publisher.

. . . perspective in the fifteenth century was sometimes seen not only as a branch of mathematics but as an almost magical process, having something of the surprise that our grandparents got from their Kodaks. Apply the method and the illusion unfolds; you press the button, we do the rest.

Robert Hughes, *The Shock of the New.*

. . . photographers do not point their cameras at everything. They select; and while we may be seduced by the impression of an open window we should never forget that out of an infinite universe of possible windows only one has been opened to us.

David Sless, *Learning and Visual Communication* (New York: Halstead Press, 1981).

And, speaking of spectacles, it often occurred to him that although man had no power to model the world as he wished, he had instead the power to grind lenses, through which we could make the world appear exactly as we pleased.

Georg Christoph Lichtenberg.

FIGURE 3–56   In part tattoos intrigue us because of their paradoxical nature. When pictures are inscribed on skin, the human figure is employed as if it were a background, and the illustrator is transformed into an illustration. In addition, two separate systems (the tattoo and the facial traits) are constantly colliding, often resulting in visual puns in which facial features are purposely mistaken for pictorial features. This picture is an apt example of that procedure, one that needs a closer look. It is a short story illustration by **Kunio Hagio,** originally published in *Playboy* in 1976 to accompany "Carny" by Harry Crews. Reproduced courtesy the artist, and by special permission of *Playboy* magazine. Copyright © 1976 by Playboy.

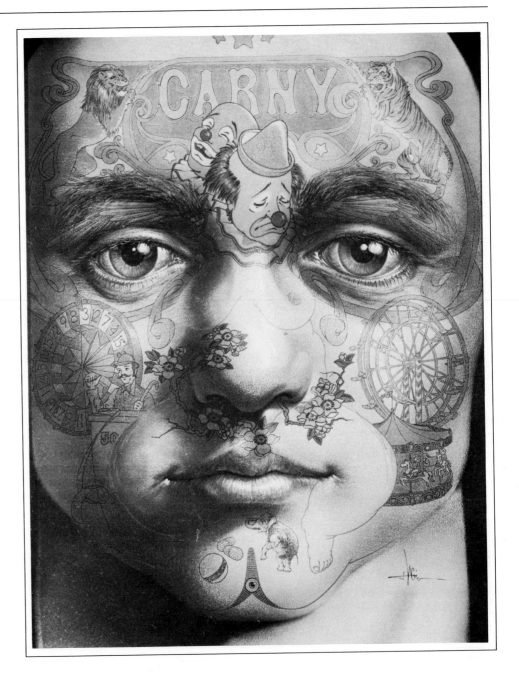

SPLIT REPRESENTATION A method of depiction in which multiple sides of an object are shown in full, somewhat as if the object were a flat, unfolded carton.

FIGURE 3–58 One of the most common ways in which representations of things differ from the things themselves is in the attribute of size. Representations are often scale models, whether smaller or larger than life. This self-portrait by **Alan E. Cober** is an exception. It is from a series of drawings of circus people and events, in which the drawings are the same size as the things that they depict—hence the series title: *Same Size Circus.* Cober developed these works in 1974, using ink and dip pens, and working on 90-inch sheets of paper. Courtesy the artist.

FIGURE 3–57 This drawing of a bear from the Tsimshian tribe of the Northwest Coast (like the preceding drawing by Tupai Kupa) is an example of **split representation.** Unlike linear perspective, this approach does not limit the picture to one point of view. Rather, all sides of the subject are shown as one flat pattern, by much the same procedure that we use when we project the spherical surface of the Earth onto the surface of a map. Reproduced from *Symbols, Signs, and Signets* by Ernst Lehner (New York: Dover Publications, 1969) from the Dover Pictorial Archives.

FIGURE 3–59 Part of this work's impact derives from its size. This huge acrylic painting by **William Nichols** is more than 10 feet wide and nearly 7 feet high. When viewed from a distance of several feet, it is a mass of abstract stains, but from farther away, it conveys a strong sensation that it is a same-size landscape, a life-sized world within the wall through which we are tempted to step. Entitled *Cedarburg Brook*, it was produced in 1982 to be displayed as a painting in galleries, museums, or private collections. It was then later reproduced as a large full-color poster, as is increasingly common today. Courtesy the artist.

FIGURE 3–60 For reasons of convenience, illustrations are usually made with paint or ink on paper. But if they could be reproduced, illustrations could be made from sand, a common way of painting among Native American groups in the Southwest. This is an anthropologist's pen and ink transcription of a Navaho colored sand painting. Round head shapes signify male figures, while rectangular heads indicate females. The central black cross represents pine logs on which gods and goddesses sit. Sprigs and rattles are employed to cause male and female rains, which in turn will bring about vegetation. Arched above this setting is the goddess of the rainbow. Compare the structure of this system of representation with that of traditional Renaissance art. Is one system more logical than the other? Is one more reliable than the other? Should only one be called "realistic," or both? Reproduced from *American Indian Design and Decoration* by Leroy H. Appleton (New York: Dover Publications, 1971) from the Dover Pictorial Archives.

. . . there is no representation of the way the world is. . . . None of them tells us the way the world is, but each of them tells us a way the world is.

Nelson Goodman, "The Way the World Is."

Art is significant deformity.

Roger Fry.

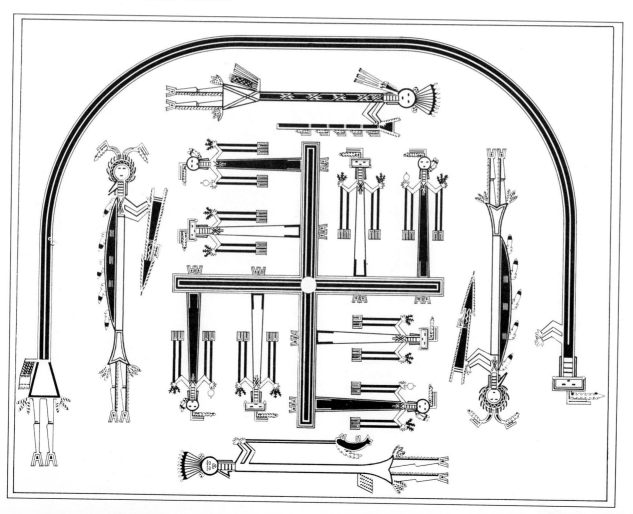

. . . what matters to us is that the correct portrait, like the useful map, is an end product on a long road through schema and correction. It is not a faithful record of a visual experience but the faithful construction of a relational model.

Sir E. H. Gombrich, *Art and Illusion* (New York: Pantheon, 1960).

FIGURE 3–61 One of the most unusual illustrators in history was the English poet and engraver, **William Blake.** Among his most intriguing works are *Songs of Innocence* (1789), *Songs of Experience* (1794), and *Illustrations for the Book of Job* (1825). Neither his art nor his writings were critical successes during his lifetime, and nearly all his books were engraved and published by himself. He was very eccentric, and it is generally believed that he was capable of *eidetic imagery.* It is not easy, nor perhaps is it of use, to decide if he was a visionary genius or (as one textbook contends) a paranoid schizophrenic, or both. Dame Edith Sitwell said of him that "he was undoubtedly 'cracked,' but that is how the light came in." This engraving represents the shadowy portion in everyone's life where sense and madness seem to blend. In an apparent paraphrase of Job 33:15–16, Blake (through Job) addresses God: "With Dreams upon my bed thou scarest me & affrightest me with Visions." Reproduced from *Medicine and the Artist* by Carl Zigrosser (New York: Dover Publications, 1970) by permission of the Philadelphia Museum of Art, from the Dover Pictorial Archives.

FIGURE 3–62 According to Freudian theory, there are two layers of structure in dreams, one of which is evident (the dream as we remember it), while the other is cleverly hidden (the dream as we interpret it). Thus, as Jacob Jastrow said, the dream "smuggles its wares by wrapping them in camouflaged packages and employing ingenious dramatic disguises. . . ." Dreaming is concealment, and the dream techniques that Freud described (condensation, symbolization, and displacement) might have been reduced to two: (1) those by which a thing is seen as being two or more, and (2) those by which two or more things are seen as being only one. These techniques are parallel to *estrangement* and *elopement* respectively, *making the familiar strange* and *making the strange familiar,* and *dazzle* and *blending* camouflage. Not surprisingly, Freud produced a book on jokes (*Jokes and Their Relation to the Unconscious*) in which he hypothesized that the same techniques are used in both dreams and humor. This acrylic painting by **Christel-Anthony Tucholke** is called *A Dreamer's Corner* (1980). As Arturo Fallico said, if we look for "an object which resembles the art-object, we will find none better than the dream." On the other hand, if we look for a thing that resembles a dream, we may not find anything better than this. It is an example of the *arranged marriage* (or radical juxtaposition) in which disparate things converge without a discernible reason to join. Courtesy the artist.

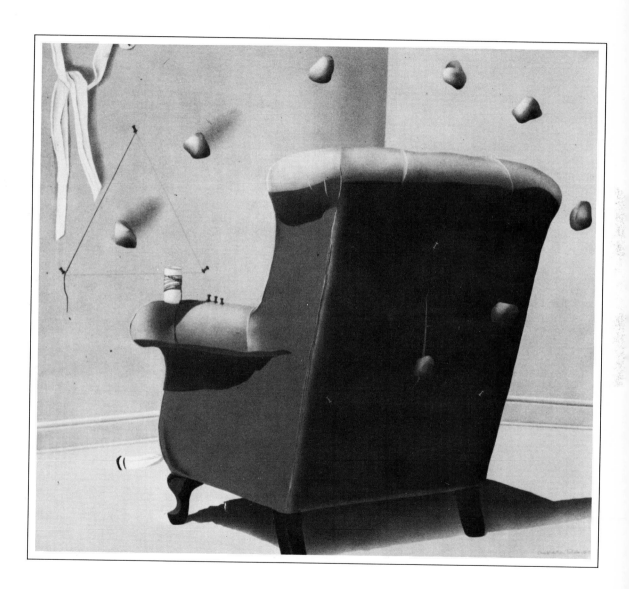

FIGURE 3–63   This lithograph by **Rockwell Kent** is entitled *Nightmare* (1941) and portrays the horrors of that dream state. The artist was a student of the American painters Robert Henri and Abbott Thayer. Throughout the first half of this century, he was extraordinarily prolific as a book illustrator (for example, Herman Melville's *Moby Dick*), lithographer, painter, and writer. The bold yet supple forms he used are especially fitting for this image of a man who (in dreams or waking states) is "on the brink" or on the verge of collapsing. This high-contrast use of light (known as *chiaroscuro,* Italian for "light-dark") is in the tradition of Caravaggio, Rembrandt, and Georges de La Tour, and has been used only since the late sixteenth century. Curiously, "night*mare*" is derived from the term that means a female horse. By metaphoric transfer, the word "mare" had come to mean an incubus, a demon that descends upon innocent virgins in their beds and makes them pregnant in the night. Apparently an incubus had certain horselike features. Reproduced from *Medicine and the Artist* by Carl Zigrosser (New York: Dover Publications, 1970) by permission of the Philadelphia Museum of Art, from the Dover Pictorial Archives.

FIGURE 3–64   Colors that are lighter (because they are mixed with white) usually seem to be nearer in space than colors that are darker (because they are mixed with black). Thus, under certain conditions, the juxtaposition of dark with light can create the illusion of depth. That is in part the reason for the keenness of this watercolor painting by **Thomas Uttech,** dated 1984. Visual rhymes are also used: the branches of the pine trees echo the foreground plants and the antlers of the moose; the tree trunks are reminders of the forelegs of the moose. In the background, a broken continuity line sets up the strong horizon and then resurfaces on the right as the backbone of the moose. Courtesy the artist.

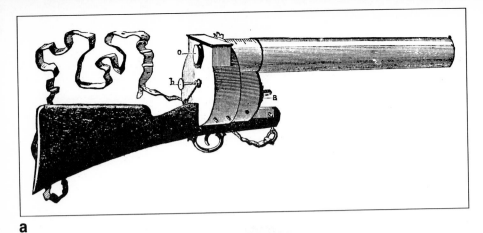

a

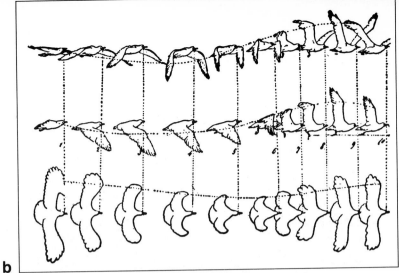

b

c

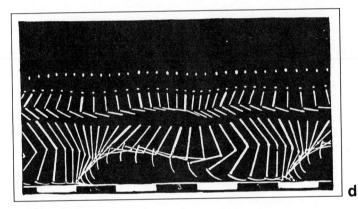

d

FIGURE 3–65 Most representations are static, while the things they portray are virtually always in motion. How should motion be represented? How can it even be observed? These were among the chief concerns of a nineteenth-century genius, the French physiologist **Étienne Jules Marey.** In his experiments after 1880, Marey used a camera gun (as shown by *a*) to record the movements of birds. Later he devised a way to photograph a flying bird from above, from the side, and from the front simultaneously (*b*). He investigated human movement by dressing his models in black tights with white stripes on their legs and arms (*c*). When photographed successively on a black background, the model's movements were reduced to a simple pattern of structural lines (*d*). It was this last procedure (which Marey referred to as *chronophotographie*) that inspired the infamous painting by Marcel Duchamp, *Nude Descending a Staircase, No. 2* (1912), by which most viewers were baffled when it appeared in the Armory Show.

FIGURE 3–66 Of all the inventions of **Étienne Jules Marey,** this may be one of the finest. This is a motion-picture machine, a spinning drum known as a *zoetrope.* Customarily, a strip of sequential photographs or drawings is placed inside the drum and then viewed from outside through the slits. When the drum is rotated, the static pictures merge into a single moving picture. But Marey took this procedure one step further, as this illustration shows. Instead of a strip of pictures, Marey used a sequential series of models of birds, sculpted in wax and painted in oils. Voila! He produced not just a motion picture of a bird in flight, but a kinetic sculpture which was, in its limited way, the first 3-D movie.

FIGURE 3–67 In stereo (3-D) photography, the subject is simultaneously chronicled by two cameras or one containing two lenses. Thus, two different views result, as shown in this antique stereo card. When viewed separately, or when both are viewed with both eyes, stereo pictures seem perfectly flat. But seen through a stereo viewer (in which one picture is seen by the right eye, the other by the left), the two views merge into one and the figures pop out from the background. The history and theory of stereoscopic representation are contained in *Foundations of the Stereoscopic Cinema* by Lenny Lipton (New York: Van Nostrand, 1982).

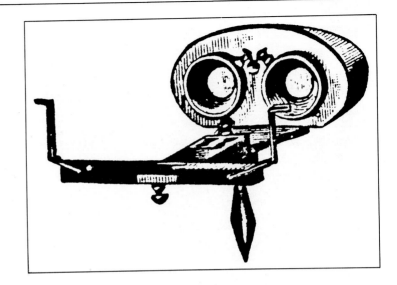

FIGURE 3–68 Until the 1950's, the most common type of 3-D viewer was this hooded stereoscope, invented by David Brewster in 1849. It was as ubiquitous as the Viewmaster, and thus it is not hard to find at antique shops, if often at an absurd price. The preceding stereo card was intended to be viewed in a Brewster stereoscope.

FIGURE 3–69 Stereo cameras can still be found (they are cameras containing two lenses), but there is no reason to bother with that. Stereo photographs can be made with any camera, as evidenced by this pair produced with a Polaroid. How is it done? Prop the camera on a table or other level support and ask the subjects not to move. Click the shutter once, then move the camera about five inches to either side and take another photograph. You now have 3-D photographs. But they cannot be properly viewed without the aid of a stereoscope. A modern plastic viewer, a stereoscope that geologists use, is currently manufactured by Hubbard Scientific Company, P.O. Box 105, Northbrook, Illinois 60062 at a cost of several dollars. In recent years, especially exciting stereograms have been produced by computer, some of which are published in *Foundations of Cyclopean Perception* by Bela Julesz (Chicago: University of Chicago Press, 1971).

FIGURE 3–70 In an engraving that **Brian Paulsen** calls *Family Television* (1983), a group of striped wooden swans, all wearing stereo glasses, is poised before a TV set. The swans appear to have been made by breeding ducks with barber poles. There is a Franz Hals on the wall, and the floor is a Mondrian update of the omnipresent checkerboard floor. Courtesy the artist.

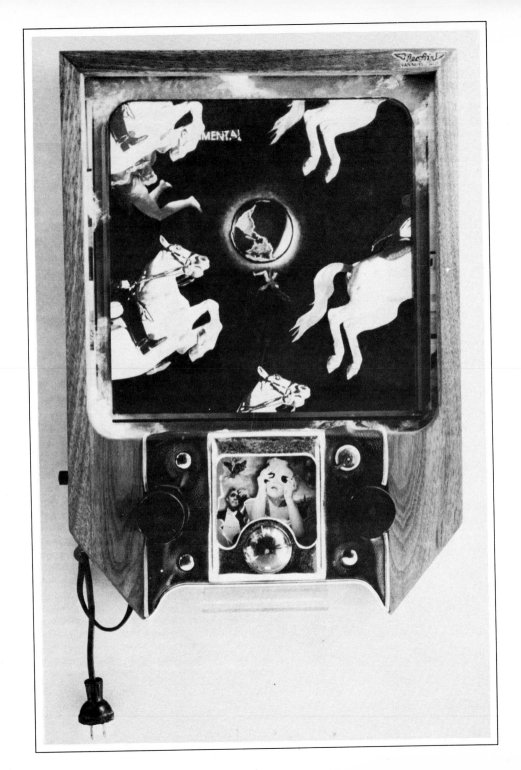

FIGURE 3–71 In the bottom central panel, a child of the 1950s is peering through stereo glasses as if to decipher the rest of the work. But even with stereo glasses, this artwork is purposely hard to decode. The artist's intention seems to be radical juxtaposition—that is, forcing the viewer to construct a constellation of emotions. The work is an assemblage by **Tom Noffsinger,** appropriately titled *Shooting Stars* (1983). Photographic reproduction has improved radically within the past few decades; an increasing number of illustrations are now produced as sculpture or assemblage, then reproduced as photographs. Courtesy the artist.

140

The Realism of Pavlov

In the second half of the nineteenth century, William Harnett was one of the best of a group of American artists who painted *trompe l'oeil* images of envelopes attached to boards, postage stamps, and playing cards (see Figure 3–72). His notable colleagues included John Haberle, John Peto, and Jefferson David Chalfant (who glued an actual two-cent stamp beside a meticulous copy of one and called the painting *Which is Which?*).

While studying painting in Munich, Harnett supposedly produced a portrait that appeared so real that one of the critics who saw it maintained that "you could walk up to it and pull the necktie from the subject's vest." When Harnett returned to live in the United States, his ability to simulate paper money was so widely talked about that Treasury agents began to suspect that he was Jack the Penman, an infamous forger of counterfeit bills.

In 1890, two years before Harnett's death, a forty-year-old Russian physiologist, Ivan Petrovich Pavlov, was appointed to direct the physiology department of the Institute for Experimental Medicine in what is now called Leningrad.

It is unlikely that Pavlov had ever heard of William Harnett, nor did Harnett know of him. Even if the two had met, they would probably have found little if any relation between the practice of representation in art and studies of gastric secretions in dogs.

In retrospect, however, Pavlov's work is seen to be central to the history and theory of illustration. It was he who proved that no resemblance is necessary between the model and the thing to cause us to respond to signs as if they were the thing itself.

In painting from still life I do not closely imitate nature. Many points I leave out and many I add.

William Harnett, interview in *New York Times*.

Before leaving Basle for England in 1526 and wishing to leave proof of his skill, the artist [Hans Holbein the Younger] painted a fly on a portrait he had just completed. The purchaser of the portrait, trying to remove the insect with a brush, discovered the jest. The story spread, and arrangements were set in motion to retain this virtuoso in the country. The painter therefore had to leave town in great secrecy.

Jurgis Baltrusaitis, *Anamorphic Art* (New York: Abrams, 1977).

FIGURE 3–72 In the late nineteenth century, it was rumored that the Treasury Department thought that an elusive counterfeiter (nicknamed Jack the Penman) was actually **William Harnett,** the American *trompe l'oeil* painter. But it was only a rumor, and less than a century later, a painting by this imitator of postage stamps (and envelopes, money, glass, and so on) was featured on a postage stamp. The Harnett painting reproduced was *Old Models* (1892), which is in the collection of the Boston Museum of Fine Arts.

FIGURE 3–73 By purposely blurring the image, the illustrator **Bill Nelson** conveys the sense of frozen motion. To incorporate this device is, in the words of the artist, "like adding another dimension to the figure. It's as if we have suddenly intruded on this figure, and he is doing his best to adjust. . . . This fellow was probably off somewhere day-dreaming about a fall day a few years back when everything was perfect—and all of a sudden we intrude upon him, and he is caught in midair as he tries to return and adjust." In this as in many of his artworks, there is a kind of theatricality, "perhaps because," as Nelson suggests, "I love the legitimate theater so much. The light in the ceilings of theaters bathes figures in wonderful ways." Colored pencil on charcoal paper, 1983. Courtesy the artist.

Fooling the Mind

Beginning in 1900 or so, Pavlov harnessed dogs in such a way that he could gauge the juices that their salivary glands released as a natural response to the presence of food. In one of his experiments, he consistently sounded a bell before presenting food to a dog. After repeated exposures, he found that at the mere sounding of the bell, without the sight or scent of food, the dog would salivate as if it had been confronted with food.

In modern psychological terms, this procedure is called *classical conditioning*. The food was an unconditioned natural stimulus, to which salivation is a natural, or unconditioned, response. The bell was a conditioned artificial stimulus, while the dog's response to it was unnatural, conditioned, or learned. Thus, it is common and proper to say that Pavlov "conditioned" his dogs to respond. But what he was doing was fooling the mind.

He was conditioning dogs to respond (by salivating) to an arbitrary sign (the bell) as if he were presenting them with food. In the terms that we have used, the bell became a "model" for food. It functioned as a substitute. It represented, or stood for, food. It was an illustration of food (a kind of menu for the ear), and it served as well as food in eliciting the normal response that would have been caused by genuine food.

For conditioned stimuli, Pavlov used not only bells but metronomes and flashing lights. For our purposes, the most interesting aspect of this **behavioral conditioning** phenomenon is that bells, lights, and metronomes have no traits whatever in common with food, that virtually *anything* can be used as a conditioned stimulus. There need not be any resemblance at all between the model (the bell, or conditioned stimulus) and the genuine thing (food, or the unconditioned stimulus) to cause dogs or people to act as if they were responding to the presence of the thing itself.

Pavlov's findings were later absorbed by J. B. Watson, E. L. Thorndike, and B. F. Skinner in their development of behavioral psychology. In behavioral therapy, *operant conditioning* methods are used as quick and expedient curatives for a range of divergent behavioral traits including alcoholism, phobias, sexual frigidity, smoking, stuttering, thumb sucking, and bronchial asthma. A fictional account of the method is found in Anthony Burgess's *A Clockwork Orange,* in which the unwilling protagonist Alex is "shaped" to respond negatively to films of sadistic behavior and the music of Beethoven by becoming horrifically ill.

BEHAVIORAL CONDITIONING   Changes in behavior brought about by contiguity grouping. In *classical* (Pavlovian) *conditioning,* a familiar reaction (salivation) is paired with something unfamiliar (the sound of a bell). In *operant* (Skinnerian) *conditioning,* an unfamiliar behavior (pressing a bar) is linked to an established need (the need for food).

Probably all artists think of their own work as realistic.

Robert Weaver, illustrator, interview in *Print* (1978).

FIGURE 3–74   This "puzzle picture" from the eighteenth century is called *The Isle of Dogs* because, especially when viewed at a distance, the island looks remarkably like a pair of snoozing mongrels. Reproduced from a book of engravings originally published by Bowles and Carver (*circa* 1970) entitled *Catchpenny Prints* (New York: Dover Publications, 1970) from the Dover Pictorial Archives.

FIGURE 3–75 A phobia is a neurosis in which a person responds to things in the environment with a fear out of proportion to the harm that the objects are likely to cause. Everyone is probably phobic to some degree, and different phobias predominate at different stages in our lives. A fear of snakes, for example, is most commonly found among twenty-year-olds, while phobic neurosis is most prevalent between the ages of forty and sixty. This acrylic painting by **John Thompson** was originally published in *Esquire* as an illustration for a novella entitled "Revenge" by Jim Harrison. The art directors were Milton Glaser and Margery Peters. The painting is a convincing likeness of the dread and despair of a phobic response. Much of the work's effectiveness is owing to the placement and intensity of the light source, from which the theatrical shadows result. Courtesy the artist.

Conditioning in Advertising

Pavlov taught his dog to sort and categorize. He trained it to arrange its world in such a way that bells and food would fall within the same suit. But Pavlov used no visual stimuli. The dog did not have to attend to shape, color, number, or relative size. The dog was deceived by **contiguity grouping,** which simply means that things will be grouped together when they recur together in time and space. It is the behavioral equivalent of radical juxtaposition, discussed in Chapter 2. Contiguity grouping predicts that things will seem to be a pair when they coincide in time. Aside from their temporal pairing, they need not have any resemblance at all.

To salivate in the presence of food is a normal and perfectly healthy response. Salivation has evolved because it lubricates the mouth and enables food to be predigested through the acts of biting and chewing. To salivate at the sound of a bell (or a metronome) is a feeble and strangely irrelevant act. Food is edible, bells are not. Dogs do not need bells to live. By making bells "the same as" food (by recurrent temporal pairing in space), Pavlov contrived an illusion of need. To use a popular marketing phrase, he set up a "viable market" for bells when he should have been selling his customers food.

As Nicholas Johnson once observed, "It used to be that people needed products to survive. Now products need people to survive." The *trompe l'oeil* misrepresentation of needs is the bread and butter of advertising. As TV commercials repeatedly prove, there need not be any resemblance at all between an esteemed but irrelevant lynx, eagle, horse, or beautiful girl (the thing itself) and a lavishly customized automobile (the model, albeit the latest model) that the ad is deceptively trying to sell.

CONTIGUITY GROUPING   A principle of perceptual organization in which it is predicted that things will appear to belong together (regardless of their visual traits) to the extent that they occur together in time. It is grouping by similarity of occurrence in time.

FIGURE 3–76   Prior to 1957 the illustration of all postage stamps issued in America was the work of artists on the staff of the Bureau of Engraving and Printing. In that year was established the Citizens Stamp Advisory Committee, consisting of historians, philatelists, and artists who make recommendations to the Postmaster General. It is not uncommon now for a civilian illustrator or other artist to be commissioned to design a postage stamp, especially a special commemorative stamp. Reproduced here are some of the recent postage stamps that have been designed by **Mark English.** In 1973, he produced a series of four stamps that honored American artists (Robinson Jeffers, poet; Henry O. Tanner, painter; Willa Cather, novelist; and George Gershwin, composer). In 1982, he designed an especially conspicuous stamp commemorating the 250th anniversary of the birth of George Washington. Compare this portrait of Washington with English's portraits of George Rogers Clark (p.33) and George Armstrong Custer (p.110), since they are similar in design. The Washington portrait is the only American stamp that makes predominant use of black, and its contrast underscores the structural lines implied by the edges of the collar and the top edge of the flag.

> . . . resemblance alone is not enough to establish a relationship of reference. In fact, representation is entirely independent of resemblance, since almost anything may stand for anything else.
>
> Suzi Gablik, *Magritte*.

> Art is illusion, not in the sense of optical illusions but in the sense that the theatre sustains an illusion. . . . For a work of art is not reality: it is a model of reality. It is a play on reality.
>
> Frederick Gore, *Painting*.

FIGURE 3–77 This page of perforated stamps is not a publication of the Bureau of Engraving and Printing. They were issued instead by Cow Town Art, the incorporated name of **Patrick Beilman,** in 1982. This artist started making stamps in 1975 because (in his own words) "I was responding to my need to distribute my artwork. . . . Stamps transcend geographic barriers, and yet they are inexpensive to send. Artists are able to reach beyond their studios without having to rely exclusively on galleries to exhibit what they make. This breaks down the isolation that many artists feel." Using various techniques, including color Xerox, Beilman makes highly unusual stamps that are to be affixed to standard mail, in addition to regular postage. "As I continued making stamps," he remembers, "I became aware of other artists and art movements, such as Fluxus, who also produced 'artists stamps'." In 1983, Beilman published a small book entitled *Artists' Postage Stamps 83* (Milwaukee: Cow Town Art, 1983), an anthology of stamps invented by twenty-five artists from Czechoslovakia, Japan, West Germany, Australia, the United States, and other countries. Each copy contains the original stamps. Courtesy the artist.

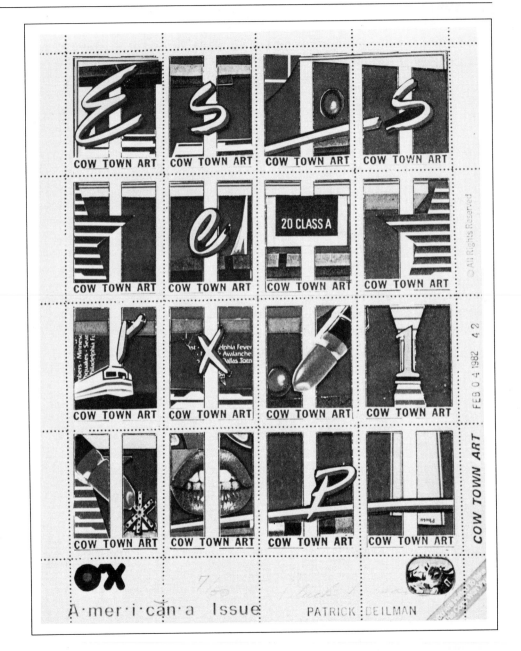

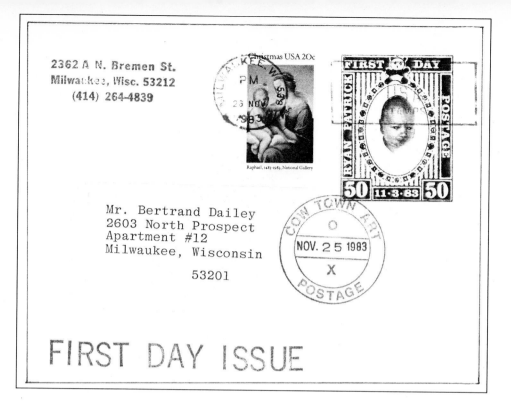

FIGURE 3–78 There are about a dozen definitions of the word *issue*. It can, of course, refer to something that is published (a postage stamp, for example), but it also refers to the birth of a child. Thus, on November 3, 1983, when Ryan Patrick Beilman was born, his father **Patrick Beilman** decided to announce his arrival by inventing a stamp, "first-day issue." The commemorative portrait was sent through the mail on envelopes, as shown here, accompanied by actual postage. Courtesy the artist.

FIGURE 3–79 The American illustrator **Gary Kelley** developed this poster illustration in 1980 to promote a season of productions at the Western Michigan University Theatre. The basic idea, as Kelley recalls, was "that of the actor's expression, emotion, and range as the very backbone of the theater. Technically, as in most of my work, I wanted the medium to be an important part of the finished artwork—thus the exposed underpainting and drawing, and the loose, gestural brushwork. Generally speaking, I wanted this to represent five emotions expressed by the same actor." The primary media are ink and acrylic. The esthetic logic of the work (its repetition with variation) derives from the juxtaposition of related but unique shapes. The line of circles on the cheeks is an especially effecive visual rhyme. Courtesy the artist.

FIGURE 3–80 The circle is the main motif in this hypothetical magazine cover illustration by student artist **Lori Svikel.** The large central targets are echoed inconspicuously by the circular joints of the body and the rows of circles on the wall. There is a visual link between the groups of ellipses and circular shapes, since ellipses are elongated circles. But ellipses are equally similar to the elongated stick-like shapes that make up the feet and the nose. Another underlying visual rhyme is found in the repetition of stripes within the magazine's logo, the figure's shorts, and the stripe on the floor. The work was completed with ad markers in 1985. Courtesy the artist.

148

As an illustrator, I am concerned with the communication of ideas that I or the client feel should be communicated. I try to find a balance between these external requirements and my own inner needs for self-expression, experiment, and play.

John Martin, illustrator, to the author (1983).

FIGURE 3–81   A richness of pattern and concept can arise from a combination of images derived from vastly different contexts. This illustration includes a painted copy of part of a sixteenth-century Mannerist work, a painting entitled *Hercules and Omphale* (*circa* 1575–1580). The artist of the quoted work was the Flemish master Bartholomeus Spranger, and the original is in Vienna. The artist of the total work is **Mara McAfee,** a contemporary New York illustrator who spent several years copying the paintings of masters in the Metropolitan Museum of Art as part of her art education. The juxtaposition of the painting on the wall and the young girl on the couch is especially powerful because of the directional cues. For example, the diagonal staff of Hercules points us toward the girl while the hand and finger of the girl guide us back toward Spranger's work. Courtesy the artist.

FIGURE 3–82 Talent does what it can, but genius does what it must, according to one aphorism. One of the consequences of the Renaissance was the pronounced distinction between the inspired creations of *art* and the pedestrian products of *craft*. With the onslaught of the Industrial Revolution (from about 1750 to 1850), inferior quality functional ware was widely mass produced. The Arts and Crafts Movement, which began in England about 1850, combatted that trend either by insisting on the abandonment of machine production (which was of course not feasible) or by proposing that artists be encouraged to design mass-produced objects. Members of the Arts and Crafts Movement aspired to the condition of the Balinese, who reportedly claim: "We have no art—we do *everything* well." The belief that art and craft are one led to the establishment of the German Bauhaus (1919–1933), the most influential art school of this century. In nineteenth-century England, one of the leaders of the Arts and Crafts Movement was **William Morris,** a poet, artist, craftsman, interior designer, and social reformer. Among the products he designed were furniture, wallpaper, stained glass, tapestries, and books. This is the initial page of the Prologue from *The Canterbury Tales*, from Morris's most remarkable book, *The Works of Geoffrey Chaucer*, published in 1896. The illustrations were derived from drawings by **Edward Burne-Jones.** They were redrawn by Morris, using black ink and white paint, then engraved on wood blocks by a master craftsman, William H. Hooper. Reproduced from *Ornamentation and Illustrations from the Kelmscott Chaucer* by William Morris (New York: Dover Publications, 1973) from the Dover Pictorial Archives.

FIGURE 3–83 The Russian artist Vladimir Tatlin traveled from Moscow to Berlin and Paris in 1913, where he observed the works of Picasso and others. On his return to Russia, he devised abstract assemblies of wood, paper, glass, plaster, and other nontraditional painting materials. Only two of these constructions survive, but photographs exist of many others. **Guy Davenport,** the American fiction writer who often illustrates his own writings, has come up with delicate versions of five of these constructions as part of his story, "Tatlin!," which is collected in his book by the same name (Baltimore: Johns Hopkins University Press, 1979). The original drawing was produced on Bristol board, using crow-quill and India ink. Regarding this drawing, Davenport said, "I drew this construct from an indistinct printed photograph, translating it from a medium in which its details were unclear into one more easily read. It is as much a part of the text of my story as the verbal." Courtesy the artist and the publisher.

FIGURE 3–84 There are those who still contend that photography conflicts directly with the traditional functions of art. That is surely not the case in the works of **Fred Otnes,** a prominent contemporary illustrator who frequently constructs his works on photosensitized linen. Through a combination of collage materials, photographic images, silkscreen, oil wash, and air brush, he produces a rich array of images that congregate and overlap. The main figure in this piece is a direct quotation (used here in a negative form) from a painting by Ingres, the nineteenth-century French master. The art director of this work was John deCesare. The client was the Art Directors' Association of Iowa. Courtesy the artist.

FIGURE 3–85 The British illustrator **Aubrey Beardsley** died in 1898 when he was just twenty-six. He was uncommonly prolific, and this drawing (an illustration for Alexander Pope's "The Rape of the Lock") is in the style of work that he fervidly produced in the last years of his life, before his death from consumption. The severity of his style (the emphatic use of line and the omission of shadow) was in part a consequence of his interest in Japanese woodcuts. Beardsley also illustrated Oscar Wilde's *Salome,* Artistophanes' *Lysistrata,* and Ben Jonson's *Volpone.*

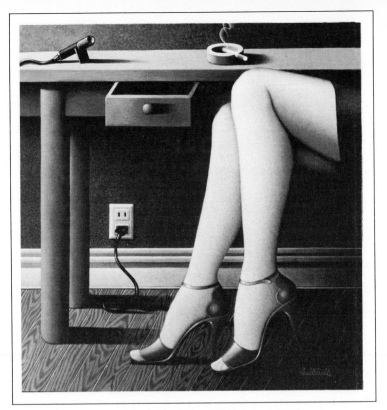

FIGURE 3–86 When Sigmund Freud was once accused of overemphasizing the role of sexual symbols, the father of psychoanalysis said, "Sometimes a cigar is just a cigar." But that is not the case in this erotic painting for an interview with an anonymous woman, originally published in *Oui* in 1981. This illustration uses popular conceptions of Freudian symbolism, in which the penis is implied by anything elongated, the vagina by any container. With that formula in mind, we may want to look again at such innocent pairs as the ashtray and the cigarette, the open drawer and microphone, and the male and female plug. We need not look too closely to find that the shape of the tops of the knees (the shape like breasts or buttocks) is precisely echoed in the shapes on the backs of the high-heeled shoes. In addition, some things occur in twos (the two legs of the woman, two table legs, two plugs, two molding strips along the wall). The odd shallowness of the space is partly the consequence of isometric perspective (as the floor boards clearly show). The artist is **Braldt Bralds,** a highly successful New York illustrator, as well as an instructor at the School of Visual Arts. Most of his paintings are made with oil on a Masonite panel. Courtesy the artist.

FIGURE 3–88 This exquisite pastel work was produced by student artist **David Lenz** to illustrate "Sudden Modeling," a short story by David Kranes that was originally published in *The North American Review* (June 1984). The story concerns the emotions and attitudes of a male artist toward the women in his life, and especially toward one of his models. Courtesy the artist and the publisher.

FIGURE 3–87 This work by **Norman Walker** was commissioned in 1982 by the Mobil Corporation for the Public Television production of *We the Accused*, the story of an Englishman who murders his wife in order to marry his lover, but who is then subverted in his attempt to fool a slow but brilliant British cop. The painting is in oil on board. The illustration was displayed on billboards, posters, and newspaper ads to promote the series. The artist has resorted to opaque overlapping in some areas, and transparency in others. The symmetry conveys a misleading simplicity; the work is quite complex in its subtle use of visual rhymes. For example, in the head of the detective the shapes that form the ears repeat those in the moustache; they also recur in the brim of the hat, the lip, and the shapes around the eyes. Courtesy the artist.

My paintings tell stories in the same way that a short story doesn't give too much information—it hits a mood, drops one or two bits of information in your lap, and then you make of those two pieces of information what you will.

Robert Weaver, illustrator, interview in *Print* (1978).

FIGURE 3–89 The American humorist S. J. Perelman was a chief scriptwriter for two films by the Marx Brothers, *Horsefeathers* and *Monkey Business.* In 1981, he published an essay in *Esquire* entitled "Going Hollywood with the Marx Brothers," recalling eventful and frustrating days, attempting to write for a comedy group that was known for its lack of compliance with scripts. This mixed-media illustration was published with Perelman's essay. On one of his first meetings with Perelman and his wife, Groucho Marx was darting about his dressing room in his underwear. **Blair Drawson** the artist has focused on that situation. The polka dots on Groucho's shorts rhyme with the light bulbs surrounding the mirror and, to a lesser degree, with the circular shapes on the shelf, the softened patterns on the dress, and the corsage on the right. The egglike eyes are also rhymes of a sort. The humor of the Marx Brothers was anarchistic and always disruptive, and precisely that feeling is conveyed by the predominance of diagonals and the inconsistent perspective. Nevertheless, this painting is highly systematic—for example, the main diagonal cuts across the background with exact symmetry, and the shapes on either side of the work (the mirror and the doorway) are symmetrically equal. The art director was Robert Priest. Courtesy the artist.

FIGURE 3–90 The range of abstract symbols associated with computerized video games communicates a modern madness in this cover illustration for *The Official I-Hate-Video-Games Handbook,* by Emily Praeger and Frank Morris, published by Pocket Books. The painting was done in acrylic by the book's co-author **Frank K. Morris,** who is also an accomplished illustrator. Courtesy the artist.

FIGURE 3–91 Of all the practitioners of what is regarded as Art Nouveau, perhaps the most exceptional was the Viennese painter **Gustav Klimt.** This is one of his pen and ink drawings, albeit not his strongest work, produced at about the turn of the century. A typically Art Nouveau product, this drawing emphasizes the innocuously overwrought rhythms of entwined female goddesses. At his best, Klimt was an important precursor to the less-pretty expressionist art of Egon Schiele and Oskar Kokoschka. Reproduced from Carol Belanger Grafton, *A Treasury of Art Nouveau Design and Ornament* (New York: Dover Publications, 1980) from the Dover Pictorial Archives.

FIGURE 3–92 Some of the most inventive effects are often the consequence of working in unorthodox ways. The idea for this anamorphic portrait occurred to student artist **David Leenhouts** while he was looking absent-mindedly at a damaged cutting board, on which he had trimmed a matt. He began to see shapes in the scars on the board, and, instead of discarding it, he used it as a painting surface. Notice the effects obtained from painting with a dry brush, as well as the deliberate use of splashes and splatters of paint. Courtesy the artist, 1984.

FIGURE 3–93 This gouache painting by student artist **Kathleen Lattyak** was an illustration for a short story by Joann Kobin, entitled "The Meat Man's Death." The story and the painting were published in the June 1984 issue of *The North American Review*. The story was concerned with the ruminations of a middle-aged woman in reaction to her father's death. Her father was a butcher (i.e., a meat man). In her state of mournful musing, she perceives the borders between different things becoming less rigid than usual, and she begins to think of her father as if he were her son, and vice versa. There is a metaphorical sense in which every son is a shadow of his grandfather. Perhaps the artist wanted us to think of that in opposing the fork to its shadow. Courtesy the publisher and the artist.

FIGURE 3–94 The illusion of depth in this painting is in part the consequence of one-point linear perspective. The convergence of lines is easily seen in the checkerboard floor, which functions as a texture gradient. By extending the vertical lines in the tiles, the point where all the lines converge (the vanishing point) can be located, but only approximately in this case because the perspective is not entirely accurate. This is probably intentional, since strictly accurate linear perspective is sometimes not convincing. In this gouache painting by **Norman Walker,** the central seated figure is Topper, the fictional character in a series of novels by Thorne Smith. The two figures at his sides are his amiable phantoms, whom only Topper is able to see. To indicate the ghostly traits of the two rear figures, the artist has cleverly shown them as being opaque (they obscure the stripes on the wallpaper) and also transparent (they do not obscure the color of the wallpaper). The work was commissioned by Ballantine Books. The art director was Donald E. Munson. Courtesy the artist.

FIGURE 3–95 One of the precursors of modern expressionist art was the Belgian painter **James Ensor.** In a way, he was also a forerunner of Surrealism. This is one of his self-portraits—an attempt to portray his neuroses, perhaps—entitled *Demons Ridicule Me* (1895). There is a gesture in his works that is especially fitting for the macabre scenes they portray. When he worked in oil paint, he made this gesture by impasto; when he was drawing or etching, he made it by lines that seem to squirm or quake. Reproduced from *Medicine and the Artist* by Carl Zigrosser (New York: Dover Publications, 1970) by permission of the Philadelphia Museum of Art, from the Dover Pictorial Archives.

Chapter 4

Techniques, Materials, Tools, and Styles

It is commonly advised (sometimes prudently, sometimes not) by artists, teachers, and students themselves, that students should be conversant with a wide range of traditional methods and tools. I do not discourage that, and it is with that goal in mind that I have included this section on techniques, materials, tools, and styles.

This is a superficial look (a handshake and a fleeting glance) at some of the countless techniques frequently employed in contemporary illustration. For serious students, this list will be much too brief; they must venture out alone to augment and to qualify the spare suggestions offered here. They will have to learn about methods and techniques by fooling around in a serious way, by watching the struggles of others, and—what is even more vital—by testing things with their own eyes and hands, a process that is now called *visual thinking*.

This book was not intended to be a handbook of technical tips. There are books that do that well and some of the better ones are listed in Chapter 5 under the heading *Techniques and Materials*.

There are two common dangers in working with illustration tools and techniques: the danger of knowing too little, and the opposite one of knowing too much. Most of us feel insecure about the first, as indeed we probably will

FIGURE 4–1 In answer to a problem to invent the box and pieces for "a game for which the rules are lost," student artist **Martin Krohne** created a wonderfully puzzling contrivance called *Adacabra* (not to be confused with abracadabra). "I try to maintain a sense of mystery in much of my work," he has stated, "I want to provide enough seduction and enough clues for someone to want to spend the time looking for them, but no solutions." Speaking of this particular work, he said that "I used to put on magic shows for my family when I was little and have always been facinated with those funny sorts of objects one finds from time to time completely divorced from their original context and hence mysterious." The moving pieces for the game were made by casting plaster in antique candy molds. "The most fascinating thing about trying to solve a problem," Krohne added, "is the attempt to understand it. The solution spoils the game so I made a game that seems to be complete, but must be missing something. It's enough to appreciate the esthetics of some things and imagine what they might be for. Knowing does not always satisfy." Courtesy the artist, 1982.

until the day we die. The second is the ominous danger of knowing what we know too well, of being too ingrown to grow. It is more subtle than the first and may require some courage to combat.

To the extent that we have learned to manipulate tools and materials in proven and proper ways, we may swiftly reach our intended goals. And yet, to that same degree, we prevent ourselves from appreciating—or even addressing—unintended results and unforeseen goals. We need to be open to *both*.

Abstract Expressionism A style of art that developed from "free association" in psychoanalysis and "automatic writing" in Surrealist literature. It was popular chiefly in the 1950s and early 1960s. It attempted to picture unconscious personality traits by unleashing spontaneous gestures. It has had a huge impact on contemporary illustration. Its best known practitioners were Arshile Gorky, Willem de Kooning, Jackson Pollack, and, more recently, Richard Diebenkorn.

Acrylic Paint in which the pigment is bound in plastic resin. Depending on its thickness and method of application, effects can be produced that more or less resemble the traditional effects of oil paint, gouache, and watercolor. It is thinned with water (although it is water resistant when set) and extended with a medium that can be purchased gloss or matte. It can be applied to nearly any surface except oil-primed boards. Virtually any brush can be used.

Adhesive Line and Pattern Tapes Printed tapes of varying widths, colors, and patterns that are used in graphic design for borders, lines, and shapes without using ink or paint. They can also be used in less orthodox ways in illustration, although, if their adhesive is weak, they do not last very long.

Adhesives All sorts of glues and tapes exist. Each is effective for certain purposes and not so good for others, depending on the weight of what is glued, its porousness, and so on. The most common adhesives for illustration are rubber cement, white glue, acrylic medium, and spray compounds. Some adhesives allow for *repositioning*—that is, carefully peeling up a piece that has been glued and relocating it. It is wise to burnish shapes—that is, cover them with a clean sheet of paper and rub the area with a wooden tongue depressor—after having glued them down, to insure that all surfaces contact.

Airbrush A painting tool that is a combination of paint brush and spray gun. It is positioned in the hand like a pencil. Various media can be used including gouache, transparent watercolor, drawing inks, and acrylic paint. It is an expensive and delicate tool, requiring practice, patience, and a considerable amount

FIGURE 4–2 In an illustration class, the students were asked to pretend that they had been commissioned by a magazine to produce a commemorative cover. Student artist **Dean Bressler** chose to simulate *Print,* the prominent journal of graphic design, and to commemorate artists. He used a variety of media in effective but largely unorthodox ways. The foreground figures on ladders, for example, were colored with airbrush and splatters, then cut out and glued to the background. The background is a reference to a pair of famous earlier works, Edouard Manet's *Luncheon on the Grass* and the painting that it parodies, Raphael's *Judgment of Paris.* Courtesy the artist.

of maintenance. At each stage, portions of the surface that are not to be sprayed have to be blocked out with paper, frisket, or a liquid mask. The process can be arduous. Some artists save time by combining airbrush with collage, by airbrushing various shapes on separate sheets of paper, trimming out the shapes, and collaging them onto a background. The chief attraction of an airbrush is that it produces a soft, graduated blending. Sometimes, however, the same result can be achieved by less expensive, simpler, and quicker means, albeit less romantic perhaps.

Alkyd A recently developed paint that has many of the tactile and visual characteristics of oil paint but dries more quickly.

Alla Prima A term referring to ways of working that are spontaneous and direct, rather than planned and belabored.

Art Deco The popular name for a streamlined style found mostly in functional objects, beginning in the 1920s and lasting nearly twenty years. It was derived from the combined influences of Cubism, Art Nouveau, Native American art, the Russian ballet, and the Bauhaus.

Art Nouveau French for "new art." An art style widely practiced in Europe and America in the 1890s. In Germany, it was known as *Jugendstil*, or "youth style." It emphasized outlines and flatness; its motifs stressed the writhing, vinelike flow of things, whether they were plants or not. It can be seen in the works of Gustav Klimt, Aubrey Beardsley, William Morris, and Alphonse Mucha.

Assemblage The technical name for sculptural collage, one that uses three-dimensional materials.

Bamboo Pens These are simply bamboo sticks that have been shaped into a pen point at both ends. To draw with them, simply dip an end in ink. Unlike technical pens, which produce austere lines, they make expressive-looking lines that vary in darkness and thickness. Bamboo pens can be purchased at art stores, but you can easily make your own.

Bauhaus The most influential art school of this century, established with government funding by the architect Walter Gropius in 1919 in Weimar, Germany. It emphasized the value of visual esthetic design in functional objects. The school was closed by Hitler in 1933. Among the Bauhaus teachers were Wassily Kandinsky, Paul Klee, Josef Albers, László Moholy-Nagy, and others.

FIGURE 4–3   The layers of Plexiglas in this collage produce several intriguing effects. Some of the shapes seem to be raised and to float in air. At the same time, their shadows become a fugitive aspect in their own right. This work, called *Aces,* was completed in 1980 by **Tom Noffsinger.** Courtesy the artist.

Blotting Making accidental forms by dabbing with a paper towel, or another blotting tool, and then refining the shapes that occur.

Bristol Board A card-weight smooth-faced drawing stock that is often used for pen and ink illustrations.

Camera Lucida A machine for tracing, sometimes called a *lucigraph* or *lucy*. It consists of an opaque projector with a table at which the artist can sit. Some kind of drawing or tracing device has been used by most western artists since the Renaissance, including Leonardo da Vinci, Dürer, Vermeer, Canaletto, and Van Gogh. Norman Rockwell used an opaque projector. He was, as he admitted once, "thoroughly ashamed of it. I hide it whenever I hear people coming." Despite the risk of feeling ashamed, most contemporary illustrators (and an increasing number of gallery artists) use a slide projector, opaque projector, artograph, or a comparable tracing machine.

Camera Obscura A venerable species of drawing machine; in essence, it is a camera with a ground glass window where the film would normally be. By placing a sheet of tracing paper on the glass, an artist can sketch the scene projected through the camera lens. It was the precursor to the photographic camera. Vermeer is thought to have painted with one.

Cartoon A humorous drawing or caricature now, but before the mid-nineteenth century (before drawing was thought to be an art), a diagram or plan from which a final work was traced. The modern meaning came about when plans for certain frescoes commissioned by the British Parliament were satirized by "cartoons" in the British humor magazine, *Punch*.

Charcoal Drawing sticks or pencils produced by charring sticks of wood. Depending on the process and the wood used, charcoal varies in hardness and thus in the sharpness of line produced. Usually made from beech or willow; vine charcoal is produced from vines. Compressed charcoal is molded powder mixed with glue. Powdered charcoal can be applied by smearing, using rolled-up paper stumps to produce softened, cloudlike shapes. A kneaded eraser works best for corrections, and a fixative is normally used on a finished charcoal work.

Collage An artwork that consists chiefly of two-dimensional materials arranged on, and glued to, a surface.

FIGURE 4–4 There is a calculated use of severe diagonal axes and a rhythmic repetition of implied elliptical shapes in this colored pencil drawing by student artist **David Hummer.** Courtesy the artist, 1983.

Colored Pencil Chalk or crayon bound in wood. They usually need to be optically mixed (crosshatched or stippled, in order to produce the right blend from a distance), and applied with patterns of delicate strokes.

Cropping The choice of where the edge should be in an illustration, photograph, or other artwork. Images often become more dramatic when distracting elements have been eliminated.

Crosshatching The use of two series of parallel lines that cross each other at an angle to create the effect of shade. Crosshatching is an especially useful procedure in pen and ink drawing.

Crow-Quill Pen A dip pen with a tiny point, normally used with India ink. It produces a very fine variant line, in contrast to the mechanical line produced by felt tip and technical pens. It is especially good for certain kinds of stippling and crosshatching.

FIGURE 4–5 Perhaps nowhere in the world is there such a high regard for the fan as in Japan and China. And because of its fan-shaped leaves, there is an equal reverence for the ginkgo tree, planted adjacent to temples because it is thought to be sacred. The shape of the leaves may also account for the fact that it is called "the maidenhair tree." By its rich employment of ginkgo leaves, combined with such ambiguous elements as the bed, a hat, and limbs, this colored pencil drawing by **Anthony Stoeveken** may prompt us to interpret it in a way that is equally complex. Courtesy the artist, 1982.

Cubism A painting style invented by Pablo Picasso and Georges Braque about 1907 and continuing to World War I. It resulted in representational works (mostly portraits and still lifes) that were challenging to read because of the breakage of typical shapes. Some Cubist works resemble World War I dazzle camouflage, and it is significant that some Cubist artists were assigned to camouflage units in the French army. Other prominent Cubists included Fernand Léger, Juan Gris, and Jacques Villon.

Dada A style of art and literature in which the aim was not to make esthetic forms but to disrupt and shock. It began as an antiwar movement of sorts at the outbreak of World War I, in Zurich, a gathering place for war resisters in neutral Switzerland. Dada emphasized chance, free association, radical juxtaposition, mistakes, and contradictions. Some of its major practitioners were Max Ernst, Hans Richter, Hans Arp, and Marcel Duchamp. It is at times called *antiart*.

Dip Pens Simple pointed split quill pens that have no reservoir for ink and thus frequently need to be dipped. All sorts of pens and points exist; a crow-quill is one such pen.

Dry-Brush Applying paint or ink with a brush with very little liquid on it in order to produce a broken, uneven effect.

Dry Transfer Letters and Symbols Printed low-adhesive shapes of all sorts and sizes that can be rubbed off a plastic sheet and transferred to an artwork. They are used in graphic design, especially by typographers, in the preparation of camera-ready layouts. They can also be used in illustrations in less-expected ways—for example, as curious details.

Embossing The use of a raised surface to make a shape, as in Braille. In this technique, a shape can be produced without inscribing a line, applying a color, and so on.

Erasers Until 1752 most erasers were pieces of bread. In that year, a substance known as *caoutchouc* was proposed in the proceedings of the French Academy. It was used to rub out marks and thus soon acquired the name of rubber. It is

FIGURE 4–6 Responding to a request to develop an overall format and image for an inventive calendar page, student artist **Dean Bressler** used a mixture of Xeroxed shapes, tinted paper, adhesive line tapes, and colored pencils. The implied diagonal lines echo the slant of the samurai swords. Courtesy the artist, 1982.

FIGURE 4–7 This work is a collage and something more. It is a two-dimensional piece for the most part, but features of the box are almost as vital as the pictures it frames. For example, the title of the work is *Three,* and on the right is a hinge attached to a strip of framing wood, which may suggest that a third of the sculpture is missing. It isn't. This is the total assemblage of an unpublished artwork by **Tom Noffsinger,** made in 1984. Courtesy the artist.

still used in the production of erasers, along with certain plastics now. Hard and abrasive erasers may damage the surface of works. Whenever possible, kneaded, or putty, erasers are preferred because they are nonabrasive and can be shaped to form a point.

Fixative A mixture of varnish and benzine that is sprayed on charcoal, chalk, and pastel works to prevent smudging. Unfortunately, some fixatives dull or darken certain hues.

French Curves Odd-shaped plastic ruling guides that look like arabesques. They are used by illustrators and other artists as guides for ruling precise curves. They are indispensible tools for drawing curves (whether French curves or the newer so-called *flexible curves*).

Frisket Any material that is used to mask a section of a work temporarily while adjacent areas are being sprayed or painted—for example, while using an airbrush. Frisket paper that is slightly adhesive on the back can be bought. Liquid frisket (which is brushed on and then peeled off) is also available.

Frottage French for "rubbing." The practice of producing shapes by placing paper on a textured surface, then rubbing the paper with pencil or chalk. (In psychology, a sexual deviation in which a person becomes excited by rubbing against other people in crowded public places.)

Fugitive Media Impermanent materials that have a tendency to fade.

Futurism A short-lived Italian art style that began in 1909 and died about 1915. Futurist painters attempted to show motion and simultaneity on a two-dimensional surface through the rhythmic repetition of lines. Although he was French, not Italian, Marcel Duchamp's famous work, *Nude Descending a Staircase* (1911–1912), is generally classed as a Futurist work.

Glazing The use of paint in such a way that a thin transparent film (consisting of the paint mixed with a medium) is applied on top of a previous coat, altering the original hue without totally blocking it out.

Gouache Also called "designer's colors" and "opaque watercolors." Gouache consists of transparent watercolors to which a white base has been added, which makes for its opacity; it is thinned with water. It may be one of the least complicated of all paint media.

Graffito The technique of making lines by scratching through an upper layer of paint to reveal the layer below. Different tools—for example, dinner forks, combs, and so on—create different effects.

Illustration Board A surface made of Bristol board with a cardboard backing. There are at least three common kinds: *Hot-press* is especially smooth, for use with detailed pen and ink. *Cold-press* is slightly textured, and thus most appropriate for water media washes and less detailed pen and ink. *Medium* is multipurpose, usually appropriate for pen and ink, watercolor, gouache, pencil, crayon, and so on.

Impasto The process of applying thick daubs or layers of pastelike paint or a comparable medium, usually with a palette knife. The pattern of knife strokes, the paint texture, and the effects of biased light are predominant concerns when working in this particular way.

Light Table A glass-covered table with a light underneath. Frosted glass is normally used to evenly diffuse the light. It permits artists to see through layers of paper in the process of planning or tracing.

Mahlstick Because of perspiration from the hands, an artist has to constantly beware of smearing the surface of a work. A mahlstick is a rod or dowel with a soft sphere on one end. By carefully propping the sphere on a dry part of the work, the artist can steady the hand holding the painting tool by leaning it against the stick.

Mixed Media The use of a variety of tools and materials from more than one medium—for example, the use of gouache and pen and ink in the same work. The concept is certainly simple enough, and yet it is surprising how often people do not think of mixing two materials because they were taught to use them separately. Also called *composite media.*

Objet Trouvé (Plural: *objets trouvés;* French for "found object.") An unaltered nonart object that has been labeled and treated as if it were art. The most famous example is Marcel Duchamp's *Fountain* (*ca.* 1917), which is a urinal mounted on a board and "signed" by R. Mutt. Sometimes called a *ready-made.*

Oil Paint in which the pigment is suspended in oil of one sort or another. For some purposes, it is an inconvenient medium in that it dries more slowly than acrylic, gouache, or watercolor. It is water resistant and must be thinned with solvents such as turpentine. Some artists still prefer it above all other kinds of paint because it has a feel and look that has not been matched exactly by newer synthetic media.

Pastels Powdered pigments molded into sticklike shapes and used somewhat like crayons. They provide an excellent means of painting with dry color. A fixative is sometimes used to protect the finished work.

Pentimento Italian for "repentance." Pentimenti are mistakes or prior trials that are still visible in a ghostly way on the surface of an artwork, even though they have been erased or painted over. As subordinate details, they add richness to a work, and in some works they are planned.

FIGURE 4–8 In his course on typographic design, Charles Vansen asked students to form an imaginary business and design a company van that would advertise its trade. In response, student artist **Beth Barber** produced this wonderfully intricate skinlike scheme for the firm of *B. A. Barber, Bugologist.* Courtesy the artist, 1981.

FIGURE 4–9 An increasing number of published illustrations are initially developed as three-dimensional sculptures, then photographed for publication. This assemblage of found objects (*objets trouvés*) by student artist **Susan Raasch** was published in the June 1982 issue of *The North American Review* to illustrate a short story by Cinda Tallent entitled "Mr. and Mrs. Smith." Courtesy the artist and the publisher.

FIGURE 4–10 One source of intrigue and complexity in this mixed media collage by the American illustrator **Fred Otnes** is the subtle collisions (or are they collusions?) between the various layers of shapes. The innuendoes that rebound are like *pentimenti* that whisper through the strata of a revised painting. Courtesy the artist.

Plein Air French for "open air." In its original sense, the term refers to landscape art completed out of doors and at the scene. It now also refers to artworks that exude a sense of freshness and immediacy.

Proportional Scale An inexpensive calculating wheel that allows an artist to easily find the percentage of enlargement or reduction when an illustration's original size differs from its reproduced size. Original illustrations are often reduced (usually by one-fourth) so that slight imperfections will be diminished. The final result is comparable to looking at the artwork from a slight distance.

Reducing Glass The opposite of a magnifying glass. It is a lens that makes things appear to be farther away. By viewing artworks through this lens, an artist can determine the visibility of an illustration when viewed from a distance, as well as how it will appear at a reduced size.

Scratchboard A white board coated with India ink. An illustration is produced by scratching the ink with various tools, producing stark, high-contrast lines.

Scumbling A technique in painting in which a surface is scuffed up with thin, dry paint. The effect is rough and cloudlike, and yet the coat beneath shows through.

Shading Screens Transparent adhesive sheets on which various patterns and shades have been printed, usually in black or white. These are used to produce grays in line art illustrations, or they can be applied to surfaces of other works to create the illusion of shadows.

Splattering Producing a visual pattern by splashing ink or paint. It is an effective way to add complexity to a work, or to give the impression of movement. Splatters can be created by rubbing a paint-filled toothbrush against a piece of window screen, or by carefully flicking a brush. Splattering can be controlled by blocking out specific parts with a frisket, just as when working with airbrush.

Sponging Making marks with a sponge. When dipped in paint or ink, different kinds of sponges produce vastly different marks.

Squaring Up A traditional, reliable way of enlarging or reducing a sketch, photograph, or other source without a projector. The original picture is divided into grids, then redrawn on a larger (or smaller) grid of the same proportion.

Stenciling Using sheets of card or paper from which shapes have been cut out. Through brushing or spraying or rubbing, the pigment is applied through the cut-out areas, while the stencil page acts as a frisket. It is a convenient way to make precise repetitive shapes.

Stippling A drawing technique that uses only dots. *Stipple board* produces much the same effect. It is an illustration board with a raised-dot texture. Marks made on a stipple board with crayon or pencil appear to be composed of dots. Commonly used in scientific illustration.

Stump A tool for smearing and blending. It is made from paper that has been tightly rolled and pointed so that it looks like a pencil. It is especially useful when working with soft pencils, pastels, and charcoal. Also called *tortillon.*

Surrealism A style of art and literature that evolved from the theories of Sigmund Freud combined with the nonsense of Dada. It officially began about 1922, under the leadership of André Breton; and while the movement no longer prevails, it is alive and healthy in that its methods are widely applied in art and advertising, especially in television commercials, which tend to be shamelessly dreamlike. Well-known Surrealist artists include René Magritte, Salvador Dalí, Paul Delvaux, and Giorgio de Chirico.

Tempera The term properly refers to powdered opaque watercolors that have been combined with distilled water and egg yolk—hence the more accurate term, *egg tempera.* It is confusing that gouache and inexpensive poster paints are also referred to as tempera at times.

Templates Plastic sheets in which various shapes have been cut out. Templates are a convenient means of drawing uniform circles, ellipses, squares, and so on.

Underpainting Because of the phenomenon of simultaneous contrast, a color will look more intense when it is placed beside a radically different color. This is one justification for the practice of underpainting, in which traces of an undercoat can be seen through gaps in the surface coat. Thus, a shape might first be painted in warm hues, and then painted over in cool. Artists who use pastels and colored pencils often work on warm- or cool-hued paper or board so that the colored board itself functions as an underpainting.

Watercolor A pigment that is bound in a water soluble gum, usually gum arabic. Unlike *gouache* (or opaque watercolor), white has not been added to what is more specifically known as *transparent watercolor*. Instead, all whites are derived from the white of the page. It can be an extremely difficult medium, especially when used in an orthodox way.

Woodcut A relief print made by carving wood on the side across the pattern of the grain. Very often, the grain is part of the design.

Wood Engraving A wood engraving differs from a woodcut in that it is carved on the cross-section end of a wood block. As a result, it is more difficult to cut, but greater detail can be achieved.

Chapter 5

Information Sources

It is always strange to hear some people advocating that art students not use libraries because "books are no substitute for experience." There is a limited logic in that, but it is more correct to say that books *are* an experience. Reading about being in Scotland is a far cry from actually traveling in Scotland, but reading itself is an experience, nevertheless, and one from which we all might learn, whether we're "verbal" or not.

As a visual artist, as one who loves things for their looks, I love the look and feel of books. I think books would interest me regardless of whether or not I could read. I could look at picture books or, if a book had no plates, I could be enchanted by the delicate shaping and placement of the type.

As it is, I have a thorough knowledge of literally thousands of volumes, and yet I am scarcely a "reader" as such. Few books deserve to be fully devoured. I rarely read a book straight through. Instead, I peruse ten at once, searching for salient answers at times, at others dipping and flitting around. But one should not misunderstand. It is not an easy search nor an aimless trail. Nevertheless, virtually all of my insights are the consequence of chance (but chance that I have *engineered*), of serendipity, of purposeful prying and probing around.

With that professional secret in mind, I have decided to offer two lists: *First,* an illustrator's list of published sources (books, magazines, and catalogs), a list that is much broader (though broad in a very intentional way) and, in the end, more practical than those that I have seen before. *Second,* a list that I have found of help as a sort of roughhewn map as I carom about in the library shelves. It is a distorted adaptation (greatly shortened, and slanted toward the visual arts) of the official outline of the Library of Congress (LC) Classification System, which most university libraries use. With this convenient guide in hand, I have yet to see a day (despite how weary and wasted I feel) when I could not unearth or spy some eccentric picture or alien fact that I could store for future use—a use that I cannot predict.

As is often true of lists, these reflect the way I think. The bias is intentional, and I hope they are deeply tinged by two very firm and unusual beliefs: (1) That only rarely do we gain from a rigid emphasis of the differences between *fine art* and *illustration*, between art that hangs on walls and art that is displayed in books. And (2) that students in our schools should be *educated* in the practice of illustrating, not just trained to fill a job.

Here is an alphabetical list of the subjects treated in the bibliography:

Advertising illustration, 184
Animation, 187
Annual collections, 190
Archaeological illustration, 186
Architectural illustration, 186
Art supply catalogs, 191
Bibliographies, 179
Biological illustration, 184
Botanical illustration, 185
Caricature, cartooning, 188
Cartographic illustration, 186
Children's book illustration, 188
Color theory, 182
Computer illustration, 187
Copyright-free sources, 191
Copyright law, 190
Creativity, ideas, 183
Design, 179
Editorial illustration, 184
Employment, 190
Esthetics, 179

Fashion illustration, 186
Graphic production skills, 189
Interior design graphics, 186
Illustrators, 189
Laws, copyright, 190
Library of Congress Classification System, 192
Magazines, journals, 190
Materials, techniques, 189
Medical illustration, 185
Pictorial content, embedded, 180
Pictorial representation, 181
Reference works: art, general, 178
Scientific illustration, 184
Technical illustration, 187
Techniques, 189
Visual rhymes, 180
Visual thinking, 183
Zoological illustration, 184

General Reference

CAVENDISH, RICHARD, ED. *Man, Myth and Magic: An Illustrated Encyclopedia of the Supernatural.* New York: Marshall Cavendish, 1970.

EDWARDS, PAUL, ED. *The Encyclopedia of Philosophy.* New York: Macmillan, 1972.

Encyclopaedia Britannica. 15th edition. Chicago: Encyclopaedia Britannica, 1974.

GALIN, SAUL, AND PETER SPEILBERG. *Reference Books: How to Select and Use Them.* New York: Vintage, 1969.

GRIZIMEK, H.C. BERNHARD, ED. *Grizimek's Animal Life Encyclopedia.* New York: Van Nostrand, 1974.

SILLS, DAVID, ED. *International Encyclopedia of the Social Sciences.* New York: Free Press, 1968.

WIENER, PHILIP, ED. *Dictionary of the History of Ideas: Studies of Selected Pivotal Ideas.* New York: Scribner's, 1973.

WOLMAN, BENJAMIN, ED. *International Encyclopedia of Psychiatry, Psychology, Psychoanalysis, and Neurology.* New York: Van Nostrand, 1977.

Art Reference

GOLDMAN, ERNARD. *Reading and Writing in the Arts: A Handbook.* Detroit: Wayne State University Press, 1978.

JONES, LOIS. *Art Research Methods and Resources: A Guide to Finding Art Information.* Dubuque, Iowa: Kendall-Hunt, 1978.

MUEHSAM, GERD. *Guide to Basic Information Sources in the Visual Arts: Where to Find the Facts in Every Art Field.* New York: Van Nostrand, 1980.

OSBORNE, HAROLD, ED. *The Oxford Companion to Art.* Oxford, Eng.: Clarendon Press, 1970.

———. *The Oxford Companion to Decorative Art.* Oxford, Eng.: Clarendon Press, 1975.

———. *The Oxford Companion to Twentieth-Century Art.* Oxford, Eng.: Clarendon Press, 1981.

PALLOTTINO, M., ED. *Encyclopedia of World Art.* New York: McGraw-Hill, 1959–1983.

STROEBEL, LESLIE, HOLLIS TODD, AND RICHARD ZAKIA. *Visual Concepts for Photographers.* New York: Focal Press, 1980.

Bibliographies

BRENNI, VITO. *Book Illustration and Decoration: A Guide to Research.* Westport, Conn.: Greenwood Press, 1980.

EMMETT, KATHLEEN, AND PETER MACHAMER. *Perception: An Annotated Bibliography.* New York: Garland Publishing, 1976.

GOLDSMITH, EVELYN. *Research into Illustration: An Approach and a Review.* Cambridge, Eng.: Cambridge University Press, 1984.

KIELL, NORMAN, ED. *Psychiatry and Psychology in the Visual Arts and Aesthetics.* Madison: University of Wisconsin Press, 1965.

KLEINBAUER, W. EUGENE, AND THOMAS SLAVENS. *Research Guide to the History of Western Art.* Chicago: American Library Association, 1982.

ROTHENBERG, ALBERT, AND BETTE GREENBERG, EDS. *The Index of Scientific Writings on Creativity.* Hamden, Conn.: Shoe String Press, 1976.

Design, Esthetics, and Anesthetics

ARNHEIM, RUDOLF. *Art and Visual Perception: The New Version.* Berkeley: University of California Press, 1974.

BEHRENS, ROY R. *Art and Camouflage: Concealment and Deception in Nature, Art, and War.* Cedar Falls, Iowa: North American Review, University of Northern Iowa, 1981.

———. *Design in the Visual Arts.* Englewood Cliffs, N.J.: Prentice-Hall, 1984.

BERLYNE, D.E. *Aesthetics and Psychobiology.* New York: Appleton-Century-Crofts, 1971.

———. *Studies in the New Experimental Aesthetics.* Washington, D.C.: Hemisphere, 1974.

BIRKHOFF, G.D. *Aesthetic Measure.* Cambridge, Mass.: Harvard University Press, 1933.

DEWEY, JOHN. *Art as Experience.* New York: Capricorn Books, 1958.

DONDIS, DONIS A. *A Primer of Visual Literacy.* Cambridge, Mass.: MIT Press, 1973.

EATON, MARCIA. *Art and Nonart: Reflections on an Orange Crate and a Moose Call.* East Brunswick, N.J.: Associated University Presses, 1983.

FALLICO, ARTURO. *Art and Existentialism.* Englewood Cliffs, N.J.: Prentice-Hall, 1962.

FISCHER, ROLAND. "A Cartography of the Ecstatic and Meditative States." *Leonardo* 6 (1973): 59–66.

GOWAN, JOHN CURTIS. *Trance, Art, and Creativity.* Buffalo, N.Y.: Creative Education Foundation, 1975.

HESSELGREN, SVEN. *The Language of Architecture.* Lund, Sweden: Studentlitterature, 1969.

KUPFER, JOSEPH. *Experience as Art.* Albany: State University of New York Press, 1983.

MASLOW, ABRAHAM. *Toward a Psychology of Being.* New York: Van Nostrand, 1968.

———. *The Farther Reaches of Human Nature.* New York: Penguin Books, 1976.

MEYER, LEONARD. *Emotion and Meaning in Music.* Chicago: University of Chicago Press, 1956.

OSBORNE, HAROLD. *Aesthetics and Art Theory.* New York: Dutton, 1970.

PICKFORD, R. W. *Psychology and Visual Aesthetics.* London: Hutchinson, 1972.

WILSON, FRANCES. "Human Nature and Aesthetic Growth." In C. E. Moustakas, ed., *The Self.* New York: Harper & Row, Pub., 1956.

ZAKIA, RICHARD. *Perception and Photography.* Rochester, N.Y.: Light Impressions, 1979.

ZUSNE, LEONARD, AND WARREN JONES. *Anomalistic Psychology.* Hillsdale, N.J.: Erlbaum, 1982.

Underlying Visual Rhymes

BOULEAU, CHARLES. *The Painter's Secret Geometry.* New York: Hacker, 1980.

DOCZI, GYORGY. *The Power of Limits: Proportional Harmonies in Nature, Art and Architecture.* Boulder, Colo.: Shambhala, 1981.

EHRENZWEIG, ANTON. *The Hidden Order of Art.* Berkeley: University of California Press, 1971.

GHYKA, MATILA. *The Geometry of Art and Life.* New York: Dover, 1978.

HAMBRIDGE, JAY. *The Elements of Dynamic Symmetry.* New York: Dover, 1967.

HOMER, W. I. *Seurat and the Science of Painting.* Ithaca, N.Y.: Cornell University Press, 1978.

HUNTLEY, H. E. *The Divine Proportion: A Study in Mathematical Beauty.* New York: Dover, 1970.

HURLBURT, ALLEN. *The Grid: A Modular System for the Design and Production of Newspapers, Magazines, and Books.* New York: Van Nostrand, 1978.

LORAN, ERLE. *Cézanne's Composition: Analysis of His Form with Diagrams and Photographs of His Motifs.* Berkeley: University of California Press, 1971.

MULLER-BROCKMANN, JOSEF. *Grid Systems in Graphic Design.* New York: Hastings House, 1981.

RICHARDSON, JOHN ADKINS. "Composition and Design." In *The Complete Book of Cartooning.* Englewood Cliffs, N.J.: Prentice-Hall, 1977.

THOMPSON, D'ARCY WENTWORTH. *On Growth and Form.* Cambridge, Eng.: Cambridge University Press, 1968.

WEISS, PAUL. "Beauty and the Beast." In *Scientific Monthly* 81 (1955): 286–99.

WILLATS, JOHN. "Unusual Pictures: An Analysis of Some Abnormal Pictorial Structures in a Painting by Juan Gris." *Leonardo* 16 (3) (1983): 188–92.

Embedded Pictorial Content

BAKER, STEPHEN. *Visual Persuasion.* New York: McGraw-Hill, 1961.

BERGER, JOHN. *Ways of Seeing.* London: Pelican, 1975.

BURLI-STORZ, CLAUDIA. *Deliberate Ambiguity in Advertising.* Bern, Switz.: Francke, 1980.

COSS, RICHARD. "The Ethological Command in Art." *Leonardo* 1 (1968): 273–87.

DIXON, N. F. *Subliminal Perception: The Nature of a Controversy.* New York: McGraw-Hill, 1971.

EDEL, LEON. *Stuff of Sleep and Dreams: Experiments in Literary Psychology.* New York: Avon, 1983.

GOFFMAN, ERVING. *Gender Advertisements.* Cambridge, Mass.: Harvard University Press, 1979.

GROTJAHN, MARTIN. *Beyond Laughter: Humor and the Subconscious.* New York: McGraw-Hill, 1966.

HAMMOND, P., AND P. HUGHES. *Upon the Pun: Dual Meanings in Words and Pictures.* London: W. H. Allen, 1978.

HESS, THOMAS B., AND JOHN ASHBERY, EDS. *Narrative Art.* Art News Annual XXXVI. New York: Macmillan/Newsweek, 1970.

KEY, WILSON BRYAN. *Subliminal Seduction: Ad Media's Manipulation of a Not So Innocent America.* Englewood Cliffs, N.J.: Prentice-Hall, 1973.

———. *Media Sexploitation.* New York: Signet, 1976.

———. *The Clam-Plate Orgy, and Other Subliminal Techniques for Manipulating Your Behavior.* Englewood Cliffs, N.J.: Prentice-Hall, 1980.

KEYSER, SAMUEL JAY. "There Is Method in Their Adness: The Formal Structure of Advertisement." *New Literary History* 14 (2) (1983): 305–34.

KRIS, ERNST. *Psychoanalytic Explorations in Art.* New York: Schocken, 1967.

LANNERS, EDI, ED. *Illusions.* New York: Holt, Rinehart & Winston, 1977.

LEACH, EDMUND. "Anthropological Aspects of Language: Animal Categories and Verbal Abuse." In Eric H. Lenneberg, ed., *New Directions in the Study of Language.* Cambridge, Mass.: MIT, 1964.

LEEMAN, FRED. *Hidden Images: Games of Perception, Anamorphic Art, and Illusion from the Renaissance to the Present.* New York: Abrams, 1976.

LEYMORE, VARDA LANGHOLZ. *Hidden Myth: Structure and Symbolism in Advertising.* London: Heinemann, 1975.

LIPMAN, JEAN, AND RICHARD MARSHALL. *Art about Art.* New York: Dutton, 1978.

MICHELL, JOHN. *Natural Likeness: Faces and Figures in Nature.* New York: Dutton, 1979.

MILLUM, TREVOR. *Images of Women: Advertising in Women's Magazines.* London: Chatto & Windus, 1975.

PACKARD, VANCE. *The Hidden Persuaders.* New York: McKay, 1957.

PHILLIPS, WILLIAM, ED. *Art and Psychoanalysis: Studies in the Application of Psychoanalytic Theory to the Creative Process.* Cleveland: Meridian, 1963.

PICKFORD, R. W. "Dream-Work, Art-Work, and Sublimation in Relation to the Psychology of Art." *British Journal of Aesthetics* 10 (1970): 275–83.

SCHRANK, JEFFREY. *Deception Detection.* Boston: Beacon, 1975.

SPECTOR, J. J. "The Method of Morelli and Its Relation to Freudian Psychoanalysis." *Diogenes* 66 (1969): 63–83.

WALKER, JOHN. "Dream-work and Art-work." *Leonardo* 16 (2) (1983): 109–14.

WICKLER, WOLFGANG. *Mimicry in Plants and Animals.* New York: McGraw-Hill, 1968.

———. *The Sexual Code: The Social Behavior of Animals and Men.* Garden City, N.Y.: Doubleday, 1973.

Pictorial Representation

BERNHEIMER, R. *The Nature of Representation.* New York: New York University Press, 1961.

BLATT, SIDNEY J. *Continuity and Change in Art: The Development of Modes of Representation.* Hillsdale, N.J.: Lawrence Erlbaum, 1984.

CROZIER, W. RAY, AND ANTHONY J. CHAPMAN, EDS. *Cognitive Processes in the Perception of Art.* Amsterdam, The Netherlands: Elsevier Science Publishers, 1984.

DEREGOWSKI, JAN. *Illusions, Patterns, and Pictures: A Cross-Cultural Perspective*. New York: Academic Press, 1980.

———. *Distortion in Art: The Eye and the Mind*. London: Routledge and Kegan Paul, 1983.

DUBERY, FRED, AND JOHN WILLATS. *Perspective and Other Drawing Systems*. New York: Van Nostrand, 1983.

FISHER, JOHN, ED. *Perceiving Artworks*. Philadelphia: Temple University Press, 1980.

FRISBY, JOHN. *Seeing: Illusion, Brain and Mind*. Oxford, Eng.: Oxford University Press, 1980.

GARDNER, HOWARD. *Artful Scribbles: The Significance of Children's Drawings*. New York: Basic Books, 1980.

GOMBRICH, E. H. *Art and Illusion: A Study in the Psychology of Pictorial Representation*. New York: Pantheon, 1960.

———. *The Image and the Eye: Further Studies in the Psychology of Pictorial Representation*. Ithaca, N.Y.: Cornell University Press, 1982.

GOODMAN, NELSON. *Languages of Art*. Indianapolis: Bobbs-Merrill, 1968.

GREGORY, R. L. *The Intelligent Eye*. New York: McGraw-Hill, 1970.

———, AND E. H. GOMBRICH, EDS. *Illusion in Nature and Art*. New York: Scribner's, 1973.

HAGEN, MARGARET, ED. *The Perception of Pictures*. New York: Academic Press, 1980.

HARRIS, ERROL. *Hypothesis and Perception*. New York: Humanities Press, 1970.

HARRISON, CHARLES, AND FRED ORTON, EDS. *Modernism, Criticism, Realism: Alternative Contexts for Art*. New York: Harper & Row, Pub., 1984.

HENLE, MARY, ED. *Vision and Artifact*. New York: Springer, 1976.

IVINS, WILLIAM M. JR. *Prints and Visual Communication*. Cambridge, Mass.: MIT, 1969.

KENNEDY, JOHN M. *A Psychology of Picture Perception*. San Francisco: Jossey-Bass, 1974.

KEPES, GYORGY. *The New Landscape in Art and Science*. Chicago: Paul Theobald, 1956.

NOVITZ, DAVID. *Pictures and Their Use in Communication*. The Hague: Martinus Nijhoff, 1977.

PIRENNE, M. H. *Optics, Painting and Photography*. Cambridge, Eng.: Cambridge University Press, 1970.

SCHAFER, HEINRICH. *Principles of Egyptian Art*. Oxford, Eng.: Clarendon Press, 1974.

SIGEL, IRVING. "The Development of Pictorial Comprehension." In Randhawa, B. S., and W. E. Coffman, eds., *Visual Learning, Thinking, and Communication*. New York: Academic Press, 1978.

SLESS, DAVID. *Learning and Visual Communication*. New York: Halstad, 1981.

STEADMAN, PHILIP. *The Evolution of Designs: Biological Analogy in Architecture and the Applied Arts*. Cambridge, Eng.: Cambridge University Press, 1979.

WEALE, R. A. "Trompe l'Oeil to Rompe l'Oeil: Vision and Art." In Don Brothwell, ed., *Beyond Aesthetics*. London: Thames and Hudson, 1976.

WRIGHT, LAWRENCE. *Perspective in Perspective*. London: Routledge and Kegan Paul, 1983.

Color Theory

ALBERS, JOSEF. *Interaction of Color*. New Haven, Conn.: Yale University Press, 1971.

BIRREN, FABER. *Color: A Survey in Words and Pictures*. New York: New York University Books, 1963.

———. *The History of Color in Painting*. New York: Van Nostrand, 1965.

CHEVREUL, M. E. *The Principles of Harmony and Contrast of Colors and Their Applications to the Arts.* New York: Reinhold, 1974.

FABRI, RALPH. *Color: A Complete Guide for Artists.* New York: Watson-Guptill, 1967.

ITTEN, JOHANNES. *The Elements of Color.* New York: Van Nostrand, Reinhold, 1971.

SHARPE, DEBORAH T. *The Psychology of Color and Design.* Totowa, N.J.: Littlefield, Adams, 1975.

STOCKTON, JAMES. *Designer's Guide to Color.* San Francisco: Chronicle Books, 1984.

VARLEY, HELEN, ED. *Color.* London: Marshall Editions, 1980.

Visual Thinking

ARNHEIM, RUDOLF. *Visual Thinking.* Berkeley: University of California Press, 1971.

BONO, EDWARD DE. *Lateral Thinking.* New York: Harper & Row, Pub., 1970.

ELFFERS, JOOST. *Tangram: The Ancient Chinese Shapes Game.* Middlesex, Eng.: Penguin, 1976.

HANKS, KURT, AND LARRY BELLISTON. *Draw! A Visual Approach to Thinking, Learning and Communicating.* Los Altos, Calif.: William Kaufmann, 1977.

————. *Rapid Viz: A New Method for the Rapid Visualization of Ideas.* Los Altos, Calif.: William Kaufmann, 1980.

————, AND DAVE EDWARDS. *Design Yourself!* Los Altos, Calif.: William Kaufmann, 1978.

MCKIM, ROBERT. *Experiences in Visual Thinking.* Monterey, Calif.: Brooks/Cole, 1972.

NELMS, HENNING. *Thinking with a Pencil.* New York: Barnes and Noble, 1964.

Creativity and Idea Production

ADAMS, JAMES. *Conceptual Blockbusting: A Pleasurable Guide to Better Problem Solving.* San Francisco: San Francisco Book Company, 1976.

BARNETT, H. G. *Innovation: The Basis of Cultural Change.* New York: McGraw-Hill, 1953.

BONO, EDWARD, ED. *Eureka!* New York: Holt, Rinehart & Winston, 1979.

GHISELIN, BREWSTER, ED. *The Creative Process.* Berkeley: University of California Press, 1952.

GORDON, WILLIAM J. J. *Synectics: The Development of Creative Capacity.* New York: Collier, 1968.

HANSON, N. R. *Perception and Discovery.* San Francisco: Freeman Cooper, 1969.

HUGHES, PATRICK. *More on Oxymoron.* New York: Penguin, 1983.

————, and GEORGE BRECHT. *Vicious Circles and Infinity.* Garden City, N.Y.: Doubleday, 1975.

JENCKS, CHARLES, AND NATHAN SILVER. *Adhocism: The Case for Improvisation.* Garden City, N.Y.: Doubleday, 1972.

KINCE, ELI. *Visual Puns in Design.* New York: Watson-Guptill, 1982.

KNELLER, GEORGE. *The Art and Science of Creativity.* New York: Holt, Rinehart & Winston, 1965.

KOBERG, DON, AND JIM BAGNALL. *The Universal Traveler.* Los Altos, Calif.: William Kaufmann, 1973.

KOESTLER, ARTHUR. *The Act of Creation.* New York: Macmillan, 1964.

O'BRIEN, JAMES. *How to Design by Accident: A Book of Accidental Effects for Artists and Designers.* New York: Dover, 1968.

ROSNER, STANLEY, AND LAWRENCE ABT, EDS. *The Creative Experience.* New York: Dell, 1980.

SHIBLES, WARREN. "The Metaphorical Method." *Journal of Aesthetic Education* (April 1974): 24–36.

TATON, R. *Reason and Chance in Scientific Discovery.* New York: Science Editions, 1962.

THOMPSON, PHILIP, and PETER DAVENPORT. *The Dictionary of Graphic Images.* New York: St. Martin's, 1980.

Editorial and Advertising Illustration

BLAND, DAVID. *A History of Book Illustration: The Illuminated Manuscript and the Printed Book.* Berkeley: University of California Press, 1969.

BOSTON MUSEUM OF FINE ARTS. *The Artist and the Book, 1860–1960: In Western Europe and the United States.* Boston: Museum of Fine Arts and Harvard College Library, 1961.

BROOKLYN MUSEUM. *A Century of American Illustration.* New York: Brooklyn Museum, 1972.

HAMILTON, EDWARD. *Graphic Communication for the Computer Age: Visual Communication for All Media.* New York: Van Nostrand, 1970.

KLEMIN, DIANA. *The Illustrated Book: Its Art and Craft.* New York: Potter, 1970.

LOIS, GEORGE. *The Art of Advertising.* New York: Abrams, 1977.

MEGGS, PHILIP. *A History of Graphic Design.* New York: Van Nostrand, 1983.

MELOT, MICHEL. *The Art of Illustration.* New York: Rizzoli, 1984.

MEYER, SUSAN. *America's Great Illustrators.* New York: Abrams, 1978.

MULLER-BROCKMANN, JOSEF. *A History of Visual Communication.* New York: Hastings House, 1981.

NELSON, ROY PAUL. *Publication Design.* Dubuque, Iowa: William Brown, 1983.

PEPPIN, BRIGID. *Dictionary of Book Illustrators, 1800–1970.* New York: Arco, 1980.

REED, WALT, ed. *The Illustrator in America, 1900–1960.* New York: Reinhold, 1967.

Scientific and Biological Illustration

CLARKE, CARL. *Illustration: Its Technique and Application to the Sciences.* Butler, Md.: Standard Arts, 1949.

DOWNEY, JOHN C., AND JAMES KELLY. *Biological Illustration: Techniques and Exercises.* Ames: Iowa State University Press, 1982.

FARR, GERALD. *Biology Illustrated.* Boston: American Press, 1979.

HAECKEL, ERNST. *Art Forms in Nature.* New York: Dover, 1974.

LESLIE, CLARE WALKER. *Nature Drawing: A Tool for Learning.* Englewood Cliffs, N.J.: Prentice-Hall, 1980.

PAPP, CHARLES. *Manual of Scientific Illustration.* Sacramento, Calif.: American Visual Aid Books, 1976.

WOOD, PHYLLIS. *Scientific Illustration: A Guide to Biological, Zoological, and Medical Rendering Techniques, Design, Printing, and Display.* New York: Van Nostrand, 1982.

ZWEIFEL, FRANCES. *Handbook of Biological Illustration.* Chicago: University of Chicago Press, 1961.

Zoological Illustration

COTT, H. B. *Adaptive Coloration in Animals.* London: Methuen, 1940.

DANCE, PETER. *The Art of Natural History: Animal Illustrators and Their Work.* New York: Overlook, 1978.

DURIN, BERNARD. *Insects, Etc.* New York: Hudson Hills, 1981.

GESNER, KONRAD. *Curious Woodcuts of Fanciful and Real Beasts.* New York: Dover, 1971.

HARTER, JIM. *Animals: 1419 Copyright-Free Illustrations of Mammals, Birds, Fish, Insects, Etc.* New York: Dover, 1979.

HYMAN, SUSAN. *Edward Lear's Birds.* New York: Morrow, 1980.

JENKINS, ALAN. *The Naturalists: Pioneers of Natural History.* New York: Mayflower, 1978.

LINSENMAIER, WALTER. *Insects of the World.* New York: McGraw-Hill, 1972.

MARCHAM, FREDERICK, ED. *Louis Agassiz Fuertes and the Singular Beauty of Birds.* New York: Harper & Row, Pub., 1971.

NORELLI, MARTINA. *American Wildlife Painting.* New York: Watson-Guptill, 1975.

PORTMANN, ADOLF. *Animal Forms and Patterns.* New York: Schocken, 1967.

RAWSON, JESSICA, ED. *Animals in Art.* London: British Museum, 1977.

SEGUY, E. A. *Seguy's Decorative Butterflies and Insects in Full Color.* New York: Dover, 1977.

THAYER, GERALD. *Concealing-Coloration in the Animal Kingdom: An Exposition of the Laws of Disguise Through Color and Pattern, Being a Summary of Abbott H. Thayer's Discoveries.* New York: Macmillan, 1909.

Botanical Illustration

BIANCHINI, F., AND F. CORBETTA. *The Complete Book of Fruits and Vegetables.* New York: Crown, 1975.

CLUSIUS, CAROLUS. *Plant and Floral Woodcuts for Designers and Craftsmen.* New York: Dover, 1974.

COATS, ALICE. *The Book of Flowers.* New York: McGraw-Hill, 1973.

COLE, REX VICAT. *The Artistic Anatomy of Trees: Their Structure and Treatment in Painting.* New York: Dover, 1951.

HARLOW, WILLIAM. *Art Forms from Plant Life.* New York: Dover, 1974.

HUTTON, PAUL, AND LAWRENCE SMITH. *Flowers in Art from East and West.* London: British Museum, 1979.

KING, RONALD. *Botanical Illustration.* New York: Crown, 1979.

LIONNI, LEO. *Parallel Botany.* New York: Knopf, 1977.

MUNTING, ABRAHAM. *Fantastic Floral Engravings.* New York: Dover, 1975.

RIX, MARTYN. *The Art of the Plant World: The Great Botanical Illustrators and Their Work.* New York: Overlook, 1981.

SWEERTS, EMANUEL. *Early Floral Engravings.* New York: Dover, 1976.

THORNTON, ROBERT. *The Temple of Flora.* Boston: New York Graphic Society, 1981.

WADSWORTH, JOHN. *Designs from Plant Forms.* New York: Universe Books, 1977.

Medical Illustration

BASKIN, LEONARD. *Ars Anatomica: A Medical Fantasia.* New York: Medicina Rara, 1972.

NAKAMURA, JULIA, AND MASSY NAKAMURA. *Your Future in Medical Illustrating, Art and Photography.* New York: Rosen Press, 1971.

ROUSSELOT, JEAN, ED. *Medicine in Art.* New York: McGraw-Hill, 1967.

SAUNDERS, J. B. DEC. M., AND CHARLES D. O'MALLEY. *The Illustrations from the Works of Andreas Vesalius of Brussels.* New York: Dover, 1950.

ZIGROSSER, CARL. *Medicine and the Artist.* New York: Dover, 1970.

Science Fiction Illustration

FREWIN, ANTONY. *One Hundred Years of Science Fiction Illustration, 1840–1940.* London: Jupiter Books, 1974.

Cartographic Illustration

GOULD, PETER, AND RODNEY WHITE. *Mental Maps.* New York: Penguin, 1974.

KEATES, J. S. *Cartographic Design and Production.* New York: Halstad, 1976.

LYNAM, EDWARD. *The Mapmaker's Art: Essays on the History of Maps.* London: Batchworth, 1953.

MONKHOUSE, FRANCIS, AND HENRY WILKINSON. *Maps and Diagrams: Their Compilation and Construction.* London: Methuen, 1971.

POST, J. B. *An Atlas of Fantasy.* Baltimore: Mirage, 1973.

ROBINSON, ARTHUR, ET AL. *Elements of Cartography.* New York: Wiley, 1978.

Archaeological Illustration

DILLON, BRIAN. *The Student's Guide to Archaeological Illustrating.* Los Angeles: UCLA Institute of Archaeology, 1983.

PIGGOTT, STUART. *Antiquity Depicted: Aspects of Archaelogical Illustration.* London: Thames and Hudson, 1978.

Architectural Illustration

CHING, FRANK. *Architectural Graphics.* New York: Van Nostrand, 1975.

COULIN, CLAUDIUS. *Step-by-Step Perspective Drawing for Architects, Draftsmen and Designers.* New York: Van Nostrand, 1971.

DUDLEY, L. *Architectural Illustration.* Englewood Cliffs, N.J.: Prentice-Hall, 1976.

EVANS, LARRY. *Illustration Guide for Architects, Designers and Students.* New York: Van Nostrand, 1982.

OLES, PAUL. *Architectural Illustration.* New York: Van Nostrand, 1979.

POWELL, HELEN, AND DAVID LEATHERBARROW, EDS. *Masterpieces of Architectural Drawing.* New York: Abbeville, 1983.

RATENSKY, ALEXANDER. *Drawing and Modelmaking: A Primer for Students of Architecture and Design.* New York: Watson-Guptill, 1983.

STAMP, GAVIN. *The Great Perspectivists.* New York: Rizzoli, 1982.

Interior Design Graphics

INFORMATION DESIGN. *Notes on Interior Design.* Los Altos, Calif.: William Kaufmann, 1981.

JONES, FREDERICK. *Interior Design Graphics.* Los Altos, Calif.: William Kaufmann, 1983.

LEACH, SID. *Techniques of Interior Design Rendering and Presentation.* New York: McGraw-Hill, 1983.

PILE, JOHN, ED. *Drawings of Architectural Interiors.* New York: Watson-Guptill, 1979.

SCHNEIDER, R. *Interior Design Careers.* Englewood Cliffs, N.J.: Prentice-Hall, 1976.

STEGEL, HERBERT. *A Guide to Business Principles and Practices for Interior Designers.* New York: Watson-Guptill, 1982.

Fashion Illustration

BARBIER, GEORGES, ET AL. *Parisian Costume Plates.* New York: Dover, 1979.

BLUM, STELLA, ED. *Eighteenth-Century French Fashion Plates in Full Color.* New York: Dover, 1982.

GINSBURG, MADELEINE. *Fashion Illustration.* Owings Mills, Md.: Stemmer House, 1982.

IRELAND, PATRICK. *Drawing and Designing Menswear.* New York: Halstad, 1976.

LEPAPE, GEORGES, ET AL. *French Fashion Plates from the Gazette du Bon Ton.* New York: Dover, 1979.

RIDLEY, PAULINE. *Fashion Illustration.* New York: Rizzoli, 1979.

SHACKELL, DORA, AND W. STUART MASTERS. *Modern Fashion Drawing.* New York: Gordon, 1978.

SLOANE, EUNICE. *Illustrating Fashion.* New York: Harper & Row, Pub., 1977.

STEPHENSON, ANN. *Introduction to Fashion Illustrating.* New York: Fairchild, 1981.

TATE, SHARON, AND MONA EDWARDS. *The Complete Book of Fashion Illustrating.* New York: Harper & Row, Pub., 1982.

Technical Illustration

BAYNES, KEN, AND FRANCIS PUGH. *The Art of the Engineer.* Surrey, Eng.: Lutherworth, 1981.

BULL, ROBERT. *Technical Illustration.* Los Altos, Calif.: William Kaufmann, 1984.

CARDAMONE, TOM. *Chart and Graph Preparation Skills.* New York: Van Nostrand, 1981.

HERGEG, WALTER. *Graphis/Diagrams: The Graphic Visualization of Abstract Data.* New York: Hastings House, 1982.

HOLMES, CLIVE. *Beginner's Guide to Technical Illustration.* New York: Focal Press, 1982.

MITCHELL, JAMES, ED. *The Random House Encyclopedia.* New Revised Edition. New York: Random House, 1983.

MRACEK, JAN. *Technical Illustration and Graphics.* Englewood Cliffs, N.J.: Prentice-Hall, 1983.

NELSON, JOHN. *Technical Illustration.* New York: Van Nostrand, 1979.

THOMAS, T. A. *Technical Illustration.* New York: McGraw-Hill, 1978.

Computer Illustration

BOLOGNESE, DON, AND ROBERT THORNTON. *Drawing and Painting with a Computer.* New York: Watts, n.d.

CLARK, DAVID. *Computers for Image-Making.* London: Pergamon, 1980.

MALINA, FRANK, ED. *Visual Art, Mathematics, and Computers.* London: Pergamon, 1979.

NEGROPONTE, NICHOLAS, ED. *Computer Aids to Design and Architecture.* New York: Van Nostrand, 1975.

PRUEITT, MELVIN. *Computer Graphics: 118 Computer-Generated Designs.* New York: Dover, 1975.

Animation

FOX, DAVID, AND MITCH WAITE. *Computer Animation Primer.* New York: McGraw-Hill, 1982.

HALAS, JOHN, AND ROGER MANVELL. *Techniques of Film Animation.* New York: Focal Press, 1976.

LAYBOURNE, KIT. *The Animation Book.* New York: Crown, 1978.

LEVITAN, ELI. *Handbook of Electronic Imaging.* New York: Van Nostrand, 1977.

———. *Handbook of Animation Techniques.* New York: Van Nostrand Reinhold, 1979.

MUYBRIDGE, EADWEARD. *The Human Figure in Motion.* New York: Dover, 1955.

———. *Animals in Motion.* New York: Dover, 1957.

SALT, BRIAN. *Basic Animation Stand Techniques.* London: Pergamon, 1977.

STARK, RON, AND CHARLES SOLOMON. *The Complete Kodak Animation Book.* Rochester, N.Y.: Eastman Kodak.

Caricature and Cartooning

BROOKS, CHARLES. *Best Editorial Cartoons of the Year.* New York: Pelican, annual publication.

CUPERIE, PIERRE, AND MAURICE HORN. *A History of the Comic Strip.* New York: Crown, 1968.

FEAVER, WILLIAM. *Masters of Caricature: From Hogarth to Gilray to Scarfe and Levine.* New York: Knopf, 1981.

HELLER, STEVE, ED. *Jules Feiffer's America from Eisenhower to Reagan.* New York: Knopf, 1982.

————. *War Heads: Cartoonists Draw the Line.* New York: Penguin, 1983.

————. *Man Bites Man: Two Decades of Satiric Art.* New York: A and W Publishers, 1981.

HILLIER, BEVIS. *Cartoons and Caricatures.* New York: Dutton, 1970.

HORN, MAURICE, ED. *The World Encyclopedia of Cartoons.* New York: Chelsea House, 1980.

————. *The World Encyclopedia of Comics.* New York: Chelsea House, 1976.

————. *Women in the Comics.* New York: Chelsea House, 1977.

KELLY, WALT. *Impollutable Pogo.* New York: Simon & Schuster, 1970.

LEVINE, DAVID. *No Known Survivors.* Boston: Gambit, 1970.

————. *The Arts of David Levine.* New York: Knopf, 1978.

————. *Pens and Needles: Literary Caricatures Introduced and Selected by John Updike.* Boston: Gambit, 1969.

LUCIE-SMITH, EDWARD. *The Art of Caricature.* Ithaca, N.Y.: Cornell University Press, 1981.

MACNELLY, JEFF. *A Shoe for All Seasons.* New York: Holt, Rinehart & Winston, 1983.

MEGLIN, NICK. *The Art of Humorous Illustration.* New York: Watson-Guptill, 1981.

MUSE, KEN. *The Secrets of Professional Cartooning.* Englewood Cliffs, N.J.: Prentice-Hall, 1981.

NELSON, ROY PAUL. *Cartooning.* Chicago: Contemporary Books, 1975.

REDMAN, LENN. *How to Draw Caricatures.* Chicago: Contemporary Books, 1983.

RICHARDSON, JOHN ADKINS. *The Complete Book of Cartooning.* Englewood Cliffs, N.J.: Prentice-Hall, 1977.

ROSENBERG, HAROLD. *Saul Steinberg.* New York: Knopf/Whitney Museum of Art, 1978.

SHIKES, RALPH. *The Indignant Eye: The Artist as a Social Critic in Prints and Drawings from the Fifteenth Century to Picasso.* Boston: Beacon, 1976.

WIESE, E., ED. *Enter: The Comics: Rudolphe Topffer's Essay on Physiognomy and the True Story of Monsieur Crepin.* Lincoln: University of Nebraska Press, 1965.

Children's Book Illustration

KLEMIN, DIANA. *The Art of Art for Children's Books.* New York: Bramhall House, 1966.

LANES, SELMA. *The Art of Maurice Sendak.* New York: Abrams, 1980.

LARKIN, DAVID, ED. *The Art of Nancy Ekholm Burkert.* New York: Bantam, 1977.

SCHWARCZ, JOSEPH. *Ways of the Illustrator: Visual Communications in Children's Literature.* Chicago: American Library Association, 1982.

VAN ALLSBURG, CHRIS. *Jumanji.* Boston: Houghton Mifflin, 1981.

WHALLEY, JOYCE IRENE. *Cobwebs to Catch Flies: Illustrated Books for the Nursery and the Schoolroom, 1700–1900.* Berkeley: University of California Press, 1975.

Illustrators

COBER, ALAN E. *Cober's Choice.* New York: Dutton, 1979.

GLASER, MILTON. *Milton Glaser's Graphic Design.* New York: Overlook, 1973.

MCMULLAN, JAMES. *Revealing Illustrations.* New York: Watson-Guptill, 1981.

The Push-Pin Style. Palo Alto, Calif.: Communication Arts, 1970.

RAND, PAUL. *Thoughts on Graphic Design.* New York: Van Nostrand, 1971.

ROCKWELL, NORMAN. *Rockwell on Rockwell: How I Make a Picture.* New York: Watson-Guptill, 1979.

SHAHN, BEN. *The Shape of Content.* Cambridge, Mass.: Harvard University Press, 1957.

SZLADITS, LOLA, AND HARVEY SIMMONDS. *Pen and Brush: The Author as Artist: An Exhibition in the Berg Collection.* New York: New York Public Library, 1969.

Graphic Production Skills

CARDAMONE, TOM. *Advertising Agency and Studio Skills.* New York: Watson-Guptill, 1981.

CRAIG, JAMES. *Production for the Graphic Designer.* New York: Watson-Guptill, 1974.

GOTTSCHALL, EDWARD. *Graphic Communication '80s.* Englewood Cliffs, N.J.: Prentice-Hall, 1981.

Graphics Master 2. Los Angeles: Dean Lem Associates, 1977.

INTERNATIONAL PAPER COMPANY. *Pocket Pal.* New York: International Paper Company, 1973.

SCHLEMMER, RICHARD. *Handbook of Advertising Art Production.* Englewood Cliffs, N.J.: Prentice-Hall, 1984.

Techniques and Materials

BORGMAN, HARRY. *Art and Illustration Techniques.* New York: Watson-Guptill, 1979.

CHAET, BERNARD. *An Artist's Notebook: Techniques and Materials.* New York: Holt, Rinehart & Winston, 1979.

CURTIS, SENG-GYE TOMBS, AND CHRISTOPHER HUNT. *The Airbrush Book.* New York: Van Nostrand, 1980.

DALLEY, TERRENCE, ED. *The Complete Guide to Illustration and Design: Techniques and Materials.* Secaucus, N.J.: Chartwell, 1980.

FIRPO, PATRICK, ET AL. *Copy Art: The First Complete Guide to the Copy Machine.* New York: Richard Marek, 1978.

GOODCHILD, JON, AND BILL HENKIN. *By Design: A Graphics Sourcebook of Materials, Equipment and Services.* New York: Quick Fox, 1980.

GRAY, BILL. *Studio Tips for Artists and Graphic Designers.* New York: Van Nostrand, 1976.

———. *More Studio Tips for Artists and Graphic Designers.* New York: Van Nostrand, 1978.

JANUSZCZAK, WALDEMAR. *Techniques of the World's Great Painters.* Secaucus, N.J.: Chartwell, 1980.

MAYER, RALPH. *The Artist's Handbook of Materials and Techniques.* New York: Viking, 1970.

MEYER, HANS. *150 Techniques in Art.* New York: Reinhold, 1963.

MILLS, JOHN FITZ-MAURICE. *Studio and Art-Room Techniques.* New York: Pitman, 1965.

PORTER, TOM, AND BOB GREENSTREET. *Manual of Graphic Techniques: 1.* New York: Scribner's, 1980.

———, AND SUE GOODMAN. *Manual of Graphic Techniques: 2.* New York: Scribner's, 1982.

———. *Manual of Graphic Techniques: 3.* New York: Scribner's, 1983.

QUICK, JOHN. *Artists' and Illustrators' Encyclopedia.* New York: McGraw-Hill, 1969.

REEKIE, FRASER. *Draughtsmanship: Drawing Techniques for Graphic Communication in Architecture and Building.* London: Edward Arnold, 1976.

SMITH, STAN, AND H. F. TEN HOLT, EDS. *The Artist's Manual: Equipment, Materials, Techniques.* New York: Mayflower, 1980.

TAUBES, FREDERIC. *The Painter's Dictionary of Materials and Methods.* New York: Watson-Guptill, 1979.

WATERMAN, ELYCE. *Air Powered: The Art of the Airbrush.* New York: Random House, 1980.

Art Law and Copyright

CHERNOFF, GEORGE, AND HERSHEL SARBIN. *Photography and the Law.* Philadelphia: Chilton, 1971.

CRAWFORD, TAD. *Legal Guide for Visual Artists.* New York: Hawthorn, 1980.

LELAND, CARYN. *The Art Law Primer.* New York: FCA Books, 1981.

LOWER, ROBERT, AND JEFFREY YOUNG. *An Artist's Handbook on Copyright.* Atlanta, Ga.: Fulton County Arts Council, 1981.

NORWICK, KENNETH, AND J. S. CHASEN. *The Rights of Authors and Artists: The Basic ACLU Guide to the Legal Rights of Authors and Artists.* New York: Bantam Books, 1984.

Getting a Job

BACHNER, JOHN, AND NARESH KHOLSA. *Marketing and Promotion for the Design Professional.* New York: Van Nostrand, 1977.

CRAIG, JAMES. *Graphic Design Career Guide.* New York: Watson-Guptill, 1983.

CRAWFORD, TAD, AND ARIE KOPELMAN. *Selling Your Graphic Design and Illustration.* New York: St. Martin's, 1981.

MARQUAND, ED. *How to Prepare Your Portfolio.* New York: Art Direction, 1983.

Magazines and Journals

Airbrush Digest

American Artist

Art Direction

Artforum

Art in America

Art International

The Artist's Magazine

Artnews

Ballast

Communication Arts

Graphic Design: USA

Graphis

Illustrator

Journal of Aesthetic Education

Journal of Aesthetics and Art Criticism

Leonardo

Print

Upper and Lower Case

Annual Collections of Exemplary Illustrations

ANNUAL OF ADVERTISING ART IN JAPAN. Art Directors' Club of Tokyo, Japan.

ART ANNUAL. *Communication Arts* magazine, Palo Alto, California.

ART DIRECTORS' ANNUAL. Art Directors' Club of New York.

CA ANNUAL. *Communication Arts* magazine, Palo Alto, California.

GRAPHIC DESIGN USA. American Institute of Graphic Arts, New York.

GRAPHIS ANNUAL. *Graphis* magazine, Zurich, Switzerland.

ILLUSTRATORS' ANNUAL. Society of Illustrators, New York.

PENROSE ANNUAL. International Revue of the Graphic Arts. New York: Hastings House.

PRINT CASEBOOKS. *Print* magazine, New York.

Copyright-Free Picture Sources

Certain effects in illustration require the use of pictures from earlier published sources. To avoid copyright violation, it is advisable to depend on "copyright-free" material. This in general is comprised of published material that has never been copyrighted, or published material for which the copyright has expired. Major revisions in the copyright law were adopted in 1978.

To make it easy to find copyright-free images, several publishers have produced bound collections of photographs, illustrations, and other artworks that, for one reason or another, are now within the public domain. For example, *The Complete Encyclopedia of Illustration* by J.G. Heck (New York: Park Lane, 1979) contains 11,725 copyright-free engravings from the nineteenth century that can now be reproduced without any payment, credit, or permission.

Undoubtedly the finest source is the Dover Pictorial Archives, a series of more than 300 volumes that contain more than 100,000 pictorial items, including a huge range of subjects and styles. Many of the illustrations in this book have been taken from that archive, as is credited in the figure captions. Other titles in the series include *Historic Costume in Pictures, Photomicrography Designs and Patterns, Early American Locomotives, Dictionary of American Portraits,* and *A Diderot Pictorial Encyclopedia of Trades and Industry.*

Regardless of whether they ever expect to use images such as these, all illustrators and students of illustration should become familiar with these books. For a free catalog, write to Dover Publications, Inc., 31 East Second Street, Mineola, New York 11501. Ask for the current edition of the *Dover Pictorial Archive Book Catalog.*

Catalogs of Art Supplies

Just as it is vital to be acquainted with a wide range of styles and manners of picturing things, it is no less essential to be aware of available tools. Since it is often inconvenient to browse in art supply stores, it is better to collect the catalogs of art supply manufacturers and retailers. Some major mail-order suppliers can be found in the following list:

A. I. Friedman
25 West 45th Street
New York, NY 10036

APA Graphics Store
1306 Washington Avenue
St. Louis, MO 63103

Artist and Display
8330 West Bluemound Road
Milwaukee, WI 53213

Central Art Supply Co., Inc.
1126 Walnut Street
Philadelphia, PA 19107

Daniel Smith, Inc.
1111 West Nickerson
Seattle, WA 98119

Dick Blick
Box 1267
Galesburg, IL 61401

Dupont Graphics, Inc.
745 Route 46
Parsippany, NJ 07054

H.R. Meininger Company
1415 Tremont Street
Denver, CO 80202

Jerry's Artarama
248–12 Union Turnpike
Bellerose, NY 11426

Palette Shop
342 North Water Street
Milwaukee, WI 53202

Rex Art Company
2263 Southwest 37th Avenue
Miami, FL 33145

Sam Flax
111 Eighth Avenue
New York, NY 10011

Texas Art Supply Company
2001 Montrose Boulevard
Houston, TX 77006

Utrecht Linens, Inc.
33 Thirty-fifth Street
Brooklyn, NY 11232

Library Guide for Illustrators:
An Abbreviated Outline of the
Library of Congress (LC)
Classification System

A	GENERAL WORKS (works too general to be grouped with any particular subject)
AE	Encyclopedias
AG	Dictionaries and other general reference works
AG 250	Pictorial works
B	PHILOSOPHY, PSYCHOLOGY, RELIGION
BF 173–175	Psychoanalysis
BF 311–499	Cognition, perception, IQ, and creativity
BH	Esthetics
C	AUXILIARY SCIENCES OF HISTORY
D	HISTORY: GENERAL AND OLD WORLD
E–F	HISTORY: AMERICAN
G	GEOGRAPHY, ANTHROPOLOGY, RECREATION
G 3160–9980	Maps
H	SOCIAL SCIENCE
HF 5801–6191	Advertising
J	POLITICAL SCIENCE
K	LAW
L	EDUCATION
M	MUSIC AND BOOKS ON MUSIC
ML 3800–3923	Philosophy and physics of music, including physiology, psychology, color and music, esthetics, ethics, therapeutics
MT 40–67	Composition, including rhythm, scales, melody, harmony, modulation, and counterpoint
N	FINE ARTS
N 400–4040	Art museums, galleries
N 4390–5098	Exhibitions
N 5198–5299	Private collections and collectors
N 5300–7418	History of art
N 7430–7433	Technique, composition, style
N 7475–7483	Art criticism
N 7575–7624	Portraits
N 7790–8199	Religious art
N 8555–8585	Examination and conservation of artworks
N 8600–8675	Economics of art
N 8700–9165	Art and the state, public art
NA	Architecture
NA 190–1613	History, historical monuments
NA 2699–2790	Architectural design and drawing
NA 2835–4050	Architectural details, motifs, decoration
NA 4100–8480	Special classes of buildings
NA 9000–9425	Esthetics of cities, city planning, and beautification
NB	Sculpture
NC	Drawing, design, illustration
NC 997–1003	Commercial art, advertising art
NC 1300–1766	Caricature. Pictorial humor and satire
NC 1800–1855	Posters
ND	Painting
ND 1290–1460	Special subjects including the human figure, landscapes, animals, still life, flowers
ND 1700–2495	Watercolor painting
ND 2550–2888	Mural painting
ND 2890–3416	Illumination of manuscripts and books
NE	Print media
NE 1–978	Printmaking and engraving
NE 1000–1352	Wood engraving, woodcuts
NE 1400–1879	Metal engraving
NE 1940–2230	Etching and aquatint
NE 2236–2239	Serigraphy
NE 2250–2570	Lithography
NE 2800–2890	Printing of engravings
NK	Decorative arts, applied arts, decoration and ornament, including antiques
NK 1135–1149	Arts and Crafts Movement
NK 1700–3505	Interior decoration, house decoration

NK 3600–9955	Other arts and art industries
NK 3700–4695	Ceramics, pottery, porcelain
NK 4700–4890	Costume and its accessories
NK 4997–6050	Enamel, glass, glyptic arts, including gems, jade, ivory, bone
NK 6400–8459	Metalwork including armor, jewelry, plate, brasses, pewter
NK 8800–9505	Textile arts and art needlework
NK 9600–9955	Woodwork including carvings, fretwork, inlaying
NX	Arts in general
NX 654–694	Religious arts
NX 700–750	Patronage of the arts
NX 798–820	Special arts centers
P	LANGUAGE AND LITERATURE
P 87–96	Communication, mass media
PN 6249–6790	Anecdotes, aphorisms, maxims, riddles, comics
Q	SCIENCE
QL 750–795	Animal behavior and psychology
R	MEDICINE
RC 321–576	Neurology and psychiatry
S	AGRICULTURE
T	TECHNOLOGY
T 351–385	Engineering graphics, mechanical drawing
TR	Photography
TT	Handicrafts, arts and crafts
U	MILITARY SCIENCE
V	NAVAL SCIENCE
Z	BIBLIOGRAPHY, LIBRARY SCIENCE

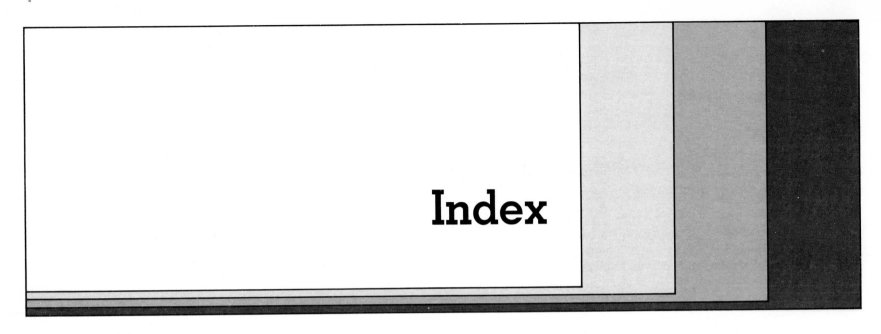

Index

Abstract Expressionism, **160**
Accent, **34**
Acrylic, 58, 60, 79–80, 107, 122, 130, 133, 144, 147, 155, **160,** 170
Adhesive tapes, 31, 99, **160,** 168
Adhesives, **160**
Advertising illustration, 184
Airbrush, 60, 102, 107, 151, **160,** 161–62
Albers, Josef, 87, 162
Alessandrini, Franco, 23
Alice's Adventures in Wonderland (Carroll), 35, 47, 55, 61
Alkyd, **162**
Alla prima, **162**
Allen, Woody, 98
Alliteration, 26–27
Allport, Gordon, 64
Ambiguity, **48,** 49–50, 166
Ambiguous figures, **49,** 50–51, 78, 103, 110, 128, 143

Ames, Adelbert, Jr., 109, 119–22, 126
Ames Distorted Room, 119–22
Ames Rotating Trapezoid Window, 126
Amin, Idi, 80
Anamorphosis, **123,** 124–26, 148,156
Anesthetic. *See* Design, anesthetic
Animation, 6, 187
Annuals, 190–91
Anthropomorphism, 69, 72, **98,** 99, 103–7
Apparent movement, **5,** 6, 72–73, 137
Arakawa, Shusaku, 113
Archaeological illustration, 186
Archimedes, 53
Architectural illustration, 186
Aristophanes, 152
Aristotle, 48, 72
Arnheim, Rudolf, 1, 4, 25, 56, 74, 83, 97

Arp, Hans, 167
Arranged marriage (radical juxtaposition), **56,** 57, 60, 62, 80, 116, 133, 140, 149
Art and Camouflage (Behrens), 19
Art Deco, **162**
Art Nouveau, 155, **162**
Art reference books, 178–79
Arts and Crafts Movement, 150
Assemblage, 140, 159, **162,** 163, 168, 172
Association, 47–49, 55
Attention, 52, **73,** 74–76, 83, 94, 107–9, 113–14, 118, 126–27
Automatic writing, 160

Baensch, Otto, 25
Balinese, 150
Baltrusaitis, Jurgis, 141
Bambi, 103–4
Bamboo pens, **162**

Barber, Beth, 171
Barbie doll, 104
Barnett, H. G., 14, 48, 56
Barnum, P. T., 104
Bateson, Gregory, 55, 57
Bauhaus, 87, 150, **162**
Baumgarten, Alexander, 25
Bayuzick, Dennis, 45
Beardsley, Aubrey, 152, 162
Beethoven, Ludwig van, 143
Behavorial conditioning, 57, 142, **143,** 144
Behrens, Mary Snyder, 93
Behrens, Roy R., 19, 43, 93, 119
Beilman, Patrick, 146–47
Bellavance, Leslie, 59
Bergmann, Mary Jane, 51
Bertalanffy, Ludwig von, 114
Bevlin, Marjorie Elliott, 6, 23, 31
Bibliographies, 179
Biological illustration, 184
Bisociation. *See* Elopement

Page numbers on which terms are defined are in boldface.

194

Blake, William, 132
Blending camouflage. *See*
    Camouflage, blending
Blotting, **164**
Botanical illustration, 185
Botticelli, Sandro, 116
Brainstorming, **53**, 67
Bralds, Braldt, 28, 152
Braque, Georges, 16, 20, 47, 167
Bressler, Dean, 72, 161, 168
Breton, André, 175
Brewster, David, 138
Bricolage, **66**
Bristol board, 151, **164**, 170
Broken continuity lines, 16, **33**,
    42, 68, 108, 110, 135, 145,
    168
Bronowski, Jacob, 63, 65
Bruner, Jerome, 52, 63–64, 71
Brunn, Lucas, 123
Buckels, James, 36, 67, 102
Burgess, Anthony, 143
Burke, Kenneth, 8, 52, 55, 68
Burne-Jones, Edward, 150
Burnham, Emilie, 24

California Conservation Corps, 31
Calligraphy, 37
Camera, 105, 118, 126–28, 136,138
Camera lucida, **164**
Camera obscura, **164**
Camouflage:
    blending, **18**, 25, 133
    dazzle, **18**, 19–21, 23, 25, 133,
      167
    military, 14, 18–20
    mimicry, **20**, 68, 89
    osnaburg, 20, **21**
Canaletto, Giovanni, 164
Caravaggio, Michelangelo da, 134
Cardano, Girolamo, 105
Caricature, 56, 67, 98, 103–6,
    164, 188
Carroll, Lewis (Charles Dodgson),
    35, 47, 55, 57, 61, 79
Carter, Jimmy, 125
Cartier, Francis, A., 48
Cartographic illustration (map
    making), 113–14, 129, 131,
    186

Cartoon, **164**, 188
Cassirer, Ernst, 114, 118
Castiglione, Giuseppe, 94
Catalogs of art supplies, 191
Categorization, 52, 54, 57, 63–65,
    67, 70–72, 105–10
Cather, Willa, 145
Cervantes, Miguel de, 54, 83
Cezanne, Paul, 39
Chalfant, Jefferson David, 141
Chance, 52, 56, 58, 60, 114, 133,
    156, 164, 167, 177. *See also*
    Arranged marriage
Chang Yen-Yuan, 90, 109
Charcoal, 28, 79, **164**, 175
Charlie Brown, 104
Chiaroscuro, 134
Children's book illustration, 93,
    188
Chirico, Giorgio de, 175
Chwast, Seymour, 81
Cisler, Jon, 31
Clark, George Rogers, 33, 145
Classical conditioning, 142–45
Closure, **11**, 13, 29, 33, 48, 77, 154
Cober, Alan E., 44, 111, 129, 189
Cocteau, Jean, 21
Collage, 4, 31, 42–44, 49, 61–62,
    72, 80, 93, 99, 103, 112,
    116, 151, 163, **164**, 173
Color blindness:
    military uses, 14
    test for, 2
Color categories, 52, 64, 107
Color theory, 182–83
Colored pencil, 27, 104, 107, 142,
    165, 166, 168, 175
Common-law bond, **57**, 142–45.
    See also Behavioral
    conditioning; Grouping,
    contiguity
Composite media. *See* Mixed
    media
Computer illustration, 187
Condensation, 133
Confusion, 6–11, 18, 49, 54, 72,
    79, 108–9, 119–22, 126,
    128, 133, 167
Constellations, 3, 10, 52, 63–64,
    108, 140

Contextualism, 119
Convergent thinking, **66**
Cook, Captain James, 127
Cooper, Heather, 29
Copyright law, 190
Copyright-Free sources, 191
Coss, Richard G., 102
Cow Town Art (Beilman), 146–47
Crazy quilt, 18, 21
Creativity, 14, 48, 52, 54–55,
    58–59, 63, 65–66, 72,
    183–84. *See also* Divergent
    thinking; Metaphor;
    Metaphorical thinking
Cropping, **164**
Crosshatching, 35, 67, 98, 129, **165**
Crow-quill pen, 36, 98, 129, 151,
    165, 167
Crystal Palace, 49
Cubism, 19–20, 23, 162, **167**
Cumming, Robert, 10–11
Custer, General George
    Armstrong, 59, 110, 145
Cuteness, 103–5

Dada, **167**, 175
Daedalus, 66
Dali, Salvador, 175
Darwin, Charles, 71
Davenport, Guy, 6, 36, 43, 151
Dazzle camouflage. *See*
    Camouflage, dazzle
de Bono, Edward, 55, 74
de Kooning, Willem, 160
Delvaux, Paul, 175
Design, 2, **4**, 6, 179–80
    anesthetic, 18, **22**, 24–25, 30,
      179–80
    elements of, **5**, 27, 179–80
    esthetic, 14, 22–32, 179–80
    defined, 23
Designer's colors. *See* Gouache
Dewey, John, 25, 31
Dickens, Charles, 67
Diebenkorn, Richard, 160
Dip pens, 36, 44, 67, 98, 111,
    129, **167**
Disney, Walt, 103–4
Displacement, 133. *See also* Shift
    of emphasis

Divergent thinking, 55, **66**, 67.
    See also Creativity;
    Metaphor; Metaphorical
    thinking
Don Quixote de la Mancha
    (Cervantes), 54, 83
Donald Duck, 98
Doré, Gustave, 54, 83
Draper, Chad, 39
Drawing machines, 94–95
Drawson, Blair, 34, 96, 154
Dreams, 132–34
Dry-brush, 157, **167**
Dry transfer letters, **167**
Duchamp, Marcel, 136, 167,
    169–70
Dürer, Albrecht, 3, 17, 43, 66, 84,
    94–95, 164

Eaton, Marcia, 11, 13, 75
Ecstatic trance. *See* Trance,
    ecstatic
Eddington, Arthur, 108
Edel, Leon, 123
Editorial illustration, 184
Egyptian Book of the Dead, 36
Eibl-Eibesfeldt, Irenaus, 98, 105
Eidetic imagery, 132
Einstein, Albert, 108
Elopement (making the strange
    familiar), **55**, 57–58, 63,
    133
Embedded figure, 13, **14**, 15–16,
    18–19, 33, 50–51, 78,
    180–81
    task (EFT), 14
Embedded pictorial content,
    180–81
Embossing, **167**
Empathy, 11, **68**
English, Mark, 33, 68, 108, 110,
    145
Ensor, James, 157
Erasers, **167**
Ernst, Max, 167
Esquire magazine, 144, 154
Esthetics. *See* Design, esthetic
Estrangement (making the
    familiar strange), **55**,
    57–58, 63, 96, 133

Etching, 38, 157
Ethology, 73–75, 94, 100–102, 118
Evil eye, 101
Evolution, 71, 77
Eyespots (ocelli), 102
Eysenck, H. J., 5

Fallico, Arturo, 22, 133
Fashion illustration, 186–87
Feat of association, 47–49. *See also* Creativity; Metaphor; Metaphorical thinking
Feldman, Edmund Burke, 5, 24, 31
Field dependence, 14
Figure-ground, 2, **4**, 6, 18, 50, 63, 76
Fisher, Mary Pat, 5
Fitzgerald, Edward, 38
Fixative, **169**, 171
Fleming, Arthur, 53
Flexible curves. *See* French curves
Footbinding, 79
Foucault, Michel, 105, 117
Free association, 63, 67, 160, 167
French curves, **169**
Freud, Sigmund, 23, 55, 133, 152, 175
Frisket, **169**, 174–75
Frost, Robert, 47
Frottage, **169**
Fry, Roger, 128
Fugitive media, **169**
Futurism, **169**

Gablik, Suzi, 117, 146
Gage-Kivlin, Constance, 103, 115
Gambale, David, 12
General reference books, 178
Gershwin, George, 145
Gersten, Gerry, 67, 98
Gestalt psychology, 1, **2**, 19, 21
Gibson, James, J., 109
Gilbert, Anne Yvonne, 32, 45, 81, 104
Glance aversion, 100–103
Glaser, Milton, 13, 81, 144, 189
Glazing, **169**
Gogel, Ken, 61

Goldberg, Rube, 66
Gombrich, Ernst H., 25, 75, 84, 131
Goodman, Nelson, 112, 128
Gordon, William J. J., 55
Gore, Frederick, 146
Gorky, Arshile, 19, 160
Gouache, 24, 50, 81, 148, 156–57, **169**, 170, 175–76
Graffito, **170**
Grandville, 124
Graphic production, 189
Gregory, Richard L., 9
Grid systems, **33**, 42, 68, 110, 125, 174
Gris, Juan, 167
Gropius, Walter, 162
Grouping:
    contiguity (temporal recurrence), 57, 63, 142–45
        defined, 145
    proximity (spatial nearness), 6–12, 56, 60–63
        defined, 7
    similarity, 1–13, 18, 22–32, 47, 52, 54–56, 63–64, 81, 94, 105–6, 117–18, 126
        defined, 1
Grouping attributes. *See* Design, elements of
Guilford, J. P., 55, 66

Haberle, John, 141
Haeckel, Ernst, 70–71, 85
Hagio, Kunio, 128
Haircuts, 52
Hall, Edward T., 86
Hals, Frans, 139
Hanson, Ken, 24
Harlequin, 21
Harnett, William, 141
Hemingway, Ernest, 107
Henri, Robert, 134
Henry the Eighth, 30, 80
Herskovits, M. J., 126
Hess, Mark, 58
Hieroglyphs. *See* Pictographs
Hitler, Adolf, 162
Hogarth, William, 89

Holbein, Hans, the Younger, 30, 80, 123, 141
Homb-Nachreiner, Ellen, 99
Hughes, Robert, 128
Humdrum and hodgepodge, 25
Hummer, David, 165
Hunter, Stephen, 69
Hyperarousal, 22–24
Hypoarousal, 22–24

Illustration board, **171**
Impasto, 157, **170**
Incubation, 50, **53**
Indiana Review, 72
Industrial Revolution, 150
Infant schema, **103**
Ingres, Jean Auguste Dominique, 151
Innate releasing mechanism (IRM) **100**–103
Interior design graphics, 186
Invention. *See* Arranged marriage; Common-law bond; Creativity; Elopement; Estrangement; Metaphorical thinking
IQ test, 5

James, William, 10–11, 14, 18, 48, 55, 58, 63–64, 68, 82, 117
Janson, H. W., 16
Jastrow, Jacob, 133
Jesperson, Otto, 48
Johns, Jasper, 117
Johnson, Nicholas, 145
Johnson, Samuel, 47, 58
Jokes, 48–49, 52–56, 133
Jonson, Ben, 152
Julesz, Bela, 138
Jungendstil. *See* Art Nouveau

Kafka, Franz, 111
Kandinsky, Wassily, 162
Kelley, Gary, 26, 30, 32, 39, 45, 69, 77, 80–81, 147
Kelly, Ellsworth, 19
Kent, Rockwell, 134
Kepes, Gyorgy, 30
Key, Wilson Bryan, 13, 16

Kierkegaard, Soren, 50, 58
King, Martin Luther, Jr., 111
Kladderadatsch, 15
Klee, Paul, 112, 162
Klimt, Gustav, 155, 162
Koch, Kenneth, 59
Koestler, Arthur, 13, 22–23, 50, 52, 55–56, 79, 108
Koffka, Kurt, 2, 21
Kohler, Wolfgang, 2, 21
Kokoschka, Oscar, 155
Kollwitz, Kathe, 38
Korzybski, Alfred, 114
Kosinski, Jerzy, 6–7, 13, 18
Kracauer, Siegfried, 119
Krone, Martin, 77, 159
Kunz, Anita, 112, 148
Kupa, Tupai, 127, 129
Kupfer, Joseph, 25, 28

Lacan, Jacques, 108
Lao-tze, 48, 55, 64
Lascaux cave, 36
Lateral thinking, 55
La Tour, Georges de, 134
Lattyak, Kathleen, 156
Lautréamont, Comte de, 56
Leach, Edmund, 52, 65, 67
Lebrun, Charles, 97, 105–6
Lebrun, Pierre, 82–83, 90, 97, 113
Le Charivari, 56
Leenhouts, David, 156
Leger, Fernand, 167
Legibility, 5, 11, 13
Lenz, David, 5, 7, 24, 29, 32, 39, 79, 87, 153
Leonardo da Vinci, 15, 86, 90, 109, 118, 123, 164
Lévi-Strauss, Claude, 66
Library guide, 192–93
Lichtenberg, Georg Christoph, 64, 69, 128
Liebermann, Max, 67
Light table, **170**
Linnaeus, Carolus, 64, 105–7
Lipton, Lenny, 137
Lithography, 37, 134
Lolita (Nabokov), 47

Lone Ranger and Tonto, 8
Long, Lenny, 46
Lorenz, Konrad, 73, 103
Louis Philippe, 55–56
Lucas, E. V., 49
Lyons, Beauvais, 37, 100

McAfee, Mara, 149
McKim, Robert, 13
McMullan, James, 189
Magazines, 190
Magleby, McRay, 11
Magritte, René, 81, 116–17, 175
Mahlstick, **170**
Mailer, Norman, 13
Manet, Edouard, 161
Mann, Thomas, 22
Marein, Amy, 121–22
Marey, Jules Étienne, 136
Marshall Islands, 114
Martin, John, 123, 149
Marx Brothers, 154
Maslow, Abraham, 28, 48
Mattelson, Marvin, 80
Medical illustration, 88–89, 185
Meditative trance. *See* Trance, meditative
Melville, Herman, 134
Mencken, H. L., 55–56
Mental set, 94
Metamorphosis, 12, 46, 71–73, 76–77
Metaphor, 47–48, 54, 58–59, 63, 69, **71**–72, 111, 134, 156
Metaphorical thinking, 55, 67
Meter, 26–27
Mickey Mouse, 98
Mimicry. *See* Camouflage, mimicry
Miro, Joan, 56
Miss Piggy, 104
Mixed media, 42–43, 103, 107, 151, 156, 159, **170,** 173
Mock-archaeology (Lyons), 37
Moholy-Nagy, Laszlo, 19, 162
Momento mori, 37
Mondrian, Piet, 139
Morris, Frank K., 79, 155
Morris, William, 150, 162

Morrow, George, 49
Motion pictures, 137
Mucha, Alphonse, 162
Muybridge, Eadweard, 6

Nabokov, Vladimir, 47
NASA, 110
National Park Service, 33
Natural selection, 77
Nelson, Bill, 27, 142
New York Magazine, 4, 34
Nicéron, Jean-Francois, 125
Nichols, William, 130
Nixon, Richard, 61
Noffsinger, Tom, 140, 163, 168
North American Review, 29, 31, 36, 43, 61, 67, 79, 99, 102–3, 153, 156, 172
Nosmo King, 9, 18

*O*bjet trouvé, **170,** 172
Oil painting, 23, 45, 62, 87, 149, 151–53, 157, 162, **170**
Opaque watercolor. *See* Gouache
Operant conditioning, 143–45
Optical diminution, **91,** 112
Ornstein, Robert, 22
Osborn, Alex, 61
Osnaburg, 20, **21**
Otnes, Fred, 42, 151, 173
Oui magazine, 28, 152
Overlapping (masking), **109,** 110, 112
Owl butterflies, 102

Paolozzi, Edward, 63, 118
Parody, 80
Parrhasius, 86, 118
Pascal, Blaise, 105
Pastels, 26, 30, 32, 153, **171,** 175
Pasteur, Louis, 52
Paulsen, Brian, 39
Pavlov, Ivan Petrovich, 141–45
Peckham, Morse, 51, 113
Peckolick, Alan, 16
Penrose, Roland, 19
Pentimento, **171,** 173
Perelman, S. J., 154

Perspective, **90,** 91, 109, 114, 120, 154
    aerial, **90**
    isometric, **90**–92, 96, 109, 114, 152
    linear, **90**–95, 109–12, 114, 120–29, 157
Peto, John, 141
Philipon, Charles, 55–56
Phobia, 100–102, 144
Photography, 118–19, 126–28, 136–39, 151
Phyiognomy, 97–98, 103–7
Picasso, Pablo, 3, 16, 19–21, 54, 57, 114, 151, 167
Pictographs, 35–36, 39–40
Picture plane, 95
Pinter, Harold, 67
Pisani, Francesco, 37
Play, 50, **64,** 67
Playboy magazine, 128
Plein air, **174**
Poetic structure, 26–27, 54, 59
Pollack, Jackson, 160
Pope, Alexander, 152
Porta, Giambattista della, 105–6
Postage stamps, 50, 141, 145–47
Pratchenko, Paul, 65
Productive thinking, 55
Projection, **17**
Proportional scale, **174**
Psychology Today, 80, 101
Pun, 59, 71–73, 79, 108, 128
Punch, 35, 49, 164
Pupil size, 101–2
Pushcart Prize, 43
Pye, David, 52

Quipu, 115

Raasch, Susan, 172
Rackstraw, Richard, 36
Radical juxtaposition. *See* Arranged marriage
Rand, Paul, 1, 189
Raphael, 161
Ray, James Earl, 111
Ray, Man, 114
Read, Herbert, 90

Ready-made. *See Objet trouvé*
Realism, **87,** 94, 100, 108, 112, 114, 117–19, 126–28, 131, 144
Rebus, 39
Redbook, 68
Reducing glass, **174**
Repetition. *See* Grouping, similarity
Rhyme, 26–32, 57, 81, 99, 108, 110, 135, 147, 153–54, 165
Richards, I. A., 63
Richter, Hans, 167
Richter, Jean Paul, 55–56
Ripeness, **65**
Robotomorphism, 69, 72
Rockwell, Norman, 164, 189
Ross, Stephen, 116
Rousseau, Henri, 114
Rubaiyat of Omar Khayyam, 38

Sancho Panza, 83
Sand painting, 131
Sausmarez, Maurice de, 6
Schiele, Egon, 155
Schlemmer, Oskar, 19
Science fiction illustration, 186
Scientific illustration, 175, 184
Scratchboard, **174**
Scumbling, **174**
Seguy, E. A., 21
Serendipity, 50, **52,** 64, 118, 177.
    See also Arranged marriage; Chance
Shading screens, 69, **174**
Shadows, 91–94, 110, 114, 134, 144, 152, 156, 174
Shakespeare, William, 63, 77–78
Shay, R. J., 59, 107
Sherlock Holmes, 50, 73–74
Shift of emphasis (displacement of attention), **50,** 63–64, 79
Siemsen, Paul, 3
Similarity grouping. *See* Grouping, similarity
Simulacrum, 17, **18**
Simultaneous contrast, 34, 175
Simultaneous inventions, 65
Singer, I. B., 96

Sitwell, Edith, 132
Skeptic magazine, 111
Skinner, B. F., 143
Smith Brothers, 9
Sontag, Susan, 63
Sort-crossing, 55
Speaking in tongues (glossalia), 22
Spencer, Stanley, 43
Splattering, 129, 156, 161, **174**
Split representation, **129**
Sponging, **174**
Squaring up, 125, **174**
Stacking, 109, 112
Steadman, Philip, 77
Stein, Gertrude, 20, 107
Steinberg, Saul, 117
Stenciling, **175**
Stereoscopic (3-D) pictures, 137–40
Stickleback fish, 73–75, 83, 94, 104, 107, 113
Stipple board, 175
Stippling, 36, 165, **175**
Stoeveken, Anthony, 166
Stump (tortillon), **175**
Subliminal perception, 13, **16,** 17
Sullivan, Edmund, 38
Sumichrast, Josef, 40
Supernormal stimuli, 86, **100**
Surrealism, 63, 116–17, 157, 160, **175**
Sylvester, John, 127
Symbolization, 133
Synectics (Gordon), 55
Sypher, Wylie, 23

Talking Heads, 8, 13, 18, 24
Tanner, Henry O., 145
Tatlin, Vladimir, 151
Tattoo, 127–28
Taylor, Warren, 41
Technical illustration, 187
Techniques and materials, 158–76, 189, 190
Telephone (parlor game), 11
Tempera, **175**
Templates, **175**
Tenniel, John, 35, 57
Texture gradients, 109
Thayer, Abbott H., 19, 134
Thiebaud, Wayne, 32
Thompson, John, 144
Thompson, Kathryn Dyble, 125
Thornedike, E. L., 143
Tinbergen, Niko, 73–75, 83, 104
Toklas, Alice B., 20, 107
Trance:
   ecstatic, **22,** 25
   meditative, **22,** 25
Translogical thinking (Bateson), 55
Tree of evolution, 70
Trompe l'oeil, 27, **83,** 86, 100, 108, 118, 141–45
Tucholke, Christel-Anthony, 60, 133
Turbayne, C. M., 55
Twain, Mark, 69, 80
Typography, 3, 5, 7, 16, 33, 36–42, 167, 171

Ubu Roi (Jarry), 10
Uebelherr, Tom, 69
Underlying visual rhymes, 16, 26, **27,** 28–32, 81, 99, 108, 110, 135, 147, 153–54, 165, 180
Underpainting, **175**
Unity with variety, **25.** *See also* Design, esthetic
Unity without variety. *See* Camouflage, blending; Design, anesthetic
Unlikeness, 113–18, 126–128, 141, 146
Unruh, Jack, 99
Uttech, Tom, 135

Van Buren, Martin, 99
Van Gogh, Vincent, 4, 108, 148, 164
Variety without unity. *See* Camouflage, dazzle; Design, anesthetic
Velazquez, Diego, 42
Verbeek, Gustave, 78
Vermeer, Jan, 164
Versalius, Andreas, 88
Villon, Jacques, 167
Visual metaphor, 58–59, 71–73, 108. *See also* Metaphor; Metaphorical thinking; Pun
Visual thinking, **5,** 158, 183
Volker, John, 119
Vries, Jan Vredeman de, 92–93

Wald, Carol, 4, 62, 116
Walker, Norman, 81, 153, 157
Washington, George, 12, 145
Watercolor, 40–41, 44, 96, 125, 135, 148, 154, 170, 175, **176**
Watergate, 61
Watson, J. B., 143
Watts, Alan, 73
Weaver, Robert, 6, 13, 34, 79, 109, 154
Wertheimer, Max, 2, 55
Wesselmann, Tom, 117
Wickler, Wolfgang, 104
Wilde, Oscar, 152
Wilson, Frances, 30, 32
Wilson, Robley, Jr., 26
Wit, 47, 55
Wood, Grant, 54
Wood, Robert Williams, 47–49, 57, 64
Woodcut, 3, 45, 66, 83, 88, 94–95, 152, **176**
Wood engraving, 15, 17, 50, 54, 83, 124, 143, 150, **176**
Woolf, Virginia, 113
Word search puzzle, 10
Wright, Lawrence, 91, 95, 126
Wyeth, N. C., 77

Zakia, Richard, 4, 6–7, 25
Zelanski, Paul, 5
Zervos, Christian, 57
Zeuxis, 86–87, 118
Zoetrope, 136
Zoological illustration, 184–85